D0998273

Greetings from
Cedrick Adams

POOR
CEDRIC'S
ALMANAC

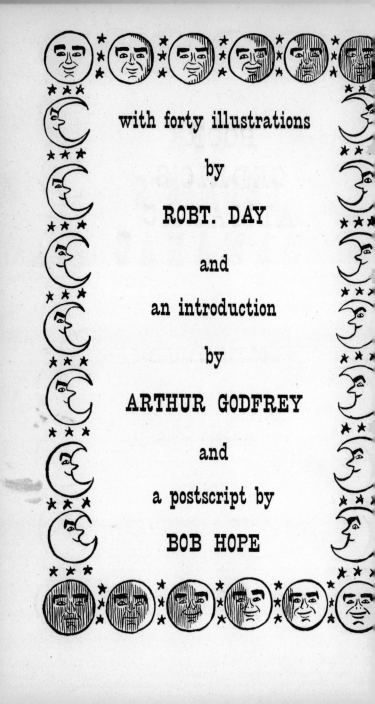

with forty illustrations

by

ROBT. DAY

and

an introduction

by

ARTHUR GODFREY

and

a postscript by

BOB HOPE

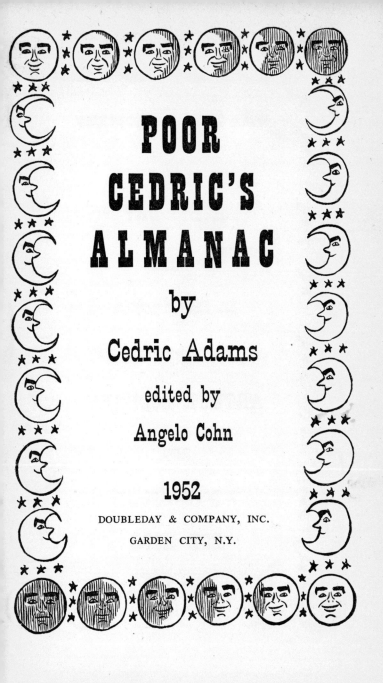

POOR CEDRIC'S ALMANAC

by

Cedric Adams

edited by

Angelo Cohn

1952

DOUBLEDAY & COMPANY, INC.

GARDEN CITY, N.Y.

Introduction
by
Arthur Godfrey

Here's a bird who wouldn't admit that the horse has passed out of American life, and he's been cleaning up ever since. Now don't get the idea that he's been following the horses. No sirree, not in any sense of the word.

What I mean is that my good friend out in Minneapolis, Cedric Adams—that's the guy I mean—is making hay on the horse-and-buggy days. Let me tell you about this Adams.

He never forgets anything. Boy, what a memory! Anything he ever did or read about, he remembers. Anything his mother or even his grandparents ever told him, he remembers. How do I know his grandparents told him? Well, he "remembers" stuff that happened a hundred years ago. And I know he can't be that old and look at his secretary the way he does.

But let's not forget the horses. Adams remembers how the hardware store used to sell buggy whips from a barrel on the sidewalk, and how the dray wagons used to squeak on winter days. He uses those memories to make items for his column in the Minneapolis *Star* and *Sunday Tribune,* or he talks about the old days over the radio on WCCO or the Columbia network. See what I mean when I say he wouldn't admit that the horse is a thing of the past?

So Adams is cleaning up on the horses, and he looks over some of the old columns and picks the best stuff to put into a book.

Now why should anybody want to share those memories? you ask. Well, if you're an old duffer of eighty you'll read stuff that makes you feel forty years younger. If you're just turning fifty, Cedric has advice that will make you want to hang around until you're eighty yourself. At thirty some of Cedric's flashbacks will make your own memories seem like pretty hot stuff; and if you're fifteen this book will give you ideas on how to live!

Take my word for it, the book is loaded with what it takes to be amusing. The guy who wrote it gives folks a run for their money in about two dozen radio spots a week, a newspaper column every day, and heaven knows how many personal appearances. He just about owns Minneapolis, that's all.

Why would anyone that busy take the time to write a book when he could be loafing on his yacht out there in Lake Minnetonka? I know he's got a yacht. He couldn't live on or off the horses all the time.

I guess he just feels like nobody really cares for him when he thinks about all those radio broadcasts going in one ear and out the other. Or that column coming in through everybody's front door with the newspaper today and going out the back way with the garbage tomorrow.

He wants something to be remembered by, and you can bet that nobody is going to toss out a book that costs three and a half bucks. But believe me, folks, this book is like everything else Adams does. That boy really knocks himself out, so you better grab a copy. It's one way you can get double your money on the horses and plenty of other subjects.

Arthur Godfrey

CONTENTS

Part One

AUTHOR, AUTHOR

If all my inhibitions were removed when I first met a person, I'd ask him about himself in this order: What do you make a month? How old are you? What is your religion? In the same approach regarding blondes, I'd ask them what they were using as a toucher-upper.

But if anybody asked me those same questions about myself, they would be just about the last ones I'd answer openly.

So in putting together this book I've left those questions unanswered. Otherwise, I hope I've given some consideration to almost everything about myself and the waggish things of the world in which I live.

This book, I keep telling myself, is not like any other . . . mainly because you don't have to read it through from start to finish like you do most books. In fact, if you read it through in that regular order you'd probably come to the end wondering what it was all about. So a word, or rather a chapter, of explanation is in order.

It's taken almost twenty years to collect the information and thoughts that now find a home in this little volume. And glad you should be that I did the collecting and saved the rest of you the chore of straining your brain on such stuff. The items, several thousand of them, are from the daily columns I've written over the years for the Minneapolis Star and Minneapolis Sunday Tribune. I like to think that I've managed to preserve a few bits of interest for almost everyone, but I hope you won't blame me for not concentrating on just one theme all the way through. After all, twenty years is a pretty long time to keep one thread of thought going.

But think of the advantage of being able to open this book and start reading an item or two wherever the fancy strikes you. Are you concerned about the weather, for instance? Well, there's a major chapter on that with weather information, hearsay and mental musings for each of our four seasons and many of the days of our year. There's a section about animals and another about their best friends, children. Also some medical gleanings—and who isn't interested in health? For the wives, a word or more that will be handy in kitchen and home; puzzles and games for your parties; out-of-the-way food hints. And, naturally, S-E-X rears its head as it does in every modern book.

To be perfectly fair, however, I think I should let you know a little about what kind of guy I am. Then you won't think I'm picking on the rest of the world. So right off the bat I'll reproduce some items from columns in which I talked about myself. Remember, if I don't seem the picture of consistency, these items come from way back when I was entirely different, even to having a longer hairline and shorter waistline. My viewpoints have changed, too. One of the surprises of gathering this material for book publication was seeing for myself how much my daily output had changed over the years. It was like gazing into a mirror that had the magic touch of reflecting the past. That would be a neat trick, indeed, if it could be accomplished, wouldn't it?

The title or heading which marks my daily newspaper column is "In This Corner," but it refers strictly to its position on the page and not to any belligerent quality. Looking into our historical mirror, here's what I had to say about myself—on November 16, 1936—back in my early years:

My city editor met me one morning with this suggestion: "Why don't you get personal in the column occasionally?" So that day I wrote about things I have and haven't done. I've never ridden a camel, worn a full dress suit, met Greta Garbo, smoked a Dunhill pipe or shot a grouse. I introduced Leatrice Joy the first time she ever broadcast, but I've never read anything by Harold Bell Wright, Zane Grey or Aristotle. Never acquired a liking for crêpes Suzette, never refused an offer of marriage, never bought any commercial bonds or securities. I've jerked sodas at the Minneapolis Chamber of Commerce, but I've never been in Mammoth Cave, never been a Boy Scout. I've never laughed at a pie-tossing comedy, written a page of copy without at least six mistakes, or bought a woman a string of pearls. I've climbed Mount Hood to watch a sunrise, but I've never played backgammon. I've never had a Turkish bath or carried a walking stick. I've never addressed a waitress as "Dearie," never bought at an auction sale, never eaten a chocolate goo; but I have slept through a third of a symphony concert. I've never slapped a sunburned back, been able to repair a light switch or smoke a cigar gracefully. I've never enjoyed a banquet where I've been on the program. I've never shaken hands with a President. I've interviewed Hinda Wausau, Mary Sunde and Lynn Fontanne in their dressing rooms, but I've never worn a straw hat, broken a mirror, been in a fight or mended my own socks. I've climbed scaffolding on a 22-floor building but I've never been usher at a wedding, learned a foreign language or attended a hockey match. I've never learned to count in bridge or said "needles and pins" when someone else and I spoke the same words simultaneously. I've never worn silk underwear, a monocle, a derby, a ring. I've never been able to finish "Anthony Adverse," "Gone With the Wind" or the Waverley Novels. I've allowed seven life insurance policies to lapse. I can't keep a checking account straight and I've never helped my wife with the dishes. I've had a manicure but I've never learned to skate, play handball or like codfish balls. I've never been psychoanalyzed. I've been swordfishing with Laurel and Hardy but never helped my wife button her dress. I've never learned to read music. I've never joined a luncheon club. I've had to ask for every pay raise I ever got but I've never ridden in a Rolls Royce. I've never asked anybody for an autograph nor have I been able to pronounce quintuplets correctly. I've played billiards with Betty Furness, chorded in E flat for Smilin' Ed McConnell and edited the first issue of Hooey Magazine, but I've never seen a woman drop her kerchief in front of me. I've never won anything in a raffle, never attended a sorority dance, taken a memory course or smoked opium. I've never eaten in a place called Dew Drop Inn. I've never bought an umbrella or carried my wife's coat. I've sold True Confessions and danced with Mrs. Morton Downey. I've never stood on my head. So there, Mr. City Editor, I hope this is what you had in mind. Oh, yes, I've never known any girl named Bridget.

The names of some of those movie stars I wrote about probably give away my age, and I must admit that my pay check and I are both fatter nowadays, but otherwise I really haven't changed too much.

If anybody ever asked me why I liked my columnist job, this would be among the top reasons: A single morning's callers included a paroled convict, a Junior Leaguer, an inventor, two would-be song writers, a bartender, two deputy sheriffs, a professional model (not bad, either) and a woman who wanted to borrow $300.

That "newspapermen meet so many interesting people" business isn't all a myth by a long shot.

DO'S AND DON'TS

Now let's shift to the dear reader's side with some Do's and Don'ts written largely from a columnist's point of view: Don't try to make a bulletin board out of a columnist by expecting him to make items out of your lodge meetings, your bazaars, your PTA gatherings, your socials and your one-act plays unless you can supply him with a twist or an angle that borders on the exceptional. Do keep in your own possession precious manuscripts, valuable clippings, original songs. A columnist's office is ordinarily one of the most disorganized places in the world and no place for anything you might value. . . . If you write to a columnist, be ready to excuse him or her if you don't receive a reply in the next mail. Legend used to have it that O. O. McIntyre, dean of them all, made a practice of answering every piece of fan mail in longhand and in lavender ink. I think that was largely myth. Inventory your own neglect of correspondence, multiply that by perhaps 100 and you'll see what position a columnist's in. . . .

DO BE A LITTLE EASY on the columnists if occasionally or periodically they fail to divert you. A writer is no different from a batter. We slip into slumps, too.

AVOID, IF YOU CAN, sending a columnist a communication

that goes something like this: "A group of us were having an argument. What time did the sun rise on April 19, 1842? Answer in your column, please." These letters are usually without a signature. Phone calls or letters are tough, too, when they make this request: "About seven or eight months ago you carried an item about such and such, could you tell me what that was?"

I've heard readers say this to columnists: "I suppose you hear this all the time, so you're probably tired of it, but I read your stuff every day. Sometimes I even turn to it first." Don't ever stop that sort of thing if you can make it sincere. That's the applause, and next to a raise in pay is probably the most welcome thing to any columnist.

OVERLOOK, IF YOU CAN, an occasional mention by any columnist of his horse, his kids, his wife, his home. In reality, we're not talking just about our horses, our kids, our wives. We're talking about yours, too, because they're perhaps not very different. It's just a little trick that we hope will sort of humanize us to our audience. . . .

Horses have I none today, but before you go too far through this book I'd better explain that the paragraph just above, written 12 years ago, is still pertinent.

Further along you'll read several essays addressed to David, who's invited to sit on my knee for each discussion. You'll also note many references to the town of Magnolia.

Both of them—David and Magnolia—are real. I hope, of course, that they will represent a person or a place just as real to you.

David, my first-born son, is a tall, lean collegian, Naval Reserve, and too rangy to sit upon my knee now. But even when he was smaller, the Father & Son Soliloquies addressed to him were really what I thought other parents were discussing with other sons.

As to Magnolia, even after 35 years in the city, I still have great love for that small town. I suppose it's really what I feel toward your home town or any other. Perhaps it's a feeling you get from having been born in a small hamlet or village. I still get a tremendous wallop out of weekly visits with one of our radio shows to smaller communities. There are pleasant experiences waiting in every one and great stories in many of our hamlets.

ON MAGNOLIA, MY HOME TOWN

One week end I visited Magnolia for the first time in about 20 years. Magnolia is a typical small town. It's down in the heart of farm-rich Rock County in southwestern Minnesota. Its population is now 270.

Well, I got the surprise of surprises. And you will, too, if you ever go back to your home town. Magnolia has gone streamlined.

On the way into Rock County, we spotted dozens of threshing rigs. Even that scene has changed. Remember how in August the old steam threshing engine with its billows of black smoke, its nearby water wagon and coal tender, used to supply power for the separator? It was one of the most picturesque of all rural scenes. The old steam engine is no more. Tractors supply the power. More economical, I suppose, but not half so colorful.

My boys had never seen a threshing crew at work, so we drove into a farmyard where they were threshing wheat. There in the yard was the same old wash bench that field hands use before every meal. The roller towel was still tacked to a tree. The bucket of water and the washbasin were about the same. Guess what was missing? It was the bar of black tar soap. You know what threshing hands are using now? The same white toilet soap that the movie stars endorse. That's what I mean by streamlining.

Just outside of Magnolia there used to be a spring alongside the road. It came out of the hillside and somebody had put a cast-iron pipe in to catch the water. The spring still flows. But that, too, has been streamlined. The WPA made a sort of rock garden out of the old spring. Fancy slabs of rock had been cemented around it; gravel paths built from the paved highway down to the spring. More practical, perhaps, but the natural beauty's gone.

Even old Tom Dean, the blacksmith at Magnolia (who

has since died), came under the modern influence. The tub, the forge, the blowers—like those made famous in the poem about the Village Smithy—were gone. In fact, the shop was renamed Dean's Machine Shop. There are hardly enough horses at Magnolia to keep the shoeing business going. It's piston reboring and welding and that sort of thing now. With that change Tom even discarded his old leather apron and grimy overalls. He was dressed in fresh denim when last I saw him.

Old Tom meant a lot to Magnolia and me. It was in his shop that I first sniffed the odor of burning hoofs. As a youngster I used to watch him pump the forge. It used to thrill me as the sparks flew from his emery wheel. Horseshoes by the dozens hung from the rafters of the shop.

SMALL TOWN CELEBRATIONS have changed a lot, too. Remember the Field and Festival days? I recall the old merry-go-round that was brought in and run by a steam engine. That's gone. The climax to all municipal celebrations in the old days was a balloon ascension. They inflated a huge canvas bag over a fire, then released it with its rider on a little seat at the bottom of the hot-air balloon. No such daring now.

Aunt Sarah, at 87, has gone streamlined with the rest of her surroundings. The roller towel that hung next to the cistern pump in the kitchen has been replaced by a paper towel roll on a bright holder. An electric range does the work of the old wood-burning stove. Milk and cream come to her house in bottles instead of little pails, and they're kept in the electric refrigerator instead of down on the basement floor.

THE NOON TRAIN has lost most of its glamor. It used to be one of those short steam locomotives with a long smokestack, shiny brass bell, a baggage car and two coaches. Bright yellow coaches. Now it's a diesel with homely stripes across the front, a harsh foghorn whistle, one car. Even the old saloon in Magnolia has been changed—into a residence. But this tiny town has its cocktail lounge with Venetian blinds and overstuffed chairs.

These are just a few of the changes. So, if you're planning a return to your home town, get set for surprises.

Whatever you do, don't long for the scenes of your childhood because I don't think you'll find them there any more.

THOUGHTS WHILE SHAVING

It's a silly notion, but I always feel like a sissy every time I dust on bath powder and yet, it's very refreshing. . . . I wonder whether most people dream in black and white or in technicolor. Guess most of my dreams have been in black and white. . . . Wish nature had been a little kinder in designing feet. There are few greater pleasures than walking barefooted in freshly cut, wet grass, or in newly turned earth, but my homely dogs inhibit me. . . . There isn't any sight much homelier than one of us fat guys in an under-

shirt. . . . Wonder if everybody gets that strange feeling of wanting to get out from under in a jiffy when driving under a viaduct when a train is passing overhead? . . . As often as I've looked at the instrument panel on my car, I don't believe I could sketch it from memory right now.

ANOTHER DAY, ANOTHER DOLLAR

Somebody once asked me how column writers worked, how columns are put together, how they're made. Well, columns are born. They're the gleam of sun on a lily pad, the dew on a petunia, the blush on a maiden's cheek. They're sheer gossamer fancy. Columnists don't work. They depend largely on inspiration. Most of us are shy woodland creatures, dwelling under ferns. Come with me today while we journey behind the scenes. Examine with me the procedure.

Columns, unlike price lists, department of agriculture bulletins or music reviews, must have "sex." So the alert columnist casts about for a good "sex" item. Babies have a universal appeal. Get a proud mother speaking about hers and you at least appeal to the mother. It's a simple matter to skim through the mail and uncover a mother-baby item; or the fact that it costs 20 cents a night to keep the word "love" lighted on a movie marquee. See how simple it all is?

Another practice in columning is what we refer to as the mooch. You spot one of the other newspaper staff members and mooch from him a paragraph. There's a sports writer, for instance, just back from a 4,989-mile jaunt to the baseball training camps. He's a generous fellow so you're apt to get a word for every mile. You cull his offer down to this: "It's now the hard 'g' in Los Angeles, and you're frowned on by natives if you say Frisco instead of the full name in that town." . . . Or you item that a pencil with an eraser on one end is rarely seen in a newspaper office.

But even more important, a column should have drama, something on how the other half lives, a tug at the heart-strings. So you offer something like this, quoted verbatim from a letter:

"Here's one for your Give Away Department. I'm a woman 53, a widow for 28 years. I spent my whole life for

*a son, but now that Mother isn't needed any more, I'm left
alone. I want to meet a man my own age. I have an equity
in some houses and apartments and no one to share my
responsibilities or my home. I work as a power machine
operator and would be willing to continue till the property
is paid up, at which time it would make two of us a comfortable living. This is no joke. I am desperate. I want
someone to belong to. Someone who needs me. He doesn't
have to have money but he must be honest and sober. I'm
no prize package, but I'm no battle-axe, either. I can't go
on alone. Please do something for me. I am not cheap nor
bold—just blue.*

(signed) "A Brokenhearted Mother."

A woman's heart crying out that sincerely always gets
me, and after carrying that item in my column there has
been no end to similar requests.

In most cases I try to switch the inquiries to columnists
who specialize in advice to the lovelorn.

But when I feel the letters make especially good copy or
have some exceptional appeal, I've never been above de-
voting my little department of the paper to encouraging
the mating instinct. Right after World War II, it seemed,
those requests reached a peak in both numbers and tragic
pleading. I'd like to recall some of the items we carried,
with most interesting results, during just the first three
months of 1948. Here's from a column in which I looked
for a mate for a woman who became a sort of symbol,
called Widow No. 1.

I am not running any kind of matrimonial bureau and
realize that as a result of the one appeal I could be flooded
with similar requests. The first letter from this woman went
back two or three months before anything was printed. She
was laying the groundwork, but I didn't know it at the time.
She wanted to know just exactly how my mail was handled.
Did I read every letter that came in? How many secretaries
opened and read the mail before it reached my desk? Did
I take letters sent in confidence and make public property
of them? Would I scoff at her intimate confessions? I had
no idea what she might be getting at. I had visions of hav-

ing some crime confessed to me. That's how far I missed
the boat. . . .

A later letter said frankly that she wanted a man. I don't
recall in all my years of newspapering such complete, un-
restrained outpouring of the human heart as this woman
gave. I couldn't reveal too much about her because she
might have been readily recognized in her home town. She
was a widow. There's one in every town. Even Magnolia
has a widow. Investments gave her a comfortable living. A
lot of widows have those. Judging from the snapshot she en-
closed, she was rather attractive, in her 40's. No Miss
America, but how many Miss Americas are there? And I've
seen many a woman in her 40's about whom you could say,
"There's a lot of miles in the old bus yet." Now then, what
to do about her? Here's the plan presented at the time:

To any bachelor or widower willing to take a chance and
write a plain, unadulterated, forthright letter about himself,
maybe include a snapshot, present this widow with the
credentials deemed proper under the circumstances, I
offered to see that his letter reached her hands. The replies
received were not to be opened, naturally. There was no
publicity about the authors of the letters. In other words,
the column served simply as a clearinghouse in an attempt
to get two kindred souls together.

A week later, like a congressman reporting to his constituents, I wrote that the mail for Widow No. 1 produced
119 applicants, if we could call them that.

One saddening thing happened. I discovered that the
widow was not a subscriber to my newspaper. That hurt, of
course. But you may imagine her surprise when she went to
her mailbox and discovered that first avalanche of letters all
marked, "The Widow." She guessed from the contents of
the letters what must have occurred, and our circulation
jumped at least one right there.

"For goodness' sakes," she wrote, "seal the next bundle
you send. I'm afraid our local post office will close while
the employes take time out for a little pleasure reading.

"So much fun I haven't had in years. I find that it isn't a
matter of the men qualifying. It is I who must meet certain
requirements. For instance, I must wear high heels, prefer-

ably gray suede, and white high-heeled overshoes with fur on the top. I must love fishing if I want another applicant. One insisted that I like trapping. It was surprising to note how many had new cars or a truck and two or three motherless children. . . .

"One woman wrote that her brother-in-law should have a wife but he's too bashful to seek one.

"Most surprising was the number of other widows who wanted my 'overflow' or 'leftovers' as they put it. So you see, Cedric, you weren't simply speaking for one, shall we say, lost soul. There are women all over with a problem similar to mine."

One of the most gratifying results of that little project was the letter from Widow No. 2. She wrote:

"Cedric, you angel, you savior of lonesome women, you are the fairy godfather to us all. In all seriousness, the project is very good. After all, what does a human need and want more than anything else? Another human for companionship. I'll tell you my wish: I need a pipe smoker in front of my fireplace, a man's socks to darn, shirts to iron and a genial host at the head of my table. I'm too young to live alone the rest of my life. I'm 33, have two lovely children (curly-haired), a home all paid for, a new Dodge and am a scrumptious cook. Wouldn't it be nice if I could meet a nice young widower with two or three small children who need a mother as much as mine need a father?

"People could live useful and happy lives together if only their paths would cross. Why don't you start a club for us?"

The interest evinced in letters to and from our Widow No. 1 and Widow No. 2, led to this last follow-up: I want to say that I'm sincerely sympathetic toward these lonesome souls. Solitude is a desirable condition now and then, but when it becomes habitual, it can be rather menacing. Those of us who are surrounded constantly by friends or families may be inclined to forget how dreadful loneliness can become. Widow No. 2 took the trouble to report on the reflection of loneliness she found in letters that were forwarded to her. She writes:

"I have just had 15 proposals of marriage. As I read the letters I am more convinced than ever that there should be a club where people might meet and find companionship. The reason that a lot of people don't meet others is because the proper opportunity isn't presented. I can't help it, Cedric, I just love all these people who wrote. I wish I could help all of them. One man wrote: 'My wife died of cancer a year ago, and I have two little boys who tease me to get them a Mama.'

"Honestly, the tears are running down my face right now as I write. I know what that is because I've heard my own children say, 'I wish we had a daddy to have fun with like the other kids do.' . . .

"Another one wrote, 'What do you mean calling Adams the savior of lonesome women? How about us men? I work hard all day, then I come home, cook supper, wash and iron, scrub the house and the kids. I find I have little time left to go out and look for a companion. And I also get tired of eating my own cooking. The kids grow a little weary of it, too. Lots of luck to you if you can, through any means, promote a club for us lonesome lost souls.' "

THE CASE OF THE UNWED COUNTESS

SO FANTASTIC, SO BIZARRE IS THE NEXT TALE that it will probably sound incredible to you. But I checked every detail carefully in this incident, also one of the 1948 items. She was probably the most woeful human being I have ever encountered. And there were reasons galore for her misery.

This is the story: A Hungarian countess had to find a husband and she would have to meet, woo and win him in two short weeks. . . .

We'll call her Illona. That isn't her name, but she needs that much protection. Her voice was soft, her accent very pleasant. It soon became obvious that she was a cultured young woman. She was 24, a Hungarian, born in Vienna, a college graduate, spent three years in the ballet. Her father was a former Hungarian minister to Austria before the family lost everything in World War II.

After the war was over, she met a GI at a party in Salzburg. They fell in love immediately. He was there for three months. They saw each other almost every night, danced together, took long walks through the countryside. He told her about America, about his family, about his ambitions. They became engaged. "As soon as I get home, I'll send for you," he promised her. "You'll like America. You'll like my home town. It's in what we call the Midwest." They planned their home, their future together. It wasn't unlike thousands of other romances.

His army hitch ended and he returned to America. For two years they wrote letters regularly, added to the attachment they had for each other. For two years she read his letters over and over again. She relived all the happiness they had had together in Salzburg. She tried to picture America. She studied English. She wondered how his family would accept her.

Finally one of his letters contained the money for her plane passage to America. He had posted the $500 bond necessary to bring her over. It took seven months to get a visa and arrange her trip to the United States. She kept writing in the meantime. So did he. Their letters were filled with plans for their marriage. Then her plane landed in Washington. She hurried to Minneapolis. She had other wartime friends in Minneapolis, a young married couple. She and her GI fiancé were to meet at the home of this couple.

SHE'LL NEVER FORGET THAT DAY. She hadn't seen him for two years, remember. She wondered if he had changed. She wondered what he'd look like in civilian clothes. She thought of what joy it would be to have him in her arms once more, to ruffle his eyebrows and pinch his chin and tweak his ears and squeeze his hands and listen to his voice again.

She gazed out the window of the home where she was staying. "Here he comes!" she shouted. Her heart danced, but not for long. She sensed something as he walked in the door. He was no longer the gay, spirited lover she had known in Salzburg. They embraced, but it was a cold, depressed embrace. She spoke intuitively. "Tell me, dear, what is it?" The scene was short. Their arms dropped to their sides. Instinctively they braced themselves—he for the blow he was about to deliver, she for the blow she was about to receive. . . .

"I've been married for three months," he told her.

"Get out of my sight," she screamed, "get out, get out!"

He left. Four weeks passed. She hardly ate. Every night was sleepless. She still looked dazed that day in my office. "I will NOT go back to Hungary," she said emphatically. "I cannot go back. My family will not have me, my country will not have me. My family disapproved of my contemplated marriage from the beginning. We are in the Russian zone. The Communists have lists of people who fraternized with the Americans. They have posted all who went to capitalistic America. I am now their enemy. I cannot go back."

Her visa set forth, however, that unless she married a former GI by a certain date, she must return to her native Hungary. That deadline was only two weeks away.

"I have come to love America even in my bitterness," she said. "Now I must marry a GI and I must do it within the next two weeks."

"What kind of husband would you like?" I asked her.

"I prefer a city man, somebody between 25 and 45. I do not like extremely young boys. Religion is not too important. I can cook. I love to dance. I am educated. I am fond of children. I would like a man of good character, a man who enjoys the nice things of life." That was her story. Illona was five feet four, weighed 120 pounds, dressed conservatively, had soft blue eyes, pretty teeth, a trim figure. A Hungarian countess wanting a husband and needing him within two weeks.

THEN CAME THE PITCH: If this young woman without a country appeals to any ex-GI or anybody who was in the war, I wrote, she would like to have the prospect get in touch with her through my office. All confidential, of course.

Within a week Illona, our Hungarian countess, probably set a world record. She's the only woman I've ever heard of who had 1,786 proposals of marriage. Illona received more than 2,000 pieces of mail, five telegrams, two bouquets of American Beauty roses, two boxes of candy and $30 in cash from three men who just wanted to lighten her burden if they could. One man who stated in his letter that he was out of work told her that he knew how hard life was and that after he had read of her misery he felt she needed the dollar more than he did.

Within the first day after I wrote about Illona, I counted 309 telephone calls. In some cases, I gave the callers Illona's telephone number in Minneapolis. They got in touch with her immediately. By nightfall she had personally interviewed five of her 1,786 prospects. By midnight that day she had two definite proposals. Both men had talked to her, looked her over carefully and said, in probably an unromantic way, "If you want to marry me, I will marry you." That probably reaches an all-time high in whirlwind romances.

Through the week, Illona accepted three dates.

THE FIRST ONE was a man of 32, an ex-army officer. After they met, he suggested a dinner. He was considerate enough to include Illona's Minneapolis host and hostess. They ate in a hotel. They danced. He was a wonderful dancer. They had a very good time. He hadn't proposed within the week.

THE SECOND DATE was a 27-year-old ex-GI. The two of them drove out of the city to Lake Minnetonka. They wound up at dinner and he proposed. He told her that if she didn't find anybody else she liked better, he'd marry her.

DATE NO. 3 was a man from outside Minneapolis. And here's a kicker: He turned out to be a personal friend of the family with whom Illona was staying. There was a little embarrassment for a moment. They all laughed about it. The two of them dined at a suburban café. He had arranged for a private dining room. The moment they had finished their dessert, he proposed. . . .

Offers weren't all for marriage. One man, 42, said he recognized her plight, offered her a job, said he would loan her money, give her legal counsel if she needed it. A group of 12 Minneapolis attorneys who eat together every noon called to offer their collective services as a sort of steering committee. A score of Hungarians living in the area wrote and offered help. . . .

Over the first week end Illona was a changed young lady. Her future seemed brighter, her appetite had returned, and when the excitement of the proposals had diminished, she began to sleep. A changed woman she was, if I ever saw one. Her spirit had been revived. She actually glowed. . . .

NOW LET'S EXAMINE SOME OF THE PROPOSALS. One young ex-GI sent her a ticket to a concert. His seat was next to hers. A pleasant surrounding to woo, indeed. Unfortunately, it didn't work because a delay in forwarding the mail brought the ticket to Illona one day too late. One young man drove 200 miles. . . .

RICHES WERE WITHIN HER REACH, TOO. One of the prospects wrote from California, offered to pay her airplane fare to California for the meeting. Business prevented him from making the trip, but wouldn't she come out? He told her of his two homes, one in Minneapolis, a beach home in California. He told her of his bank balance, that his business was sound, his income sufficient to make them very comfortable and, he hoped, happy. . . .

There was gratitude in Illona's heart. She couldn't physically answer all the letters she received. She had a time just reading them. The spokesman for the group of attorneys called a few days later to report that her permanent residence in the United States would be established. Out of the 1,786 proposals, she selected one.

It was quite a week for me, too, with men sidling up to me and surreptitiously asking for information about her. We had a couple of laughs out of it, though. This telegram came from Rochester, Minnesota: "Dear Cupid—As long as you're in the business, how about a helping hand here? —Gert, Elaine and Celeste."

Illona married a native of North Dakota who was a graduate of the University of Minnesota. He had been a captain in the army, became a mechanical engineer. The two of them had a brief and quiet honeymoon, are now living quietly in one of our northern cities. Strong, indeed, was their desire to keep out of the limelight. *LOOK* Magazine sent two representatives out to get the complete story. *LOOK'S* rates for that sort of thing are very attractive, too. The pair turned the offer down. The radio program, "We the People," was extremely anxious to have the two of them appear on the network. It could have meant a honeymoon trip into New York, lavish entertainment for them and a tidy little sum. That was rejected also, and any number of other offers that might have made it harder to live happily ever after.

Not all of a columnist's work consists of bringing lovers together. Sometimes I have to pause to change a typewriter ribbon. Ugh, how I hate that job, even though a new ribbon makes so much difference that it's a shame to cling to the old one. Just for fun this time I measured the length of the ribbon—25 feet of the stuff. The experts claim a typewriter ribbon should be changed in exactly 16 seconds. They also say that only a chump gets ink-stained fingers in the process. Give your steno the test and be sure to look at her paws when she's through. This Rotund Reporter has been changing typewriter ribbons for more than 25 years and I still can't make it in less than 15 minutes. And I always have to add another 10 minutes for cleaning up. Well, I just noticed for the first time that there are two units in the type machine keyboard that come in alphabetical sequence—*fgh* and *jkl*. Enjoy writing *property* on a typewriter because the *erty* are or is in a line. But look what you have to do to write *opq*. The *p* and *q* are miles apart. A guy could sit all day and figure out stuff. Guess I'd better quit, though, and do some work.

INTELLIGENCE

The most uninteresting chap
I think I ever knew
Had thousands of remarks on tap
And all of them were true.
He bored me to a final tear
Before he went away
Because he didn't care to hear
The things I had to say.

The woman I've enjoyed the most
Had neither charm nor wit;
She didn't even have the ghost
Of knowledge to transmit.
But with what grace she gently bent—
A flower on its stalk—
And listened meek and reverent
When I desired to talk.

The dullest people, as a rule,
Possess the largest brains;
The cleverest man may be a fool
Because the fact remains
That brilliance not at all descends
From erudition's tree—
One joins my group of clever friends
By listening to ME!

SELF-DEFENSE DEPT.

Four hundred and nineteen miles of driving in swirling snow with visibility at times extending about as far as the car's radiator ornament. That was what our little traveling unit had in going down to Luverne, Minnesota, to help celebrate the 25th anniversary of the Rock County Co-operative Oil company. We missed the noon broadcast by 15 minutes and weren't able to get back to Minneapolis for the 10 p.m., but out of something like 19 hours of travel I learned several things. After we had put on our show and were trying to decide whether to head back or stay over, a Rock County resident got me off in a corner. He was a sincere guy. He wasn't trying to butt into somebody else's business. His conversation went something like this: "What do you do this for? Why do you take all these chances? Are you money-hungry or are you shy a few marbles?" Unfortunately I didn't have time to give him a full explanation. But his query did start me thinking along those lines as we bucked our way home. . . .

That money-hungry expression sort of got me. I don't know why so many persons translate work into that single term. I'm sure that if they examined their own lives they'd find dough isn't their only compensation. Then why do they charge others with that motivation? If I were going to say to myself, how much is it going to be worth to fight a storm for nearly 24 hours or to take chances of night travel or even walk from the parking lot to the office, I'm confident that no employer would be willing to pay what I thought it would be worth in the dollars of today. That trip in the snowstorm is one of those things that cannot and should not be reduced to monetary terms. Walking out on that stage in Luverne to be met by the warm applause of a thousand farmers and friends right from my old home county is something you can't hang a dollar sign on. . . .

There was a spirit in others which I observed that was a very compensating thing. When we got as far as Mankato, less than halfway, I felt maybe we should have a little conference among the troupe. If they were nervous I didn't want to subject them to real or imagined dangers of the rest of the journey. This was the sentiment they expressed: "Don't forget, those people down there are expecting us. They all did some driving to get there. We can't disappoint them. Let's keep going." That we did, and there again is that curious kind of compensation. The troupe wasn't thinking of money. They had a job to do and they wanted to do it. Even under strenuous conditions, they found their major satisfaction in keeping their obligations. Maybe it's the ham in all of us. Maybe we like to get out in front of our fellowmen, perform and then hear that applause. Could be that it's like a pat on the back from the boss or a gold watch or a plaque that workers get at the end of 25 years of service. Or—maybe we are shy a few marbles. . . .

IF'S

We all like to project ourselves into somebody else's business, personality or habits. That is what I'm going to do now with some "If's." For instance, if I were a waitress and had to wear a short-sleeved uniform, I'd be extremely careful about keeping my elbows clean. And I'd have to have a pretty set of pins, if I were a young girl, before I could let myself go for those white overshoes.

If I were a society editor on a metropolitan daily, once in a great while I'd go hog-wild on reporting a wedding. I'd function just like a sports writer does, for instance, or a movie or dramatic critic. They don't heap praise on every event they witness, and there is no reason why a society editor should. All brides simply do not look lovely. And society notes would have more avid readers if, occasionally, a drop of frankness were put in. When Mr. and Mrs. John Johnson entertain friends from Kansas City over the week end, if I were society editor, I'd add, "and they hope they don't stay any longer." If I were a big shot or even a junior executive I doubt whether I'd ever have a secretary start my phone calls. And if I did, I'd be sure to be right on the line and waiting for the party I had asked her to get.

If I were a restaurant proprietor, I'd print up a bunch of fake menu cards, label them as such and hand them to patrons just to toy with after they ordered from the real menu.

If ever I progress in the field of writing to the point where I'm writing the wordage for insurance policies, I vow that I shall change every paragraph beginning with: "If, at the death of the insured." There's no special need for insurance policies to imply that they've been brooding for years on the unalterable fact that I am going to die.

If I ever run across a good psychiatrist, I'm going to ask him why it is that every time I go in a strange bathroom where there are scales and guest towels I always test the scales, even though I know my exact bedside weight, and always pass up the guest towels to use a corner of a nearby bath towel.

If I were a movie, dramatic, book or art critic, I'd remember this before I took my place on the well-known limb. The Chicago Times back in 1865 evaluated Lincoln's Gettysburg Address and commented thusly on it the next day: "The cheek of every American must tingle with shame as he reads the silly, flat and dishwatery utterances of a

man who has to be pointed out to intelligent foreigners as the President of the United States."

Suppressed Desire: To see a hotel manager swiping a towel at a patron's home.

THINGS THAT I CAN GET ALONG WITHOUT

● The crease that's left across the knees of my trousers after Ma hangs them over one of those wire hangers.

● The movie usher who grabs at my coat tails as I enter a theater to hand me those useless little stubs.

● Woman who, in mixed company, sits toying with a cigaret, obviously too lazy to light it and waiting for somebody to help her.

● Golf partners, whose score is only slightly better than mine, who inform me after every shot that I'm either gripping the club too tightly or too loosely.

● Beach playboys whose self-expression takes the form of gymnastics in the sand, including grappling, cartwheels, handstands, heel kicking.

● Magazine editors who either conceal or omit page numbers after the first five pages.

● Hotel clerks who greet you with, "What sort of room would you like?" But they don't even give you the slightest hint of their rates or what they have to offer.

● Sopranos with no more than six vocal lessons who organize a little group singing at parties as a ruse to get their own pipes heard above the rest.

● Yes, I can get along without all these folks, but without them I'd just have to work harder to fill another column.

A COLUMN TALKS TO ITSELF

Whuuups, here I go off the press. I'm quite a bit like a human—I never know where I'm going to wind up. My fate is uncertain, indeed. This mail room is a nice airy place. Wouldn't mind staying right here. No such luck. Here I go into the wiring machine. Gosh, they really pack us into these bundles. What a strong arm gee he was. He pitched me out of there as though he thought I had no feelings at all. Oh, we're going for a ride. Springs in this truck aren't too hot. This fresh air feels good after that stuffy pressroom. I hope I get out into South Dakota some place. Oh, dear, another disappointment. That ride was so short I didn't even get a chance to relax and enjoy it. So this is what they mean by a newsstand, huh? Here I am, right on top of the stack. I'd like to take a squint at the outside world. I wish I were Page One. That guy really knows what's going on. I can hear voices, though.

Imagine that, I'm going to the football game. I hope he turns me around so I can get a glimpse of the game. This must be an overcoat pocket I'm in now. Sounds like he's with his wife. She's doing all the talking and all he does is grunt. Now he's shoving a package in here along with me. Why didn't he put that on the other side? Wow. I think it's cheese. Why in the world would he be taking cheese to a football game? I get it. She's been shopping and she found a bargain in cheese so she bought it and she's making him carry it. That's probably what he was grunting about. It's sure stuffy in here now. Oh, we're going over by streetcar.

Are we ever packed in here. Me and the cheese. I'm glad I'm not getting this cozy with a dozen eggs. We'd have albumen all over the place. Come to think of it, I'm a little sore at that Adams guy. I make his living for him and what does he do but get me into some gent's overcoat pocket snuggled up against a batch of cheese. I could be dining with some beautiful girl if I got the right breaks. But I don't suppose that would last long, either. You get a glance or two and you're tossed aside. I remember one of my brothers got into an apartment where they had a dog. His was a miserable life. I'll take this cheese and like it, I guess.

We must be near the stadium. I can hear the tramp of feet and the far-off band music. The Old Girl wants a chrysanthemum. Did he let out a grunt on that one. That's telling her, Bub. He said he could get a bushel of flowers on the way home for a buck. And she says, "But Homecoming comes only once a year." And he says, "Yeah, but them bucks don't grow on bushes." Pretty intelligent conversation I got into. Then she says, "You spend 5 cents for a paper, 10 cents for a streetcar token and you think you're giving me the time of my life." And he says, "These football tickets ain't sent out to you for box tops, don't forget." It was the Old Girl who grunted that time. I'm out of the pocket, anyway.

What a relief to get away from that cheese. Neither one of them has given me a tumble yet. He's reading the lineup on Page One. I wish Adams had put something in here about football. Maybe I'd get a break. She's on her high horse again. "You could at least give me part of that paper to sit on," she mumbles. I knew it. Here I go. Right down underneath her. Ooooohhh, she must weigh a ton. Now I'm glad I'm not Page One. That fur coat of hers must be mighty ticklish. I've never been so squeezed in my life.

There goes the kickoff. I wish they had one of those every four seconds. It's my only chance to get a little air. What a relief when she stands up and takes her weight off me. Whuups, she hit bottom again. I don't think I can take four quarters of this. And besides she's such an old wigglesticks. Every time she moves she tears me. There goes part of me underneath the seat. There goes a hunk fluttering through the air. One more move and I'm finished. Yup, there it is. . . . It's odd to think we might have been Sun, Moon, and Stars unto each other—only I turned down one little street as you went up another. Fate.

FEARS & PHOBIAS

Wonder if anybody else gets the fidgets while standing near the railroad tracks when a locomotive whizzes by. When I was a child somebody told me that if I stood too close to the engine when it passed it would suck me right into it, and I've had the phobia ever since.

It always irritates me considerably to push an elevator button and then have another customer, who just watched me push the button, come up and give the same button another push. Makes me think he doesn't trust me.

Wonder if all humans have the same sensation of trembling that I get every time I board or get off an escalator?

THE CELLAR STEPS

Now, then, I want to take you back again to Magnolia where we had a cellar. There was a little back hall and off that hall were the cellar stairs. Even the hall had a sort of romance to it. Some pots and pans and the lantern hung on the wall. On the floor in the hall we kept the five-gallon can of kerosene with the potato in the snout. And if it hadn't been for the cellar stairs in Magnolia's homes, I don't believe the weekly paper would have ever had any front page news. A week that went by without some woman falling down her cellar steps was a pretty dull week. But I loved those cellar stairs. Carpeting? I should say not. The carpenter took a plank, see, and he sawed down and then over and then down and over and put boards where the notches came and that made the steps down into the cellar. . . . You got down there with a little providential help, but that was when you began to enjoy the cellar. It didn't go under the whole house. It was just a hole that was dug under maybe two or three rooms. The walls went up so high and then there was a sort of shelf that led over to the window.

It was the stuff you found down in the cellar that made it interesting. There were always two or three five-gallon crocks of pickles. Each crock had a white slime on top of it that had bubbles in it, and atop the pickles was a big plate with a rock on it. A nice clean rock.

Over in another corner were the potatoes that used to sprout along about April. Some carrots and rutabagas were buried in a box of sand in another corner. . . . There was a table where we used to put the milk. We always kept it in pans so you could skim the cream off easily. Even on the hottest July day it always was fairly cool down there in the cellar.

There was a dampness to the air, but after you'd been down there a minute you got so you liked it. Our dog used to go down there a lot in the summertime. There was always a sort of mystery as to what was back of our cellar steps. I never did probe around back there. I used to have to clean out the cellar a couple of times a year, but I never got back there. I think maybe it was the cobwebs that kept me out more than anything. But I'll bet to this day the same stuff is back of those cellar steps that was there 35 years ago. We kept a lot of preserves and that kind of stuff on shelves made out of old orange crates. All the empty fruit jars were down there, too. . . . There lurks in me a yearning for the simple things. I guess that's why, in planning my postwar home, I'm going to brush aside any plans for a modern basement. Away with rumpus rooms and machine-run heating plants and square-tubbed laundries. Give me the damp, the earthy smell, the dust-laden crevices of a cellar. Won't you join me? I'll help you dig yours.

Other things I haven't thought about for years: The fancy-handled buttonhook that was part of my mother's dresser set . . . Those chimes that were made out of thin pieces of glass suspended on threads and made music when the wind swayed the glass . . . That medicinal smell that old Doc Sullivan always had about his person . . . The green-visored white caps that kids always got free in the spring with a flour ad printed across the front . . . The horse-chawed hitching posts that used to line the main street in Magnolia . . . The soap ad that always asked, "Have you a little fairy in your home?" . . . The isinglass doors on the old base-burner whose ruddy glow gave the finest welcome in a home you could possibly have . . . The lumps my long underwear used to make underneath my black-ribbed stockings when I had to fold it around the ankles in wintertime.

More Flashbacks: Of course you recall the huge coffee grinders with two big wheels and the bell-shaped top into which the coffee beans were poured by the grocer for grinding. Candy hearts with such stirring messages as "Oh, You Kid!" printed on them. Doorbells with a handle on them you had to turn to make the bell function. The thrill you got when you moved into the third grade and got a desk with an inkwell in it. The sofa pillows that pictured either the White House steps or an ocean wave. The forerunner of the electric pad—a bag of hot fried onions placed on your chest. When the small-town editor met all trains and asked every departing townsman where he was going and when he would return. When after every meal the dishes were washed and put right back in their places on the table ready for the next meal and the "set" table was covered with a cloth in the interim. The milliner who always had a "trimmer" come out from the city every fall and spring to make pattern hats. The huge ash pile that collected at the back of every house during the winter. Familiar, are they?

THINGS I CONSIDER IMPORTANT

Any time you're introduced to a blind person, you should speak first. This places you for the sightless one and also tells him in what direction to hold out his hand.

There's something about an elderly man who spills cigar ashes on his vest that I like. Maybe it's that his spilled ashes indicate a casual method of living. . . .

Can't remember any woman with dimples whom I wouldn't call attractive.

BONER DEPT.

Don't get the idea from some of the foregoing items that a columnist's life is all beer, skittles and memories to replace digging for facts. Each day opens up brand-new possibilities in this column-writing and news-broadcasting business of mine for offending someone.

At least once I had a whole industry up in arms. On a news broadcast one evening I interviewed a young lady who had just been made stewardess for a crack train. In the course of our chatter I suggested that there should be a law against children having bananas on trains. Now, on the face of that remark, you wouldn't think there was any dynamite in it, would you? But it was a bombshell as far as the banana industry was concerned. Early next morning I was called and informed that I shouldn't be going around trying to dissuade kids from gnawing on the yellow fruit delicacy. Bananas, I was told, are exceptionally good for kids. They are considered by medical authorities to be one of the most energizing and healthful of foods. Mashed ripe bananas, the industry also told me, make up the very first solid food for most babies. Mr. Banana Fellow, I apologize.

One of the toppers in the Adams Boner Department came when I listed the number of the Division of Employment and Security (for defense registration purposes) as Room 400 in our Transportation Building. That happened to be the Ladies' Rest Room.

There's one other thing about this job. When you get jumped on, those who do the jumping do it thoroughly. In a little Thought While Shaving once I remarked that I couldn't remember having made a practical application of geometry since I went through the stuff in high school. You'd never dream there were so many geometry lovers, people who worship those angles and those parallelograms or whatever they were. You say one word against the right side of a triangle and those geometricians are ready to crawl down your throat dragging an obtuse angle behind them. Most uncomfortable that is, too. Here's a typical example of the type of letter that came in as a protest. And you can see how sensitive this geometry lover is.

"When I used to be a schoolteacher, I taught geometry in high school. It was such a pleasure to be unfolding that beautiful study to young boys and girls. Geometry is representative of the high degree of civilization attained by the Greek empire. Nor has it been changed appreciably since it was first so beautifully organized by the great Greek teacher, Euclid. Do you not admire the modern geometric designs in our various tiled and linoleum floors? Don't the arrangements of triangles and beams and parallels in our modern bridges and skyscrapers intrigue you? You must have viewed cities and the countryside from a plane to note the squares and the triangles and the patterns? Indeed, geometry ranks very high in our educational system today and may it always remain, you columnists notwithstanding."

I must have had algebra and geometry and physics all right after lunch in high school and probably dozed through those sessions. I took a special look at the tile on our bathroom floor. I was unmoved.

FATHER & SON SOLILOQUY ON FATHER'S DAY

Come on, boys, let's the four of us get down on the floor and we'll have a little visit together. This is Father's Day, you know. Remember awhile ago it was Mother's Day. It's Pa's turn now. I know your mother has told you that I am supposed to be the kingpin around here today and that she has schooled you in the speeches you'll make when you hand me your little gifts. This is one day when your mother is very obvious. On all other days mothers are pretty subtle. That means they're cunning like a fox. When they're nice to us fathers, we don't know what they might have up their sleeves. But today, mothers and children all over the land are going to be nice to their fathers as a sort of tradition.

I don't expect your mother to hold out, though. Along about 4:30 this afternoon I expect her to say, "Hasn't this been a glorious Father's Day?"

Then the next breath will sound something like this: "I saw the best washing machine advertised in the paper today," or "Do you think those printed slacks would look nice on me?" . . .

And Pa, having been made a lot of all day, will probably go for those or similar items. Anyway, it's a good day for fathers to sort of take stock of themselves, to look back over the year, to see what kind of fathers we've been. That's what I want to do with you boys for just a little while this morning. But, first of all, I want to tell the washing-machine salesmen not to come trotting out tomorrow morning, because maybe it won't be washing machines that she'll pick on. . . .

Now, let's go back over the year and see how things stack up. Ric, you remember the other morning when you caught Pa just as he was going to work. I recall how you asked, "Pa, will you fix my trike?" And I told you that I couldn't then because I had to go to work. Remember that? Well, that was a pretty big mistake for Pa to make. I should have realized that the trike is the biggest thing in your life now and a whole day without it means a lot more than Pa's getting to work five or ten minutes later. Just the other day Pa took his car in to get it fixed and, when the mechanic said he couldn't do it right away, I remember that I didn't like it any too well. That day with the trike got me, if you must know. I could see Ric's blue eyes looking up at me asking for that one little favor. And his look of disappointment haunted me all day.

And, David, that trick of yours of waiting till Pa gets sprawled out reading the paper and then coming up and asking me to read Dick Tracy to you. Several times I've sent you to your mother to let her read the comics. That's a bum deal. I'm not going to do it any more. If you've shown enough interest in Pa to ask him to do something, then I'm not going to alienate that affection by sidetracking you to your mother.

I think maybe if fathers forgot some of their own problems when they're around their kids and considered more deeply the problems that, at the moment, concern the youngsters, we'd be better off all around.

Now here's a secret I want to let you boys in on, too. Not even your mother knows about this yet. You know how she saved those first little booties of yours. Somehow mothers always have a sentimental attachment for babies' booties. Well, down in Pa's desk at the office I have tucked away three pairs of old shoes that you boys have worn. The laces are out, the shoes are scuffed, the heels run over. They're no good to anyone except Pa. And when the going gets a little rough or things seem to be breaking on the dark side, I open that drawer for a long look at those shoes. That does something to me. Those old shoes pep me up when I imagine you boys running and playing and living life with scarcely a care.

Maybe if all fathers had some kind of symbolism that would function for them, it'd help. For instance, if a father were speeding across Forty-fourth Street and suddenly he thought of a pair of shoes, maybe that would remind him of a boy who might be darting out into the street and he'd slow down to a safer speed.

Well, that's what I mean when I said that Father's Day

is a good time to take inventory. This business of being a father is a pretty serious matter, and sometimes we don't give it quite the attention we should. I don't want you guys to get the idea that Pa is going to be a pushover for any little thing you boys might want, but I will promise you right here and now that I will be more considerate of what you suggest.

This Father's Day is a good time to bring this up, too. Your mother does all the wrestling in connection with getting you boys to bed. She handles the neck and ear scrubbing department. And then Pa comes along and cashes in the kisses. You don't know it, but every night before I go to bed I sneak into your rooms and give each of you a smack on the cheek, and if there's a father who has neglected or quit that custom, let him revive it tonight. It's the one way that any father can get his full compensation.

And remember this: Today is a sacred day. It's Father's Day, so no fist fights.

You may consider all those things I've written about myself and my more personal attitudes a sample of what lies ahead. So plunge right in and read wherever your interest happens to be. The rest of this book, I keep telling myself, has plenty of information in 9,872 items, numerous laughs, 352 pages, 40 cartoons and almost anything you'd care to consider. But for plot, frankly, it isn't worth the price. Don't say I didn't warn you, but please read on anyway.

Oh, yes, I always like to end each day's column, if possible, with a good sock item. So here it is for this chapter: Whales travel in pods, not schools.

Part Two

WEATHER

"You never know you have a stomach," the wise old Chinese used to say, "until something goes wrong with it." And I suppose the same thing could be said about the weather. Weather talk is never out of season, but we're never much aware of the weather until something goes wrong with it. The worse it is, the more it gets talked about.

That seems like a pretty negative approach, however, and someday I hope to start a crusade to glorify the "usual" weather instead of always dwelling on the unusual. If we looked at it honestly, I suppose we'd have to admit that most of the weather is really pretty decent for most people. So why the hypochondriac approach?

Weather is important stuff, too. It's the weather that serves as the common ground where man meets nature.

I suppose that's why some of the smartest guys in history spent their lives studying the weather. Up to this point, however, they've had a lot more success classifying it than controlling it. And classify it they did, into days, weeks, months and seasons that the rest of us with ordinary brain equipment can retain in our noodles.

For all the scientific effort over the centuries, however, most people recognize just two kinds of weather—good and bad. And about all the attention they really give it is to curse it when it's bad. That's why I think there ought to be a movement to emphasize the "usual" as far as weather is concerned.

In our present scheme of things, for instance, suppose that the weather on the official first day of spring were all that it was supposed to be. The kind of spring day poets sing about. A clear sky with just wisps of clouds being blown across by brisk but warm wind and plenty of sunshine to make everything look bright and bring out the first bits of fresh greenery. What would happen? Just exactly nothing in this negative world of ours. Certainly no managing editor would ever ask his headline writers to go into typographic ecstasy heralding the perfect spring day.

But just let a few out-of-season snowflakes find their way down after the calendar says it is supposed to be spring, and the newspaper is full of copy emphasizing the freak weather.

Or take another example that just about all of you experience in the extreme of two seasons, summer and winter. Hardly a man is now alive who hasn't been pestered by some wag who picks a day when the mercury is at 20 below zero to ask, "Is it cold enough for you?" Or the summer opposite, "Is it hot enough for you?" when the thermometer is boiling up around 100 degrees.

But did anybody ever open weather talk by asking, "Is it usual enough for you?" Not on your life.

Yet there are good things about every season, and a lot of human activity is tied to the changing weather in different parts of the year.

Butter and egg men (the down-on-the-farm variety, not the Broadway song, skirt and step boys) literally live by the seasons, as do clothing manufacturers, athletes, department-store Santa Clauses and sports writers.

Weatherwise, however, the housewife has more interest in conditions than most of those people who make or lose money on weather.

In 180 American cities there's cloudy or partly cloudy weather on an average of 70 per cent of the time. No wonder our nightshirts have that tattletale gray. The average number of clear days per week is only about 2.007. No wonder hanging out clothes is such a chore.

Mother Nature is a queer duck at times. Cones of some species of pine trees require the heat of a forest fire to open them to release the seeds. Therefore, vast amounts of good seed are accumulated through the years which automatically reseed burned-over areas after a forest fire causes the cones to open. . . .

If you're too impatient to wait for the reports from the Weather Bureau, you can make yourself a good barometer with only a bottle of shark oil. When a storm's a-brewing the stuff turns murky; for good weather it's clear.

Quick, what's an anemoscope? It's the highbrow name for the common weather vane.

Bet you didn't know that, which illustrates my point about our indifference to the really important things in weather.

In the highly organized life that we call civilization, much of the weather information that has been collected over the centuries is codified in what we call the calendar. But you have to look beyond the girl picture to discover it. And the same information has been the inspiration for many other common objects.

For instance, there are 52 cards to a deck because a deck was fashioned after the calendar—52 cards, 52 weeks; four suits, four seasons; red and black, day and night; add the points of the cards with the Jack as 11, the Queen 12 and the King 13, and they'll total 365, the number of days in a year. Count one for the Joker.

How do you suppose this comes about: The fourth day of the fourth month, the sixth day of the sixth month, the eighth day of the eighth month and the twelfth day of the twelfth month always agree and are always on the same day of the week.

Another calendar puzzler: The year 1900, though divisible by four, wasn't a Leap Year. But the year 2,000 will be—if there's anything left of the world by then.

While we're at it, here's a method for indicating which of the months have 31 days. I'm sure you'll want to take off a month or two to memorize this simple formula: Count on the knuckles of your hand, like so: The knuckle of your first finger is January—31 days. The space between the first finger and the second finger is February—28 or 29 days. The second knuckle is March—31 days. The next space is April—30 days. The next knuckle is May—31 days. The next space is June—30 days. And the fourth knuckle is July—31 days. You think we're stuck, huh? No siree. You simply start over again on the first knuckle, which is August—31 days. The first space is September—30 days. Second knuckle this time around is October—31 days— and the second space is November—30 days. The third knuckle is December—31 days—and there you are with knuckles and spaces left over. Quite a few people, of course, carry calendars, which is also satisfactory.

Quite a few people, I'm sure, don't give a darn. That may be the best idea.

But you can't escape the weather, and the calendar makers and farmers don't want you to ignore the seasons, so what can a columnist do but give in to that kind of pressure and write about weather. Before you read on, however, let me give you a few warnings. You'll see some items that sound as if they should be in the HEALTH chapter, or in our ANIMAL section, or someplace else. But the mixture is deliberate. If I didn't borrow some items about colds, wet feet and such, I'd never have been able to find enough stuff to fill the SPRING section. In the spring, frankly, a columnist's fancy turns away from work, and I was up against it in collecting copy, so I borrowed related items. To be specific, you'll find in the SPRING listings a warning about the sniffle dangers in March. Now, suppose I had been medically logical and put those in the HEALTH section. You might not read that until sometime in August, when you don't need the advice, and you'd be sure to forget it by next March.

And another warning. With everybody talking so much about the weather, there aren't so many original ideas along that line at this late date. So you might be reading stuff that seems to you as old as the valleys (they're just as old as the hills, you know). One notable example is the WINTER story about lumberman T. B. Walker and the bank directors' meeting. The same yarn, with different bankers, is told about famed New York blizzards of 1888 and 1949, the San Francisco earthquake, the Chicago fire and any number of other disturbances, so it's more or less common property. (See page 123.)

Honestly, I make no claim for originality on that story or many others. After all, I didn't invent the weather. I'm just writing about it.

Just one more point. While our calendar year both starts

and ends in winter, I've lined up my seasons beginning with SPRING, which always seems like the real start of the year because that is when I feel as if I really begin to live again.

SPRING

Leave us greet the spring, should we? I love *spring!* Bursting buds and peeping flowers and the songs of birds. Winter one day and spring the next. And rain, lots of good old rain. *Spring!* Of which the poets sing and don't ask me why. And lovers stroll down the woodland paths, between rainstorms. *Spring!* With its coughs and sneezes and pneumonia and bronchitis. And heaps of leaves in every nook and cranny of the dadbloomed yard. It wasn't my fault. The rake broke. And thunderstorms and winds and pleurisy. And rain. Don't forget the rain. *Spring,* beautiful spring. You can have it. It shouldn't happen to a dog. And I will shoot the weatherman on sight.

Of all the poetic lines that have been written about March, perhaps the most comforting are those that go, "Ah, March! we know thou art kind-hearted, 'spite of ugly looks and threats, and, out of sight, art nursing April's violets." . . .

Frankly, it's hard, at times, to achieve the poet's point of view. One wrote of spring, I remember, in these words: "Now begins the housewife's happiest season of the year, the ground, already broken by the spade—the beds made level by the passing rake."

Those are pretty words, but a housewife tugging with a mattress, a husband applying liniment to an aching back, a teen-ager forsaking his hot rod for a rake bring nameless pathos to the air of spring. Is it not better that we face it? . . . I suppose, though, that a tulip bursting through the damp earth, the softness of a pussy willow, the industry of the nest-building robins dissipate what hardships spring may bring.

MARCH

March is with us and provides
C. J. Caesar's well-known Ides,

Which with caution and with care
Well-read people should beware. . . .

Every little Ide, 'twas shown
Has a meaning all its own.

March is here; upon its axis
Turns the globe, and daylight waxes
And we shiver and pay taxes——

Yes, for one and thirty days,
Every Burgher pays and pays. . . .

March, when Winter, brazen thing,
Lingers in the lap of Spring,
Thereby staying, so 'tis said,
Always just a lap ahead.

March that comes with merry breezes,
Buttercups and sudden freezes,

Romping robins, icy sleet,
Early rhubarb and wet feet.
March that loves to loaf and tarry,
Not dash past like February;

Here you are, you fallen arch—
Make it snappy, Forward March!

WATCH YOUR STEP & YOUR HEALTH

Beware of March: Surveys made over the last 10 years show that infections such as septic sore throats, scarlet fever, epidemic meningitis, respiratory infections all reach their highest incidence during the month of March. Maybe we should have stayed in bed.

Watch the kids the early spring days, health authorities urge, and be sure that they don't run with their coats open during premature warm weather. Exposure of that type is a quick and thorough method of contracting a cold that might jump readily into pneumonia. Nor should adults be too eager to flip up a window or loiter in a draft.

A tree surgeon tells me that mid-March is the very best time of year to do tree transplanting. Seems the professionals take the tree, roots and all, while the ground is still frozen and the job's a fairly simple one. . . .

Don't go clipping your evergreens in springtime on the assumption that because they've turned brown during the winter they're dead. Wait until June 1, at least, urges George Luxton, photographic Nature Boy. The "dead" limbs may revive or may not even be dead, which means you may be trimming live wood.

Keep your eyes, ears, nose and throat open for the first thunder of the year. Six months later, to the day, you'll get the first frost, according to an old belief.

I consider this one of the best words ever coined by any contributor to my column: It's *"sloppery"* and refers to weather that's a combination of slippery and sloppy . . . typical of spring.

It's always amusing to see girls jumping the season by doffing their fur coats and getting into the more springlike toppers. You know very well they're chilled to the bone, but the penalty must be worth it. Fashion rules all.

WHITHER GOEST, ICE?

Ask a silly question and you get a silly answer. Here's the question: When the ice goes out of a lake, where does it go? Most northern lake residents will tell you that it sinks. A few will aver that it simply melts away. Some say that it becomes porous, water gathers on top of it and forces it out of sight. Those against the "sinking" theory argue that ice floats, so therefore it couldn't sink. There must be a scientific explanation for the disappearance, I thought, so one spring I raised the question of what actually happens when the winter accumulation of ice leaves our lakes.

This reply came from the aquatic biologist of the Minnesota game and fish department: "Some ice melts. That is, it changes from trihydrol (ice) to dihydrol (true water). A lot of it doesn't go anywhere. It breaks up into particles of molecular size. These are dissolved in water. Ice, as it comes from the iceman, is a mixture of ice and water in which there is more ice than water. Water, as it runs from the tap, is a similar mixture in which water predominates. The number of molecular steam particles increases as the water warms, and that is where the ice goes."

SIGNS OF SPRING

The ball park has this sign over its entrance: "Tickets for Opening Game Now on Sale."

Wonder if kids still bring pussy willows to their school-teachers in the spring?

Unless it's the smell of bacon frying on a Sunday morning, there isn't an odor to compare with that of a spring bonfire. And young moderns can't have the full thrill of spring because they don't have an old base-burner to dismantle and store in the woodshed, come the balmy days.

SENTIMENTAL JOURNEY UPSTAIRS

Let's go browsing up in the attic today. Smelly old place, isn't it? But some of the smells are kind of good. Good if you like musty smells.

The stairway that led up to our attic in Magnolia was an interesting approach. I don't know how we ever happened to have a stairway to the attic. Most of the homes had a ladder that led up to a trap door. The ladder made the entrance to the attic more dramatic, but its inaccessibility was a handicap. It had to be an event before a kid could get out the ladder and open the trap door. A stairway, though, made a trip into the attic a weekly occurrence if you wanted to do it that frequently.

Our attic stairway used to be a catch-all. Down at the bottom was the basket for dirty clothes. Then on every step above that, as far as a human could reach, was junk to be saved. When traffic up and down the stairs was finally halted by a six-month accumulation, the junk was moved to the attic proper with one grand gesture.

I used to marvel at the thoughtfulness of carpenters in those days. There wasn't an attic stairway that ever saw so much as a drop of paint or a dab of varnish. I suppose that was a little money saver. The steps were no dreams, either. Rough pine and splintery. I also marveled at the sudden change in temperature you always found on the way up the attic stairs. In the summertime, you'd leave the room temperature of the bedroom, and if it were 85 you'd suddenly strike a warm spot going up the attic stairs, and by the time you reached the top, it could be 120 degrees of extremely dry heat. In the winter just the opposite was true. You'd leave the warm air of the bedroom and then hit a blast of frigid temperature that would chill you to the bone. It was these temperature changes that always made you glad to get down out of the attic.

The attic floor right around the stairway was always a mess. That came from family laziness, I suppose, in most instances. Stuff slated for the attic would always wind up there first. There'd be old shoes, little bundles of discarded clothes, a broken dish, beat-up magazines, pictures with frames that had sprung, an odd piece of cracked pottery, if you know what I mean. There were always mysterious, cavernlike sections in the attic back where the eaves came down. I was always a little timid about getting back in some of those dark corners. Many of them in our house remained completely unexplored as long as I lived there. I wish sometimes now that I'd been a little more courageous. Those corners might have yielded untold treasure.

THE TRUNK SECTION WAS A LULU. Ever notice how all trunks, when you open them in the attic, smell the same? It's a dry, spiritless smell. I remember our No. 1 trunk. You lifted up the top and there was a sort of compartment arrangement that had a wallpaper lining which had browned a bit from age. Over on one side of this tray arrangement was a lidded section. In there were great bundles of old letters. One bundle, I recall, was very neatly tied in blue ribbon. I got into the bundle one day. There were letters my mother and father had exchanged during their courtship. They used to get pretty mushy in those days, too. But what thought went into those precious documents. I wondered, at the time, if they had ever gone over them together. I wondered if letters like those could stand the test of time or whether they'd ring a little bit foolish some 10 or 12 years after they'd been written. I never made an actual count, but it always seemed to me that there were more letters from my mother to my father than there were from my father to my mother. In fact, I've speculated some as to whether mother, like most women, might have been doing the pursuing. . . . Beneath the tray compartments were things that represented the culmination of the love letters. Mother's complete wedding attire, the outfit that father wore. The deeper down into the trunk one got, the mustier the smell, the crinklier the contents. Had I been caught I probably would have had my hide tanned, but I remember four or five of us kids got up in the attic one day, got into that trunk, hauled out all that old wedding stuff and staged quite a fashion parade. Hat, dress, 15 pounds of petticoat, pantalettes, high-buttoned shoes and all the duds my dad had donned. How he ever got into those pants, I can't imagine. They weren't much wider at the bottom than coat sleeves are today. That's a strange custom, saving your wedding clothes. The next generation is the only one to benefit, and then only in case of a costume or hard-time party.

The book section interested me. We had some shelves that had been built up near the window where our discarded books were stored, and what disorder there was on those shelves. And dust, too. There was one volume that always intrigued me. My family referred to it as "the doctor book." I had been told on many occasions never to look at that volume. Strangely enough, that was the one I headed for first. Furtively I'd thumb through it, listening for a footstep on the stair, ready to toss the book into a corner if anyone approached. I didn't understand much of the content but I remember some of the pictures were rather revealing. The book section bothered me just as the wedding clothes did. I could find no good reason for storing those old volumes in the attic.

The window in the attic was an engaging thing. It had a border of little square panes of colored glass—greens, reds, yellows, purples, oranges. Used to be fun looking out at the snow or the green-leafed trees through those panes. Over in the corners of the window were great spider webs. In the spring spiders would catch those big green bottle flies in their webs. I often wondered what those spiders lived on after flytime. There was a little penny pinching in our attic I could never understand. The attic floor extended only over the center section of the bungalow. Back to where the kitchen started below, there was no attic floor. Every time we kids went up there we were warned not to walk out over that unfinished section. But we did. In fact, we made quite a balancing game out of it. We'd walk back and forth across those two-by-fours, and rather skillfully, too. We never had a fall-over. One little misstep though, and some guy would have plunged down through the lath, the plaster, the wallpaper, and probably into a pot of baked beans on the kitchen range. For six or seven bucks more, at the time the house was built, that section of the attic could have been floored and all of those dangers eliminated.

Did you have a miscellaneous corner in your attic? I can remember some of the items in ours: the little chair with the hole in it that stayed there through the years waiting for a brother or sister who never came; the lithographed picture of the Battle of Vicksburg; a bird cage; dishes that had been inherited from Grandma Hitchens; two striking clocks that looked as though they had struck their last the day Lincoln was slain; Etude songbooks, covers torn, edges tattered; a pillow with a picture of a guy and a gal in a canoe painted on its face. These and hundreds more of useless, yet cherished items. Yes, bless the attic as a place to play, but deliver me on cleaning day.

ABOUT SPRING

Precious spring, thou comest apace
With whispering winds and sunny skies,
Thou lead'st my feet to many a place
Where the first violet shyly lies.
Likewise, thy brilliant sun revealeth
The spots where the wallpaper peeleth.

Impetuous spring! Thou showest me
New beauties in familiar scenes—
The yard, the shrub and then the tree
Newly attired in tender greens.
Thou showest also, near and far,
The shabbiness of my old car.

O spring! Thou bringest many things—
The daffodil, the lark, the linnet—
And happily the poet sings
An average of an ode a minute.
I hear a voice say: "Listen, you!
These curtains simply will not do!"

I know what you wives really go through with your spring cleaning ever since I first had decorators in my office. Messy fellows they are. They throw everything in a heap and then put a canvas over it. So on D (for Decorator) Day I just sort of sneak under the canvas to let what will come out.

Here's a little har-har item hanging right here on the edge. It says the young lady who calls periodically to report that the checking account is overdrawn is a Miss Joy. Wonder how these walls got so black. No wonder I've been getting beefs at home about my shirts. Well, for gosh sakes, there's that bathrobe my wife gave me last Christmas that I was supposed to exchange. Say, I'm glad these painters got in here after all.

ALL OF WHICH LEADS UP TO CLEANING TIME: Spring house cleaning doesn't seem to be the job it used to be.

And I for one miss the old form. I suppose it's the vacuum cleaner that has wrought the change. Housewives do their cleaning from week to week instead of the intense seasonal cleaning we used to have.

SPRING CLEANING

You wash all the windows,
*   You scrub all the floors,*
You polish up the handles on
*   The front and back doors.*
You take down the curtains,
*   You take up the rugs,*
You clean the old fruit jars
*   And vinegar jugs.*

You scour out the icebox,
*   You put up the screens.*
You paint the kitchen furniture
*   Lavenders and greens.*
You take out the tin cans
*   And dump them in a hole.*
You sweep out the coal bin—
*   There isn't any coal.*

You get out the mothballs,
*   The chest made of cedar,*
Busy as the bee in
*   McGuffey's Third Reader;*
You slosh down the porches,
*   You rake up the yard,*
Dogs are in the tulip bed—
*   Turn out the guard!*

You clean up after
*   The painter and the plumber,*
Everything's in shape now
*   Ready for the summer.*
You've aches in your fingers
*   And pains in your toes.*
The place is tidied up now—
*   **So next day it snows!***

Housewives engaged in spring house cleaning may get some comfort out of this comparison: The rug in the central lobby of the Waldorf-Astoria Hotel in New York measures 69 by 49 feet and weighs 3,500 pounds. How would you like to put that baby up on the line in the back yard?

And speaking of the rug chore in house cleaning, many husbands will welcome this announcement from a home economics expert who says, "Never beat a rug. It may snap the fibers and loosen the foundation." . . .

Something else to remember when you're doing house cleaning: An ounce of spider's web would extend 350 miles if straightened out.

MILDEW'S ABROAD in spring's balmy days, so after church of a Sunday or some afternoon maybe you'd better skip out in the yard and lift the winter covering from your rosebushes and your perennials. Part of the covering of earth should be removed as it grows warmer, but some should be left and stirred up with the soil to prevent mildew action.

If you can hold off putting up the awnings until mid-June, you'll escape having them wrecked by squirrels. The animals won't nest after that, and it's the nest building that raises the devil with your canvas.

When the sun gets higher in spring, you should think about keeping a pan of fresh water out on the lawn available for the birds and dogs. They'll appreciate it.

If you're doing over a room this spring, here's something to remember: A red room looks smaller than a room painted blue.

Here's a hint to keep in mind when it comes to painting your radiators: A radiator freshly painted white will radiate heat about 25 per cent better than one done in a dark color.

If you believe your house-painting job is a little on the expensive side, think of our Capitol's dome in Washington, D.C. It takes 2,000 gallons to give the dome one coat of paint.

If the odor of turpentine annoys you during your annual painting, here's a little gimmick for relief. Simply add a dash of vanilla to the paint. It cuts the aroma of turpentine, I'm told. Or don't you care for vanilla, either?

Maybe it's an old gag, but for a sweet-smelling closet take a fresh orange, puncture its entire surface with cloves and hang it up where you hang your clothes.

A pretty timely spring suggestion for you mothers: For safe and easy storage of youngster's snow suits, mittens, overshoes, sweaters and the like, get yourself a brand-new garbage can. The covers are tight enough to keep out moths.

That million-dollar pest, the moth, is out to get you as the weather warms, and the clothing experts are advising frequent brushing, beating, sunning, and cleaning of garments that appeal to Mr. Moth's ferocious appetite. Rayon and linen aren't exempt. Many housewives have overlooked that fact.

House-cleaning hint: Have a good look at the felt in your piano. Moth worms and eggs find these pads a comfortable resting place, and the damage can be quite severe if precautions aren't taken. It's a place frequently overlooked in de-mothing.

I haven't tried it because I don't get around to taking off storm windows till the Fourth of July, but for you prompt birds, this stunt sounds like a dilly. It's a method for washing the first-floor windows on the outside before putting up screens. You take a pail of hot water and dump in two or three handfuls of soap flakes. Borrow Ma's mopstick with a nice clean rag on it. Swish the mop around in the soapsuds and then slosh the rag full of suds on the window. Apply as you would your shaving lather, giving the corners a few extra pokes. In other words, cover the entire window, sills and all. Then turn your garden hose on the window. If the day is warm (that's why I wait till July) the window will come out shining and sparkly before you even get to the next one. You don't even have to do any wiping. Of course, if you have a ladder and a good sense of balance, you can use the same stunt on the second-floor jobs, but don't blame me for any spills. I warned you.

April is the worst time of the year to begin a diet, so be careful. It takes more food to sustain the human body in that month, according to a survey conducted by the University of Buffalo, than at any other time of the year.

Here's a pathologist's explanation why we get spring fever. It's the weather that does it. Every period of passing cold is associated with an increase in blood pressure and is experienced as "stimulation." Later, a reaction sets in, leaving a feeling of fatigue. The repeated cold waves of our climate swing an individual's metabolism back and forth between stimulation and fatigue until, come spring, many individuals suffer the characteristic lethargy known as spring fever.

Too bad women can't enjoy the wonderful feeling of getting rid of a vest come spring. Gives a man a new freedom.

I'm never quite convinced that it's spring until I've seen one of those big bluebottle flies. I'm glad when they're late in appearing, though, because they sort of scare me.

Do you want a pretty fair weather prophet? Watch a spider. When rainy weather's due, he'll shorten the threads supporting his web, and he'll lengthen them when good weather is in store. If he fails to repair his web after it rains, it's a good sign there's more rain to come.

FATHER & SON SOLILOQUY ON MOVING DAY

"Pa, why do we have to keep moving from one house to another practically every spring?"

"Well, David, climb up here on Pa's lap and I'll tell you about that. It's largely your mother's idea. She's like practically every other woman. She's what we nature lovers often refer to as a migratory bird. It started the very first year we were married. Like many another young couple, we began our married life in a one-room furnished apartment. We had what they called a roll-away bed. In the daytime we folded it up and put it in the closet. There were just the two of us and it seemed to me there was ample room. One night—just before our lease was up incidentally—your mother hinted that she was getting a little tired of rolling the bed out every night and putting it away every morning. It didn't seem like an awful chore to me, but you know how your mother is. So the next week we were living in an apartment that had a bedroom. That was quite a year. I remember that year very well. That was the year we spent only $12 more a month than Pa was making.

"Not having to roll the bed out every morning and night gave your mother more time, so she started thinking about buying some furniture of our own. And if Grand Rapids has had a depression since then, it's certainly not our fault. For about 10 months we stayed rather stationary. You were scheduled to arrive shortly, and your mother thought it would be nice if we quit apartment life and found ourselves a little two-bedroom bungalow. She could raise you and some flowers. And I could take care of the storm windows and the screens and shovel the walks. And we could also buy some more furniture. That bungalow idea was a lot of fun. I remember I spent Fourth of July morning taking off the storm windows. I don't know what ever happened to that flower-raising idea. Just some of your mother's whimsy, I guess. . . .

"Some people get hay fever. Others break out in a rash at a certain time of the year. Your mother was afflicted with the moving bug annually. I could look forward every May 1 to finding myself up on the driver's seat in a moving van. I knew the boys by their first names and many a pleasant ride we had from one part of town to another each year. Your brother's arrival was the excuse one year. We had to have a third bedroom. After we got that, I bade the moving boys good-by and told them I probably wouldn't see them for a few years. Oh! How wrong I was. The very next spring a real estate man got hold of your mother. He told your mother that it was silly for us to be paying rent every month. All you do is wind up with a bunch of receipts. And besides, he had a place he'd like to have her see. . . .

"That was the year that your mother went closet-batty. There was a bedroom in the house that had two big closets. She has imagination, you know that. One closet would be hers exclusively. And point ninety-nine of the second would be hers. I don't think it was more than a day or two after she had seen those closets that Pa was down at the real estate company's office signing some sort of papers; and the real estate man was slapping me on the back and congratulating me on the fact that in 20 years I would be a homeowner. I remember I heaved a little sigh. It was probably for those days when I was only overspending my income $12 a month. That was a great year, though. That was the year we joined the Venetian blind set. That's probably the only social distinction that Pa will ever have. . . .

"This move we just made into our new house, I guess, I'll have to take some of the blame for. You see, when we bought that first house, your mother was so busy looking at the closets that she overlooked one important point—the fact that there was only one bathroom. Ordinarily, that'd be enough. But now that you have two brothers, which makes five in our family, and your mother had five or six pair of stockings hung up to dry in the bathroom plus some lingerie and your bath towels and four guest towels, it didn't leave Pa any place for his towel. I moved the stockings once, but that didn't work; and, of course, nobody is supposed to touch a guest towel. So I was left with but one alternative—buy a house with two bathrooms. Now just the other night I found some stockings drying in my bathroom, so it may be that I'll have to move down in the laundry. Apparently that's never used. . . .

"Well, that, David, is the background of our having moved so often and I guess it happens in just about every family. . . . Just don't ever write your address in ink."

"Pa, what is a mortgage?"

"That's the only thing your father has plenty of, dear. Now you run along and play with your train."

You movers might do well to remember that insurance policies should be changed accordingly. Fire, wind, hail, tornado and the rest of the coverage doesn't apply unless your agent or the company has made the address change. So, if you've overlooked it, get busy first thing tomorrow. . . .

GOD'S ODDS

This is what you call an "on-the-nose" paragraph. It occurred at a certain church service early one May, in the words of the minister himself:

"Obviously I made the mistake of misjudging mental capacity of my congregation. Around Kentucky Derby time, I reasoned, certain members might be horse-race conscious. With that in mind, I used the Derby figuratively in my collection appeal. The members of our church, I told them, should keep in mind that right now the church is running a sweepstakes in which the horse 'Justice and Charity' will indubitably pay 100-to-1 for every cent put up. You may imagine my surprise when the next day a woman came into my study with a $2 bill in her hand and said that she had come to make sure of the right name of that horse. She wanted to bet on it."

Grasshoppers can't leap unless the temperature is at least 62 degrees.

FLOWERS THAT BLOOM IN THE . . .

I'm a softie for lilacs. You can have your orchids, your long-stem red roses, your gardenias. With their looks and scent, lilacs do something to me. Harbingers of warmth, beautiful in bud and blossom, generous of fragrance, the lilac is a joy, believe me.

For an honest-to-goodness whiff of real spring there isn't much that can beat a bouquet of lilacs in home or office.

Too bad lilacs don't stay with us longer, but if you want to get the most out of them when they're cut, smash the ends of the stems in a ruthless manner with a hammer. Sounds vicious, doesn't it, but the lilacs love it and will stay fresh ages longer.

Somehow a tulip always disappoints me. It's so beautiful a flower but completely lacking in odor. Invariably I stick my schnozzola into the bud in expectancy and nothing ever happens. Why don't I learn?

BUCOLIC

Spring is shyly waiting
Her allotted term;
Birds are congregating
Near the early worm.

And where quagmires harden,
Rid of melting snow,
Once again my garden
Promises to grow.

Plastic its condition,
Soft its fertile floor,
Ready for the mission
Of the dog next door.

Who, to dig a bone up,
Excavates to boot
Bulbs that aren't grown up—
Seed and plant and root.

Spring in green and fair dales,
Waits to bless the ground
So do all the Airedales
For a mile around.

Gardening, best of all games,
Burgeons with the aid
Of all the urchins' ball games
And my awkward spade.

Here's a clever little detail for flowerpots. Whenever a plant dies, pull the dead posy out and substitute the foliage part of fresh pineapple. It just fits into the smaller type household flowerpot, somewhat resembles a cactus and lasts for months. Try it sometime.

When fresh breezes make good kite weather, you might want to heed this warning issued by the Electrical Industries. Mothers and fathers should examine carefully Junior's kite, particularly if it's an army or navy surplus kite equipped with a wire cord. The wire should be replaced with cotton or linen twine. This really goes for any type of kite. If that wire, covered or otherwise, should come in contact with overhead transmission lines or lines of high voltage, a very serious, perhaps even a fatal accident might occur. Life is full of strange hazards, isn't it?

A SPADE'S A SPADE

At moments like the present
My farming instinct grows;
I find no task so pleasant
As planting things in rows.
There's just one thing detains me,
One cramping rule that's made—
No lack of land restrains me,
But first I have to spade.

It's fun to choose the spaces
That June will fill with blooms,
And to allot their places
To root crops and legumes.

To set out plants and tend them
    Are jobs that never irk;
I stoutly recommend them—
    But spading—that's just work.

The man who seeks no leisure,
    Who craves no boon but toil,
May find a certain pleasure
    In wrestling with the soil;
But I've my private notions
    Of clean and wholesome fun,
Including various motions—
    But spading isn't one.

THOUGHTS ON MOTHERS

Those of us wearing white carnations on Mother's Day will have to dig back into memory for recollections of Mother. But isn't it strange how vivid those memories remain. An inmate up at the state reformatory in St. Cloud, Minnesota, once did quite a piece on mothers for the *Reformatory Pillar,* the prison paper.

He objected to the memory of Mother sitting in a rocking chair, her specs on, a shawl draped over her shoulders. There was no place in his mother's life for a rocking chair. She was too busy. He remembered her as cleaning and dressing the kids, carrying in the coal for the stove, rubbing sore muscles, taking care of ailing tots, stirring something in the skillet. Rarely did he ever see her in a rocking chair. And I think that's true of most mothers. I remember some worries that my mother had. I remember when she reached 30 she started to get a little fat. I remember when she reached 40 she was developing a few wrinkles. When she hit 60, she had a lot of gray in her hair. All of those things concerned her. But somehow, to me, they added something to Mother. As she took on weight, she was lots more fun to hug. The few wrinkles she had developed seemed to soften her face. The silver in her hair made a better frame for it, too.

Young mothers always are a sweet sight. I remember particularly the war days when so many young mothers were not only mothers but fathers also, with the father perhaps overseas. Seeing those young mothers in their double roles you could see bravery in their faces. I think it was Joaquin Miller who once wrote, "The bravest battle that was ever fought; shall I tell you where and when? On the maps of the world, you will find it not; it was fought by the mothers of men."

Do little incidents in connection with your mother remain with you through the years? I have one picture of my mother that never leaves me. Strangely enough, she was bent over the oven of our kitchen range. She had in her hand one of those little holders that the Ladies' Aid Society used to sell at their bazaars and she was pulling from the oven a hot pan of fresh cinnamon rolls. There was Mother at her best. Mother did an awfully good job in the church choir, too. I call it a choir, though there weren't enough people in all of our town of Magnolia to make a choir. It was really a quartet; Mother sang the alto. Somehow, she always looked her prettiest on Sunday. Naturally, she'd wear her best dress to church, but she had a sort of glow on Sunday morning that she didn't have at any other time. She'd get up in front with this quartet, right alongside the foot-pedal organ. It was her perfect opportunity for self-expression and she sang right from her soul. I can hear her now holding some of those notes of a hymn, her face lifted just a little, her tone as mellow as a bell.

She even looked saintly. One amusing thing happened to Mother that I'll never forget. We were still living down in Magnolia and she decided that her bedroom ought to be done over. I guess every mother has that same idea every once in a while. So she threw out all the old furniture— the bed, the bureau, the commode and the chest of drawers —and she got a new set. The new one was a pretty fancy deal. I've always admired Mother's vision in connection with that bedroom set because that set had the first dressing table that was ever brought into Magnolia. It had a flat top, three little drawers underneath and long legs. Then there was a mirror fastened on at the back. The dressing table took the place of the commode and bureau. But you know, there was one thing lacking in that set. There was no place for the what you may call it. If you remember, those old-fashioned commodes, or sometimes the bureau, had a kind of big compartment with a door on it for the—you know. Well, there was Mother with her brand-new bedroom furniture, just a little too far ahead of her time.

The mother theme has played its part in literature, certainly. Thackeray wrote this line: "Mother is the name for God in the lips and hearts of little children." Remember this verse? "Who ran to help me when I fell, and would some pretty story tell, or kiss the place to make it well? My mother." Poe in his "To My Mother" expressed it this way: "I feel that in the heavens above, the angels, whispering to one another, can find, among their burning terms of love, none so devotional as that of 'Mother.' " I always liked this line: "God could not be everywhere and therefore he made mothers." Maybe this isn't the day to bring it up, but there's a little warning in this passage: "Simply having children does not make mothers."

The inmate of St. Cloud wound up his little piece with this: "I've found out that Mother must have had to learn a lot of things the hard way. A whole lot of this (you know what I mean) would have been unnecessary had I but listened to Mother. I know that Mother's the one who comes to visit. Mother's the one who writes faithfully. Mother still sends her hard-earned money to me for cigarets. Everyone else might change, but Mother won't. Mother loves you."

- o -

You June brides wear bridal veils as a carry-over from an ancient belief that the veils protected brides from evil spirits.

Do you want to make something of it? . . . Twenty-two presidents of the United States were conceived in the first six months of the year and only nine in the latter half of the annum. . . .

The most practical Father's-Day gift I've heard of was one used by a family in the East. Mama and the kiddies chipped in and paid off the second instalment of Papa's income tax, due around the date of Father's Day. . . .

SUMMER

Summer is when the starch goes out of your shirt, the crease goes out of your pants and the kids get into your hair.

I just discovered that cows and columnists have at least one thing in common in hot weather. Because the bossies refuse to move about, preferring, when possible, to stand in water, their production is reduced as much as 50 per cent.

Wonder what the supreme court justices do on their three-month vacations? They probably need that long to air out after listening to lawyers for nine months.

Restaurant owners, I'll wager, never call it the good old summertime. Appetites are fussier and people more irritable during the hot months. . . .

A veterinarian offers this summertime advice to dog owners: When the first hot weather comes, dogs should be given broth and milk, with their solid food being gradually cut down as the mercury moves up into the 90's. It's solid food and changes in the weather that cause sickness in dogs, especially the large ones like collies and German shepherds.

VEXANS AND VEXATIONS

Wonder what good a *mosquito* is anyway?

It won't up your love for the pests, but you might as well take a few facts about the mosquito from John Palmer of McGregor, Minnesota, up in the lake country where they thrive. The mosquito's nose and ears are located on her antennae and the mosquito's voice or piping is not produced by the vibrations of the wings but by tiny tracheae or tubes located on her body. Thus the lady mosquito, intent on a meal of your warm blood, gives you as the intended victim fair warning, proving she's a bold highwaywoman rather than a cowardly sneak thief.

Mosquitoes won't go for a sun-tanned skin half as quickly as they'll move in on a lily-white patch.

With the season on us, though, you might be interested in this: After a mosquito bites you (and it's always a female that does the chewing) it shoots its own saliva into the wound, and that's what makes the bite itch and swell.

Mosquitoes are going to be a major menace this summer, as usual, so you might as well know this simple treatment for their itch: Get a cake of yellow laundry soap, the yellower the better, make a thin lather over the bite, then let the lather dry. It removes the sting in our family. I hope it works in yours.

A little citronella spread around your pillow at night, they tell me, will keep the buzzing mosquitoes at their proper distance.

SUMMER MONDAY

She was stringing a deucedly interesting line
As I happened to stroll by the way.
   For you see it was Monday
   and all of the undi-
world there was hanging that day.

There were brassières and scanties
   and stockings and panties
And teddies with trimmings of lace;
   And the slips and chemises
   That blew in the breezes
Would soon bring a blush to your face.

There were scanty creations in rare combinations
   of camisoles, bloomers and such;
And some nice summer frocks
And some little blue smocks
   That smacked of a feminine touch.

And the nightie she slept in, a vest and a step-in,
And a negligee trimmed with real fur.
She was stringing a deucedly interesting line
And I learned about women from her.

YOU CAN BE SUMMER-IZED

You probably never realized it, but you're actually hotter than a 1,000-watt electric light bulb. That frame of yours when it's relaxed gives off approximately 400 BTU's while a 1,000-watter gives up a measly 360.

Hot weather affects me in a curious way. I can't stand it when the humidity takes the gimp out of the scratching surface of paper matches. It's like trying to strike a match on a piece of cocoanut cream pie.

I almost forgot to mention the antidote. Next time the humidity or the heat softens the scratch surface of your pack of matches, try rubbing the moist part of the scratching surface across a pane of glass. Window glass will do. The surface returns to normal immediately.

A shout in July will travel further and faster than a similar shout in January, in case you're the hollering type.

Although the Hawaiian Islands are just north of the equator, Weather Bureau records show the weather there is cooler in the summer than at Portland, Maine, Denver, Colo. or Los Angeles, Calif. The maximum temperature for Honolulu is about 83 degrees.

Weathermen probably would scoff at the idea, I know, but the simplest system of weather forecasting in the summer is to watch how the sun goes down.

Every time it goes down behind cloud banks, the next day is a cinch as a cloudy day. And a clear sunset invariably points to a pretty next day.

Hot-weather tip to users of electric shavers: Cool the face first with a couple of ice cubes, dry your face and then shave. The ice-cube treatment takes out all the pull and stickiness.

You more fortunate souls whose houses are air-conditioned might find a pleasant little comparison between all of your air-conditioning equipment and that big or little nose of yours. The schnozzola is really one of the scientific marvels of all time. In the course of a day, your nasal passages, approximately three inches long and less than two inches wide, air-condition at least 500 cubic feet of air that enters your lungs.

I've always wondered why women during a heat wave can look so fresh and flip with dry brows, linens crisp, hair in perfect place. Nature's helping the little dears and hindering us males, I learn. While the thermometer hovers around 80 degrees, both sexes fare the same degree of discomfort. But when Old Sol shoots the mercury up beyond that, the weaker sex drops in the heat production of their bodies, while men go on generating more warmth.

Don't curse summer's heat waves too much, girls. You might as well know that there's at least one beauty aid in all that warmth and humidity. They create perspiration, which makes your skin soft, so there.

Want to have some fun all by yourself? On the next hot

day—I mean one of those swelterers—stick a portion of your perspiring skin under a microscope. You'll note that the perspiration doesn't flow gently sweet Afton to the surface, but instead it actually squirts out as though each pore might be a tiny little fountain.

The average adult perspires from a pint and a half to five pints a day. And about two per cent of that perspiration is solid matter, chiefly salt, fatty and neutral acids. . . .

It's not the heat, and it's not the humidity, either. To set the record straight, I consulted a heating engineer at Minneapolis-Honeywell Regulator Co., and he told me it's vapor pressure that causes our major discomfort on the hottest days. Vapor pressure representing the actual humidity, rather than relative humidity, is the true method of computing climatic effects on the human body. Relative humidity, which is usually blamed, but unfairly so, is just another way of saying that the air around us at any temperature is holding a percentage of the maximum amount of water it could hold at that temperature. An 80-per-cent humidity when the temperature is up in the 90's is insufferable. But a 98-per-cent relative humidity at zero degrees isn't bad at all. In fact, it feels dry in that situation.

Vapor pressure, on the other hand, is a scientific measurement of the actual amount of moisture in the air at a given time. Here's the way it works. Vapor, you know, is actually water. Water has weight. The more water in the air, the greater the weight. The greater the weight, the greater the pressure. There are several things to do when the pressure's high, said the heat engineer. One might sit in a vacuum, but that's hard on human life and it's hard to find a nice vacuum. Reason why air-conditioned stores or theaters are so comfortable is because the moisture has been taken way down in the chilled air and the vapor pressure has been reduced. Even though the heating engineer has been calling it vapor pressure, you and I probably have other names for it, which we won't go into now.

Vapor pressure or not, there are the days when it's pleasant to stand under a pump, primed or not.

Airline pilots have found out some interesting things

about flying temperatures on hot days. At 3,000 feet up the temperature is about the same as it is on the ground, but during our sweltering, up at 9,000 feet they enjoy 65 degrees. About 9 o'clock at night, though, if they're up around 1,000 feet the mercury stands at about where it was during the hottest part of the afternoon. Our hot air of the afternoon rises up in a body after sunset.

FATHER & SON SOLILOQUY:
A WARNING
ABOUT THE OL' SWIMMIN' HOLE

Well, David, it's been a long time since you and Pa had a little session, so climb up here while I talk to you about the beach. Pretty soon you and Bruce and Bobby and Joan and lots of others will be going down to swim and play on the sand. And just as sure as anything, the papers this summer will carry pictures and stories about children and even older people drowning.

I remember last summer when one of our photographers got out to a beach right after a little boy had drowned. The little boy was lying on the beach and his father was bent over him. The little boy was dead, and I'll never forget the picture of that father's face. The little boy was about your age, too.

So maybe if we sort of talk this thing over now, both you and Pa will be a little more careful this summer and head off any serious trouble. It's a funny thing—states and cities and countries all spend a lot of money and go to a lot of trouble to make our highways safe. They put up signs and guard rails and fix speed limits and all that sort of thing, but they haven't gone nearly as far toward making our lakes and beaches really safe. A man came into my office the other day. He had just finished going around to several hundred beaches in our state, which is so proud of its 10,-000 lakes, and he sounded like he knew what he was talking about. He said right here in Minnesota we can expect 200 or more drownings every summer. Some of those will be the fault of parents and some of them will be the fault of the children. So everybody should be careful.

About two-thirds of the children who drown are drowned on farms, many in stock watering tanks. Other youngsters fall into crocks or vats.

Another thing you have to guard against is falling into garden pools. Remember the time I told you about the father who found his little girl drowned in their pool? And there was only about a foot of water in it. So you want to watch out when you're playing around water. And keep an eye on your little brother, too, because he doesn't understand about the danger of slipping in. When parents take their children down to the beach there should be as much responsibility on them as though they were taking the kids through a factory where there are lots of machines running, because the dangers are just as great.

It's a pretty tough thing to drown. A lot of people think it's an "easy" death. Your lungs fill up with water and you choke and you can't get your breath. I can't understand how they'd think that was easy, can you? You probably won't be diving for a year or two, but this fellow said that 23 per cent, that's nearly a fourth of our drownings, come from diving. And more than half of those came from divers striking the bottom or a submerged log or something like that. Your mother does most of the diving in our family, so maybe we'd better tell her to be careful, huh? The amateur diver, this fellow said, should always keep his hands and arms stiffly stretched out in front of him until he has lost the momentum of the dive.

When the man was going around to look over the beaches, he found the guarded beaches were the safest. The so-called neighborhood beaches and the private beaches were the worst. Lots of times they have weedy bottoms or they're covered with broken glass or old tin cans. And many have drop-offs, too.

You also have to be pretty careful when you're on a dock. It isn't a very good idea ever to play on a dock. Especially when you're barefoot. The boards on a dock, if they're wet, get slippery and you're liable to fall off in water that's way over your head. Even when you're wading out into the water you have to be careful. When you find that you're out too far and the water starts to get deep, you get scared and that's bad because you usually walk the wrong way and get where it's still deeper.

It'd be a fine thing if we could have uniform regulations all over so our beaches could be made safe. Maybe some day we will have, because it isn't a very good thing to have all these drownings.

It's a fine thing for all of us to be able to enjoy our lakes, and Pa will see to it that you get down to the beach a lot this summer. But I just wanted you to know that water can be dangerous even unto death. That means that careless swimming can be just as dangerous as walking across the street without looking. I know what a terrible shock it was for that father last summer as he bent over the limp form of his little boy. So let's you and Pa be awfully, awfully careful every time we go for a swim, shall we?

BEAUTY AIN'T THE BEACH

Park cleaners collect bushels of bottles (many of them broken) from our beaches every morning. Strangely enough, the bottles aren't all left by the hard-drinking people. Picnickers are almost as careless as the roister-doisters when it comes to leaving debris of the glass variety.

Guess what! Men with their beer and liquor bottles tossed into the lakes aren't the only cause of broken glass hazards at beaches. The women are leaving their sun-tan and lotion bottles around to be broken and cause injuries. So both sexes might exert a little more care.

How've you been getting along with your "apricating" lately? I'll save you a trip to the dictionary. It means to bask in the sun, sunbathe.

I don't know why we go so crazy over sunshine. The Eskimos get virtually no ultraviolet rays and seem to be a pretty healthy lot.

And while you golfers and bathers and sun-tan addicts are strutting your berry-brown skins, remember this—a heavy coat of tan prevents sunlight from penetrating your skin, thereby robbing you of that very important Mr. Vitamin D. . . .

It's the ultraviolet rays of the sun that cause sunburn and not the sun's heat. These rays come directly from the sun or indirectly through clouds, which sometimes act as burning glasses, making it possible to receive more sunburn on a partly cloudy day than on a clear day.

Baby chick eyes are very similar to human eyes, and you can be thankful they are. Scientific studies on baby chicks have been used to demonstrate the evil effects of ultraviolet rays on the eyes.

Better be careful about the type of sunglasses you wear. An eye specialist tells me that cracks, lines or fissures, frequently found in the cheaper glasses, may easily lead to or develop a serious astigmatism. Green, he says, is the best color, and the lenses really should be ground to fit your particular eyes.

A doctor on the staff of a TB sanatorium, addressing a group of public health nurses on the subject of heliotherapy in the treatment of TB, told them that patients with blond coloring who burn instead of tan can acquire a good coat of tan by eating large quantities of carrots. So for that bronzed look this summer, go heavy on the carrots.

Bald-headed gents should particularly guard their bald spot against sunburn. A bad case of it on a bald noggin may cause congestion in and around the brain. . . .

This comes from one of the best skin specialists I know and should be passed on after some of the sights you see around town as a result of week-end blisterings. After sunburn, rub on butesin picrate. Any good druggist carries it, and the stuff takes out pain almost instantly.

I wouldn't worry about it, but hogs sunburn very easily and never tan. And speaking of sunburn, when the time arrives where you cover your tires to protect them from summer heat, you might also throw an old gunny sack over your gasoline tank. Old Sol's rays evaporate gasoline at a rapid rate on hot days.

It's fun to watch girls at the beach with corns on their feet. They seem to have a hundred trick ways of hiding their feet. And I don't blame them. I still think there's nothing uglier than the average human tootsie.

Cool Hint to the Ladies: You know how hard it is, after you've had your hair "set" and waved, to pull on a bathing cap for a swim or a shower. Well, to avoid the trouble simply put on one of those heavy mesh hair nets first. The bathing or shower cap will then slip on like a darn.

HOT HEADS

Funny how heat exhaustion and sunstroke require such vastly different treatment. If it's exhausted from the heat you are, you should be wrapped up warmly and given hot coffee; but if it's sunstroke that's bothering you, a shady spot is the place and cold water should be applied to your skin.

Once you've been a victim of sunstroke—and lived through it—you're oftentimes so sensitive to heat that a temperature of 80 degrees will cause you extreme discomfort. . . .

What to do in a summer storm when lightning streaks across the sky: Get into your automobile if it's handy. Its all-steel body gives excellent protection. Get into a house, barn or building, but stay away from walls, doors, windows, chimneys. A steel building is safest. Avoid open spaces, water, trees, hilltops, masts, wire fences, metal objects, machinery, stoves, telephones, radios and electric wiring. Low trees are less dangerous than high ones. And forget that business about being in a draft. That won't cause lightning to strike you. It is true that strong currents of air change the direction of lightning, but those same currents of air are as apt to blow it away from you as to move it in your direction. A steel building gives you a sort of umbrella protection to an area within a radius about equal to the building's height. And the same is true of a building with lightning rods. There is proof that lightning does strike twice in the same place. So don't run for a place that has been hit assuming you'll be safe.

If you have doubts about your car being safe, here's a report from a Westinghouse laboratory. A researcher got into a sedan, had fellow workers toss 3,000,000 volts of artificial lightning at him and came out unscathed. Only a small scorched spot on the car's metal top remained as evidence of the bolt.

NEAT TRICK DEPARTMENT: "Mrs. Nellis Gammett who was struck by lightning in the mountains is doing as well as can be expected, according to her doctor, who said the lightning burned the skin from one to five inches along her leg and then followed a water pipe and came out of a faucet."—DENVER POST

Talking about lightning, be assuaged by this dope from one of the world authorities on electric bolts: If you heard the thunder, the lightning missed you. If you saw the lightning, it missed you. If it should strike you, you'd never know it anyhow.

It's a good thing, however, that we don't know when lightning hits us. Here's a little description of what might take place following a flash that found its human mark: The skin may be turned black but otherwise remain quite intact, but the whole interior of the body may be reduced to ashes or liquefied, and the bones splintered as though the marrow in them had exploded. Cheery little hunk of reading, isn't it?

The lightning of thunderstorms does good as well as harm, nevertheless. Each flash combines some atmospheric nitrogen and oxygen to form ammonia which, when carried to the soil by rain, adds fertility. Ammonia is an important source of increased fertility in the regions where thunderstorms are common.

The American Medical Journal was the source for this, but maybe you'd better have your family surgeon give you a demonstration before you go trying it yourself. Anyway, here's what the Journal has to say about removing fishhooks, which any of us may have to do in summer. The "push-through" method is best when the barb has gone through the skin. But when the hook would require going through a curved path for a considerable distance, as has happened in a lot of cases, the Journal suggests it might be better to make a small incision down to the barb and then pull it out backward. Kind of makes you shudder just to think about it, doesn't it?

Warning: When the hot spells are lengthy, you might as well know that iced or chilled fruit eaten in warm weather may lie like lead in your tummy.

Watermelon season may be a joy to you, but it's a pain in the neck to the garbage men. It makes the heaviest garbage of the whole year.

The postman walked in without ringing once to deliver this: "I made a personal survey during a hot spell and it was a 2½ to 1 chance that every woman driver going up the avenue was sitting at the wheel with her skirts up well beyond her kneecaps."

There aren't very many typically midsummer smells.

PLEASE PASS THE GRASS

I can't be too particular on a sizzling hot day, so I might as well toss this one in: The combined length of clippings removed from a single blade of grass by a lawn mower in the course of a year may add up to as much as 36 inches.

And have you heard about the lazy fellow who planted sword grass on his lawn so that every time the wind blew the grass would cut itself?

TIPS ON LAWN MOWING FROM AN EXPERT: Once a year is often enough to have your mower sharpened. Oil the mower after every time you use it. Keep the machine in a dry place. If grass has become attached to the lawn mower during cutting, turn the hose on it after you're through. Best time to cut the grass, says the expert, is when it's dry. Leave it at least an inch long. If you cut it once a week or oftener, let the cuttings remain on the lawn. In good growing weather, cut it twice a week.

Cuss the dandelion we all do, but I'll bet you didn't know that it's a commercial crop in Salem, Oregon. Its roots are used for compounding medicines; its leaves are sold for salads, its heads are turned into wine, and several thousand pounds of seed are gathered yearly to be manufactured into dyes. Friends of the weed like to refer to it as "the lawn dahlia." Here's something to remember: An established dandelion plant produces two mature seed heads a week, each head bearing more than 125 seeds. It has possibilities of 12,000 seeds a year.

If dandelion eradicators do their job too well, dandelions will probably become so rare that they'll be sold as corsages. And strangely enough, they wouldn't make too bad a lapel piece. . . .

How are your warts? Reason I ask is that a friend offered this midsummer wart treatment (not tested as yet in my own wart laboratory): "You can remove warts during the summer months with milk from milkweed. Two or three applications a day will make the most stubborn wart disappear. The milkweed's at its best in July and August. And it's also an excellent bleach for moles."

This is for aster growers only: To keep your plants from turning yellow in midseason and developing "witches" bloom, shove an unlighted kitchen match into the ground about two inches from the stem. It will generally work. The match does away with the gray plant lice that gnaw at the small roots.

Dog days always had a rather curious significance down around Magnolia, and perhaps in your locality too. We always associated the spell with dogs "going mad" from the heat, running into the pond where we swam and thus contaminating the water. The term, however, was applied by the ancients to the 40-day period that commonly was the hottest of the year. And four-footed canines had nothing to do with the period. Or did you know that all the time? The period was supposed to be the time of the heliacal rising of Sirius, the Dog Star. The heat, which is usually most oppressive at this season, was formerly ascribed to the conjunction of this star with the sun.

A TALL COOL ONE, OR MORE

Help for Ma: If you thoroughly heat a lemon (hot water'll do it) just before squeezing it, the fruit will yield almost double the amount of juice, and that's certainly welcome in this lemonade season.

Or, sometime, try adding two or three dashes of salt to a glass of buttermilk. Very refreshing.

For a summer cooler try this: A tall glass of milk, a liberal dash of honey tossed in and a raw egg beaten into that. It's nourishing enough to suffice for a lunch.

Perhaps with the heat and all, "the bath" could be a timely subject. Babylonian kings used bathtubs 5,600 years ago. Recent Iraq excavations unearthed bathtubs. At least 1,200 years before Christ, excavations of the small palace of Rameses III revealed that the young ladies of the harem had four-room apartments—a living room, bedroom, clothes closet and a bathroom. Some of the wealthy Egyptians rebuilt and redecorated their bathrooms no less than 12 times in the life of a house. The grandeur that was Rome was partly built around the gigantic public baths and the social life that centered around them. One was a mile square and accommodated 3,200 people at a time.

First English-speaking publicity man for baths and tubs was King Henry I of England. It was he who instituted the Knights of the Bath. The ritual required each noble to scrub himself thoroughly before he was made a knight. Several knights returning from encounters with the enemy guilelessly presented themselves, dirty and bloodstained, before the king. The King saw the practical need and instituted the Order of the Bath. . . . Kings of England to this day, at their coronation, go through a bathing ceremonial. In the 15th century, Englishmen began to dunk themselves in wooden tubs and casks, and there soon sprang into popularity social bath picnics sponsored by the merrie gentlemen and ladies of the era. It was quite the thing at these parties for the ladies to sit in tubs, toss off a bit of lunch and talk about how strange men looked without their beards. It seems that Henry IV introduced shaving along with popular bathing.

The French created the slipper bath, a tub which greatly resembled an old shoe. Some even had wheels to permit moving them from room to room. Benjamin Franklin fell for one and brought it home from France. He sat for hours in it catching up on his reading. There was a spigot drain in the toe and a place to heat the water in the heel.

If you take an occasional shower, you should thank a Union commander in the Civil War. Muldoon by name, he was the first to perforate the bottom of a suspended bucket to let the water run out for a shower bath. The bucket was hung in a tree, and Union soldiers carried water to let their fighting comrades bathe.

For a cooling and cleansing summer relief try applications of just plain old-fashioned witch hazel, but cool it before you rub it on.

LAST THROES OF SUMMER

I hate the month of August. It's the tail end of the season. People are irritable. They go away. It's a sticky month. Business isn't any too thriving. I think August and February should be ripped right off the calendar. I'm sure that anybody in the columning business will agree that those two periods are the toughest of the year.

A full year after I had jotted down those notes on my aversion to August I was still stewing about it and in it. After all that time, I decided that if I controlled the weather calendar I'd knock August out completely.

There are a lot of things that combine to make August, shall we say, a poor month. Ma's tan always looks terrible in August. She's a deep mahogany in July, but in August the effect is jaundiced. And that sort of fading is symbolic. The season fades. The memories of summer fade. Fall fashions arrive and the summer savings fade. August should be nothing more than a man's name. . . .

Nature's at her worst in August, too. She deals out some of her hottest days. Days when we'd like to do nothing but loll in a hammock. But Nature will permit none of that. She fixes it so that the fly's bite is most vicious in August. She ripens all of her berries in August. And at a time when kitchens should be cool we find jams and jellies and preserves stewing on the hot stove for hours. . . .

AUGUST IS A MONTH OF WEAK RESOLVE. It's the month when every dictate of conscience says, "Go over now and see about your football season ticket." But the month does something to man. Nobody but a goon would order football tickets in August. I think I really developed my hate for August during the days when I was a renter. (I didn't know what a mortgage was then.) But I remember it was Aug. 1 when I was supposed to give notice of our moving as of Sept. 1. Invariably I forgot it and the landlord held us to another year.

White shoe cleaner always runs out in August. You hesitate about buying another bottle so late in season because most of it is bound to dry up before next summer. So for the last 10 days you're a hopeless mess trying to keep your shoes clean.

KIDS ARE INFLUENCED BY AUGUST, TOO. It's a forerunner of school. Even as this is written our 7-year-old is squawking for a pair of long pants. August has done something to the child.

The telephone naturally is a great asset to me. I obtain a lot of information for my work over the telephone. I communicate with friends constantly, and I draw great joy from the instrument. Except in August. One of these years I'm going to have the phone disconnected for the entire month of August. Anyway, the only calls I ever receive during this lethargic month start out with: "Would you like to have your furnace cleaned? During August we have a 2 per cent discount on all furnace work." Don't misunderstand me. I enjoy having my furnace cleaned. And I think the furnace enjoys it, too. If a furnace is going to be efficient in January, it probably should be cleaned. But August is the one month that I simply will not discuss our heating plant with even our closest friends. May? Yes. June or July? Okay. But flytime is not furnacetime in the Adams menage. . . .

Ask people when they're going to take vacations, and what do they tell you? Half of them say they're going the last two weeks of July. The other half say they're going the first two weeks in August. And what does that mean? Simply this—the first two weeks in August you hear nothing but chatter about the birds who went in July; and the last two weeks in August you have to listen to the klunks who vacationed the first two weeks of the month. Ear muffs are the only preventive, and they get awfully hot.

Vacation talk is always in the extreme. The cabin was either lovely or lousy. They met either the grandest people or the world's greatest goofs. They either got a lobster red or the days were so cloudy they did nothing but play bridge. It's nothing more than August that makes people that way. NOTE: if you will, the cadence of this: "May, June, July, September." Notice that pleasant rise? Now try, "May, June, July, August, September." Did you feel that drop when you hit August? It's the nuts. . . .

INTO EACH LIFE A LITTLE RAIN MUST FALL

I had built up an unshakable attachment for the waters of Minnetonka over a period of about 10 years during which the Adams family lived afloat each summer. There has always been a delightful escape in the 20-minute drive from the hot city to the narrow streets of Wayzata and the leafy shores of Minnetonka and then into the fresh lake winds.

As vacationtime approached one year, however, there came the annual question, "What shall we do?" but with more insistence. We'd been homebodies for a year and a half. Maybe this was the summer to travel. We studied the resort ads in the paper. Their lure was strong. Rest and relaxation. Pine air. Kindly climate. Sports that you could take standing up or sitting down. Summer pleasures at their finest. Riding trails. Tennis courts. Outdoor dancing. Sandy beaches. Terrace dining. Friendly atmosphere. Phrases probably born in an advertising office, yet meaningful to the person with three weeks without work.

I pondered for a long time. Wasn't there some way to distinguish this vacation from those of the past? Forty-nine weeks of the year represent quite an investment to attain the dividend of a three-week vacation. And out of the vacation, of course, must come revived strength with which to face the next 49 weeks. Vicious circle, isn't it?

In the midst of that reasoning I decided that this was the year to do nothing but—sit. So I picked Lake Minnetonka for my sitting . . . ashore or on the deck of our boat.

A very discouraged boy I was the first day. I had looked forward to that first Monday when I could wake up whenever I wanted to and face the whole day without a thing to do. What a feeling that was going to be.

What made it so I do not know, but I awoke even ahead of my regular rising time. "Go back to sleep," I said to myself, "you're on vacation, now make the most of it." But sleep I couldn't. I had longed to be idle. Now idleness was proving to be most unattractive.

Perhaps I had better set up a new chain of responsibility,

lay out a program of daily chores. No, that would defeat the purpose. I was going to do nothing but—sit.

Just sitting is an art. Nor does one learn it in a day. And there is more irony. At the end of three weeks you have become a highly accomplished sitter, when the call to work interrupts. If employers were going to be strictly fair about the whole business of vacations, they'd add three or four days during which the readjustments of returning to work could be made. After all, the employee is, during the first three or four days of vacation, still thinking about his job, making some kind of mental contribution to his work. . . .

Minnesota is blessed in having all its lakes. There's nothing like a lake scene for sitting. It's easy to understand why people from Kansas and Nebraska and other less-watered areas flock to our lakeland. Even on familiar Minnetonka there are vistas that will linger always. Sit in a boat in the middle of a bay and you may gaze across at great stretches of well-kept lawns. Trees, although often trimmed high to improve the view, cast cooling shadow patterns over the landscape. A gardener pauses in the sun to wipe his brow with his fist. Laughter of the college set home for the summer comes from a private beach. A runabout cuts a great white "V" and leaves a churning wake behind. There can be an unearthly stillness, too. Summer insects amaze you with the length of their flight from shore. And they always seem so busy. . . .

Ever stretch out on your back in the middle of a lake and for an hour or two do nothing but gaze up at the sky? The light and heat of the sun changes as the clouds go by. Shadows strike you, then move on across the water to vanish in the woods on shore. Clouds are fascinating. There are days when their formations resemble the fluff that gathers beneath a bed. At other times, the far-off ones look like great mountain ranges. Ominous they can become, too, with their accompanying dull blasts of thunder, their slate-colored rolls, their swift movements across the sky. One becomes conscious, indeed, of nature's bigness and the minuteness of man. . . .

SO IT WENT FOR THREE WEEKS—NOTHING TO DO BUT SIT. Mary Olson, receptionist at the radio station, received a

call about the middle point of my holiday. A man's voice on the other end asked, "Is Cedric Adams actually on his vacation?" She told him I was. "My wife is a member of the W.C.T.U.," he went on, "and at their meeting last night the women discussed Mr. Adams. They decided that he wasn't actually on his vacation but instead was not giving his news broadcasts because he was at an institute taking the cure. I don't want to pry into his private life, but I thought if he was taking the cure I wanted to send him some flowers." . . . Yes, into each life a little rain must fall. . . .
Please omit flowers.

HAY—HAY—HAY—CHOO-OO

If hay fever hits you, you might as well go highbrow and describe ragweed by its right name, Ambrosia artemisifolia.

You hay-fever victims may take a bow today. Clinical tests at a New York hospital showed that those who suffered from hay fever, asthma, hives and other allergies had also leadership, poise, go-getting qualities markedly in excess of a similar group free of those allergic annoyances.

Another survey made at Bryn Mawr College and an IQ test indicated that hay-fever victims were just a shade brighter than those who didn't have it.

TIP TO HAY-FEVER SUFFERERS (but you'd better consult your physician first): A woman caller said she and several of her friends had tried this with marked success. When the schnozzola fills up and breathing becomes almost impossible, simply fill the nose with oxide of zinc and, she said, it'll clear up immediately. . . .

When and if your hay fever starts, remember this: Sufferers in a section of Texas discovered that they improved markedly when they ate honey made by bees of that immediate neighborhood. The pollen in the honey, it was reasoned, fought back the irritations from the pollen breathed in by the victims. . . .

It takes from 25,000 to 40,000 golf balls to operate a large driving tee all summer.

Golf links really derive their name from Scotch thrift. Scotchmen first used their waste lands (links) as golf courses. . . .

AUTUMN

FATHER & SON SOLILOQUY ON SCHOOL OPENING

Well, David, tomorrow you and thousands of other little youngsters start school for the first time. Climb up here on Pa's knee while he tells you a little about it. Having a boy in school means a lot to Mother and Pa. It means that we're getting older, that we're pretty well placed in the middle-age bracket now. Tomorrow for you and for us a new set of responsibilities begins. From now on for you the days that used to start with play are just about over. . . .

But you know, the thing that worries me right now is the bathroom in the morning. Pa has always been Kingpin when it came to the bathroom in the morning. I always had to get to the office and the rest of you could wait. But, starting tomorrow, you and Pa will have to vie for bathroom honors; just about the time I'm getting up to shave and get ready for work, you'll be washing your face and hands and neck and ears. . . . And those ears and neck, from now on, will have to have special attention, too. It isn't that you'll be any smarter in school with clean ears. In fact, you won't be the one who suffers in case you're caught with dirty ones. It'll be Mother and Pa who suffer. The teacher will wonder what kind of folks we are to have a boy with dirty ears. . . . There's a little handicap I want to mention, too. Unfortunately, your last name begins with "A." That means you'll probably always be seated right up in the front row, smack under the teacher's nose, and it will mean also that you'll have to recite first because they often call on you alphabetically. There's nothing much we can do about that, but I thought you should be warned. . . .

Your mother is going to be a changed woman, too, with you in school. Already the PTA has called her up to ask if she'd take the job as publicity chairman. You see, they figure that because Pa is on a newspaper, she can get all the PTA notices on Page One. Well, when they find their first notice back with the want ads and the second one probably left out entirely, Pa isn't going to rate any too well with the parents and teachers, and that's where you'll take the rap, indirectly. . . .

If there happens to be a pretty little girl in your room, I want you to be especially nice to her. There's many a romance that has had its start in kindergarten. You might find a little girl that some day will turn out to be your wife. Heaven knows that even a lifetime isn't any too long to get to know very much about women, so the sooner you begin the better off you'll be. That's why, I say, it's the smart thing to start looking them over the day you start school. . . .

It's tomorrow, too, that you start your exposure to things in life that some day may shape your entire career. If I were you, I'd be extremely careful about developing any strong liking for newspaper work. You might turn out to be a managing editor, and Pa certainly wouldn't want that to happen. . . .

You'll start widening your circle of friends when you start school. You'll meet a lot of new boys and girls. You'll want them to like you, so you have to be good to them. Be polite, share your things with them, but don't let them beat you down. I mean, don't let them take advantage of you, but try your very best to keep friendly. . . .

I don't know just who your teacher will be, but no doubt she's been picked for her ability, she's been trained for her work and she knows how to run things in school. You might as well get it into your noggin right now that she's the boss, and then do the things she tells you to do. Some days she'll feel a little owly, but she'll get over it. In the long run I think you'll find teachers are usually pretty good eggs. . . .

Another thing, this is the first time you're being sent any

place alone, so Pa wants you to be extremely careful about crossing the streets on your way to school. Don't ever cross in the middle of the block. When the school police are out, wait for them to wave you across. If a car is coming, wait till it gets by, because not all the motorists are careful about youngsters. They think more of getting someplace in a hurry than they do about the lives and limbs of little boys and girls. So remember, son, always cross the street very carefully.

I think you're going to like school. You'd better because you have 16 years of it ahead of you. Pa doesn't necessarily want you to be the smartest one in your class, nor does he want you to be where your mother was, either. If you hit around the high-middle you'll be okay. Good luck to you, Son. Make Pa proud of you, will you?

It is indeed a thrilling sight while driving down to work on the opening morning of school to see young mothers walking along with their tots as they make their way to the first sessions of kindergarten. It's a big step for both. The mother, for the first time in five years, is going to have the youngster out from under her feet, and the youngster is out to make his first big adjustment in a world of people.

It's a good thing the kids don't realize what a long trek they're starting, the hours of study ahead of them, the problems, mathematical and otherwise, that will face them from now on. Most of the mothers, too, who are taking youngsters to school for the first time undoubtedly are unfamiliar with the tribulations, the hazards, the heartaches and the thrills that lie ahead. I hope nothing happened to any tot who started school for the first time. I hope either the mother or the teacher made it very clear how to get to the bathroom. Believe me, that's more important than singing, "Good morning, dear teacher."

NEAT TRICK DEPARTMENT: "Paris gowns, fashion designers have indicated, are so sheer this fall that virtually every wearer of them will have to have a slap of some sort underneath them."—PORTLAND OREGONIAN

Graphic description: "This resort town after Labor Day," writes Rosie from northern Minnesota, "is so dead that even the earthworms walk around on tiptoe."

DIRECT TO THE CONSUMER

I like to go out among rural scenes
As soon as the crops are in,
And purchase potatoes and squash and beans
From the farmer who in his home-spun jeans
Welcomes the transient tin.

I love to pile on the flivver's floor
The things that the farmer grows,
For they cost me only a little more
Than what I pay at the corner store
And that is enough, Lord knows!

The farmer cheerfully digs and delves,
And after his work is done
He spreads his produce on wayside shelves
And the customers carry it home themselves
And think they are having fun.

Oh, city folks are the cleverest folks
And their ways are terribly sly,
So the farmer laughs at their funny jokes
As he loads cull apples into their pokes
Where the automobiles go by.

Fuel experts say that the early autumn weeks are the toughest when it comes to wasting fuel. So if you want to keep expenses down, heed a few simple instructions: when the temperature drops to below zero, you don't have to be warned to keep your windows shut, but now you do. Plenty of heat flows out the windows on chilly autumn days, and September is a good time to remember, the minute your furnace is on at night, be sure to pull your shades.

If you lake dwellers, on your last trip to your cabin or cottage, will remove the stovepipes, you'll effect a saving.

Removal of the pipes will forestall rust to your stove and pipes caused by rain and snow. Plug up the chimney hole, of course.

Wonder if people who move to California miss the joy of an October morning's frost?

By golly, comes a morning when you can see your breath and that's a better sign of fall than the state fair.

Why is it that you couldn't think of putting away a stack of buckwheat cakes on a humid August morning, but the minute there's a chill in the air, they begin to have appeal?

NOT SO DOGGONE

You call these melancholy days?
Oh, la, la, la, what folly!
The gent who pulled that solemn line
Was slightly off his trolley.
What's sad about a chimney place
Where chestnut logs are snapping
So cheerfully that even Ma
and Pa lay off their scrapping?

What though the summer blooms depart
And trees grow starkly nude?
Who cares that gentle breezes now
Grow boisterous and rude?
The pumpkin pie is on the shelf—
Is that a cause for moaning?
Green sausage in the market stalls—
Is that a cause for groaning?

Nuts to the melancholy dope!
It gives a guy the willies.
What though we've gooseflesh now and then
And cat skins drape the fillies?
A guy can neck without a mop
To sop up perspiration,
And any way you look at that,
It's ample compensation.

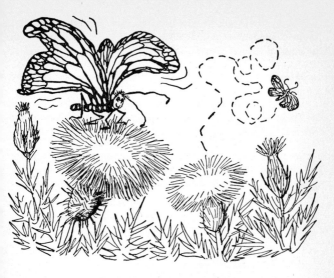

NATURE IN THE RAW

Before it's too late in the fall, try to catch a butterfly squatting on a thistle—the winged creature actually gets a little cockeyed on the nectar therefrom.

A friend of mine, thoroughly reliable in his storytelling, relates this dilly:

"My wife and I decided to do a little bird hunting one week end. Before turning in for the night at our cabin, I soaked a cob of corn in my old bonded standby and then tossed the cob to the edge of the cornfield. Next morning, to my surprise, I looked out the window and saw two pheasants supporting a third one between them, taking him home from the night before on the liquored corncob. Out came my trusted shotgun and, believe it or not, I got the three tipsy birds with one shot."

FALL LAWN TREATMENT should be a good item these days. An expert on such stuff forwards these tips: Use the catcher on the last mowing to prevent matting and smothering and to pick up crab, quack and weed seed heads which have escaped earlier routings. And after your leaves have fallen, and all those from your neighbors blow over, rake most of them up. They sog and smother the healthiest of lawns over winter and spring. Excellent seeding conditions prevail in mid-October, and seed may be sown as late as the soil can be worked. Seed may remain dormant over winter and will jump the gun next spring.

It's okay to leave moderate amounts of any kind of leaves on your lawn for fertilizer, except oak leaves. They have an acid content that raises ned with most grass.

October is the time of year, say the experts, when you should eliminate the dandelion plants from your lawn, particularly in the northern part of the country.

Don't become startled when the needles of your pine trees drop off in the fall. It's a natural function of pines. True pines retain their needles for only two or three years, spruce and balsam from three to five years. New needles appear on new growth each spring. . . .

Pine cones are never planted. Each scale of the cone contains two seeds. The seeds are extracted from these scales. It takes two years for pine cones to mature. Many trees won't produce seeds for 35 to 40 years. You don't have to cover pruning wounds of evergreen trees. Natural resin of the tree will protect it. Broadleaf tree wounds should be painted though. It's slow suicide to cut into birch, aspen, cottonwood and willow—there are so many diseases that attack them. Winterkill, common among pine trees, isn't due to freezing. It's really drouth that gets them. That's why watering of pines just before the winter freeze-up is so important.

The last week or so before the freeze-up is expected, drench your shrubs, and particularly your evergreens. By drenching, I really mean that. Let the hose run at the base of each tree or shrub for a good 10 or 15 minutes. If fall rains haven't been plentiful, trees, without the thorough late watering, are very apt to suffer and perhaps die.

If you belong to the birdbath set, don't forget to take the gadget in this fall. Cold weather's very apt to crack it.

AN INDIAN SHOULD KNOW when Indian summer occurs, so let's take the word of one who says we're usually wrong in calling a few nice days of late September or October Indian summer. Actually Indian summer doesn't arrive until after the first hard frosts along about the time of the full hunter's moon.

CARE TODAY, HERE TOMORROW

Always anxious to save your necks, I give you this little fall driving hint: Be careful of bridges. The temperature of bridges changes much more rapidly than the temperature of paved roads. Consequently, you're apt to be driving along on a perfectly dry pavement, start blithely across a bridge, and wham! The surface is slippier than a trombone slide because the early dew hasn't evaporated yet. Keep that in mind, will you.

Harping on safe driving perhaps isn't the thing to do, but every fall there are a couple of things all of us should remember. NO. 1: On rainy days be extremely careful when driving over pavement covered with wet leaves. Leaves when dampened make a slime that's impossible to stop on. NO. 2: Long twilights call for earlier turning on of lights. If we all made it a point to turn on our headlights the minute we start for home, driving conditions would be vastly improved. Remember—leaves and lights. That's easy, isn't it?

Dampen a rag with a little water and kerosene, rub it over your car windows and windshield and then rub them dry and you've got excellent protection against fog and mist.

Parents, give your kids a quickie warning about the dangers of walking on the ice when it first forms in the fall of the year. Drownings are plentiful at this season and rivers or lakes where snow has covered the early ice present a great danger. Just a little talking about it at the dinner table today might prevent a tragedy in your home.

A woman who golfs with my wife suggests to all of you women golfers that you go into your golf bag when the playing season is all over to search for a little extra change you stuck in there during the summer. Many a woman, she says, puts a coin purse in her golf bag and then forgets it by season's end in the fall. Always a pleasant surprise when you find the unexpected kitty.

If your kids are picking up a little more weight in the year's last quarter than you wish they would, think nothing of it. It's the fall and winter months when the poundage is added and the spring and summer when the tots increase their height more rapidly.

FATHER & SON SOLILOQUY
ON ONE MAN'S THANKFULNESS

Well, David, this is Thanksgiving Day, and maybe Pa had better tell you a little bit about Thanksgiving. It's a day when once a year we take a little special time out to express our thanks to God for what He's given us during the past year. God is probably a little hard for you to understand. But He's the Fellow who is sort of the boss. He runs things. . . .

Well, you and Pa have quite a lot to be thankful for this year. In the first place, Pa's pay checks have been coming in pretty regularly and that's important. A lot of fathers haven't had jobs this year of 1938 so we'd better be thankful for ours. . . .

I'm thankful, too, that we got through this last summer without any water tragedy and that last Fourth of July you didn't blow a finger off or an eye out. And outside of a bellyache or two, you and your brothers have remained healthy. We'd better be thankful for that, don't you think? You have a new brother this year, too, and it was pretty nice to have him born a normal baby. . . .

Pa's thankful that your mother is earning her last year's fur coat and that the payments on the water heater are nearly done. . . . I got a letter the other day from the mother of a little six-year-old girl, who is just a year older than you. That's why what the mother wrote about her hit home so strongly. In the letter the mother told how her little daughter came home from school one day with a fever and how that fever later developed into that dreaded disease of infantile paralysis. You could tell all through the letter that the mother was writing from an aching heart. How she visualized the once normal, healthy limbs of her child being withered perhaps to dangle helplessly through the remainder of her daughter's life. . . . She couldn't understand, she wrote, why such a catastrophe should be visited upon her. And it is a pretty difficult thing. We don't know, for instance, why some innocent pedestrian meets with sudden death, victim of a hit-run driver. Nor is it easy to understand why a community should be ravaged by floods, families by disease, homes by disaster of any kind. . . .

Those things happen. But it's when they don't happen to us that we must express our thanksgiving. . . . There are all sorts of little things that we ought to be thankful for. Remember the time brother Ric fell and cut that gash over his eye? And you remember that time last summer when you darted out into the street and forgot all about what Pa had told you about running into the street, and that car almost smacked you? Well, that's what this day is for—to remember those incidents and be thankful they weren't any more serious than they were. . . . You might mention sometime to your mother that she'd better be thankful she didn't marry that fellow from her home town.

In just a little while now we're going to eat. It isn't every family that can be together on Thanksgiving Day. There are some mothers who are in hospitals today. There are some fathers who are in jail. There are still others who have to work on holidays. All in all, we really have a lot to make us happy today. . . .

So, while you're still sitting here on my lap, let's you and Pa bow our heads for just a minute and say, "Thanks, God."

- o -

Might as well take a bit of time to talk turkey. A little background of the drumstick you gnawed on shouldn't hurt. The turkey is of the pheasant family and our domesticated bird is derived from the Mexican variety. Despite four centuries of domestication, the turkey we enjoy is still a half-wild creature. Those erectile structures you may have noted on its neck are called wattles, and under excitement vary in tint and hue. The bird's the marrying kind, too, and a gobbler in the spring will fight furiously for its mate. Turkey hens, usually three, frequently share the same nest and deposit from 10 to 25 eggs. Flocks of the birds, under a bad scare, often actually go nuts.

Not that it'll make your holiday any brighter, but a turkey has approximately 40,000 feathers, according to a Department of Agriculture bulletin, and you can start plucking them 90 seconds after the bird is dead. . . . It doesn't make much difference whether you gulp or even bolt your holiday dinner. It still takes about six seconds for the food to pass from the mouth to the stomach.

NOVEMBER MEMORY

Have Thanksgivings changed some in your life? I got to thinking about some of the festive holidays we used to celebrate at Aunt Sarah's house. Thanksgiving was a sort of reunion for a lot of relatives. As many as 18 or 20, counting all the kids, would be there for the turkey dinner. Our entrance was always the same. There was usually snow by Thanksgiving in Magnolia, and we'd march up onto Aunt Sarah's glazed porch and begin stamping our feet so we would not track in. There was always a little rag rug in front of the door and we'd wipe our shoes on that. While my mother and father were taking off their overshoes, I'd ring the doorbell. That was one of the big treats of the day. Aunt Sarah had one of those doorbells where you turned the handle to make it ring. After the hellos were exchanged, there was always an argument about the overshoes. "Bring them inside, they'll freeze out there," Aunt Sarah would warn. "No, they're all right out here," my mother would say, "we don't want to make a mess in the house. . . ."

The womenfolks would take their wraps upstairs and the menfolks would hang theirs on the hall tree and then we'd all go in the parlor. Some one of the kids would hit for a rocking chair and get it rocking as fast as it'd go.

The parlor capacity was reached very suddenly, so chairs from the dining room had to be brought in. After the women had exchanged greetings, some of them would go to the kitchen to help, but first Aunt Sarah would equip each one with a dressy little apron. The conversation in the parlor never got very heavy. One of the relatives would say, "Well, how you been, Charlie?" And Charlie would say, "Well, I been pretty good. How you been?" Then somebody else would liven it up with, "My, your kids are gettin' big, ain't they?" and so it went. . . .

I'll never forget Aunt Sarah's Thanksgiving table. It took all her extra leaves to make it big enough for the crowd. The holiday tablecloth always had an extra amount of starch in it, I think, which made it glisten. She had quite a time finding enough water glasses. At some of the youngsters' plates there were plain jelly glasses. The dinner-plate situation was about the same. But nobody minded. Aunt Sarah was proud of her carving set. The knife, the fork and the steel sharpener all had huge bone handles, and the box for them was lined with purple velvet. She put the box on the table, too, for adding a little color. What really added color, though, were three or four shivering plates of jelly.

About the time one of the womenfolk would start filling up the water glasses, you'd also get the aroma of rutabagas, turkey and gravy coming from the kitchen. That did something to some of the kids. They'd trot to their mothers with, "Mommy, I'm hungry." That whine was placated by an encouraging word from Mother like this, "Yes, we're all going to eat in a little while. Now you be good and play with your cousins till we call you." You finally knew you were getting right up to the starting gun when Uncle Bill took the carving knife out to the kitchen and gave it a little whetstoning. The minute Aunt Sarah said, "Well, I guess everything's on now," we hit for the dining room.

There was quite a pause while the mothers tucked the napkins or bibs under the chins of their youngsters, and then some kid would probably shout, "Mama, I don't want any rutabagas. I don't like rutabagas, Mama." Just about then some kid at the other end of the table had dipped his sleeve in cranberries while reaching for his water, and the mother would yank him out to the kitchen for the clean-up job.

Well, we ate, and we ate, and we ate—right down to the last nibble of pumpkin pie. The men would surreptitiously loosen two or three buttons on the tops of their trousers. The women, I imagine, sighed for similar relief. Then developed the argument that went like this among the women: "Now you go in and sit down, we'll do the dishes." "No, you go in and sit down, we'll do them." Eventually the dishes were done. Everybody sat around in the parlor for a while and talked about the relations who were not there. Aunt Sarah was probably the most thankful one in the whole crowd—thankful that Thanksgiving came but once a year.

- o -

Every time I see snow on a little green bud at the start of cold weather it makes me feel like I'm standing on the back porch in December in a nightshirt.

THOUGHTS WHILE SHAVING: Fall is the only season I can stand to think of myself in a cemetery. Lying under the beautiful autumnal foliage might not be so bad. But winter wouldn't be so far away, so that thought is spoiled.

WINTER

Was it a proverb that said, "An early winter is a surly winter"?

OUT OF SEASON

(Lines written after receiving and browsing through a new edition of Northrup, King & Company's seed catalog the first day of winter.)

When the frost king is doing his darnedest,
When the wind through the icicles hums,
And the meadows are sere, it's the time of the year
When the hardy seed catalog comes.

Its rubicund beets and tomatoes,
Its corpulent carrots and corn,
Its mammoth sweet peas bring a tropical breeze
To a month that is bleak and forlorn.

Then I take out my pencil and paper,
I lay out my plots with a rule
And a long piece of string I have found is the thing
To use as a gardening tool.
My garden is lush and prolific
As soon as the seeds have been sown,
And my peas and my beans and my various greens
Are the finest that ever were grown.

I know (for experience teaches)
That dark disappointment is sure,
That summer and spring disillusion will bring
And that most of my crops will be poor.
But now being knee-deep in winter,
I dig and I hoe with a song
For the catalog (seed) never mentions a weed,
And a catalog cannot be wrong.

Let's have a little visit today, shall we? I'm sitting here in
what we call our den, writing this. The room looks out on
our back yard where two sparrows are playing skittishly
in the snow. Our little suburb is growing. Two years ago I
could sit here and look out over a great wooded tract, completely undeveloped. Now there are three full streets of new
houses, changing the entire pattern of the landscape. It's
fun to leave the office early in the afternoon and work at
home. Not enough of us husbands enjoy our homes in the
daytime. One's whole neighborhood has an entirely different aspect in the sunlight. We get used to seeing our homes
only in the early morning or at twilight, dusk or after dark.
The lilac bushes and the birches and the oaks and the
apple trees seem so peaceful in their winter's sleep. Maybe
it's because they have so little to do. There's a delightful
pinkness to a December sky in the afternoon. You'd never
dream, looking at it now, that on occasions it can grow so

ugly and give us blizzards and cloudbursts and crashing thunder and lightning. I wonder if Minnesotans who have migrated to Florida and California ever long for a December afternoon?

Winter twilight is settling down over the back yard now. Lights have gone on in windows across the old wooded tract. The boys have just come puffing in from school. I wonder where those sparrows that were playing about on the snow have gone. My, it won't be long till the lilacs and the birches and the oaks are budding again. December afternoon, I have enjoyed you!

WINTER WHEELING

Ever notice on these crispy mornings that the exhaust on some cars shoots out steam that turns to the left, while other cars send it twirling to the right? How come, scientists?

It's this time of year when you should be reminded not to race your motor to warm it up. It not only wastes gasoline but it's also bad for the engine.

Keep this in mind next time your car stalls during a winter weather blitz: Frequently it's a short circuit in the ignition that stops the motor, so get out and with your handkerchief wipe carefully around the porcelain portions of all your spark plugs. Snow gets in there, melts and causes the short that causes the halt.

While we're in the helpful hint department, here's a dandy for motorists to forestall that kind of ignition trouble. A man I know gets from his drugstore enough nursing bottle nipples to cover his spark plugs. He cuts a hole in one end of each nipple just large enough to permit the cord to slip through, and then slips the nipple down over the plug. Keeps them dry regardless of weather, he says, and prevents many a stall.

And another tip for better starting when the mercury dips. Have your garage mechanic or your oil station attendant close the gap a trifle on your car's spark plugs. It makes for snappier starting in the winter.

Adding half a cup of alcohol to your automobile gas tank now and then in winter will prevent gas line freeze-ups.

One of our state highway patrol officers called with a good tip for winter driving. The tiny filaments in the head and tail lights of cars grow more sensitive during cold weather. To prevent frequent burnouts, turn your car lights on before the engine shoots too heavy a charge through the battery into the light circuit.

Car doors are always hard to close in the wintertime. They'll slam, but not clear shut all the time. They'll close on the first pull, however, if you remember to roll down a window about a quarter of an inch. It's the release of inside air pressure that permits an immediate closing.

Next time your car gets stuck on an icy patch, deflate your rear tires 10 or 15 pounds for more traction surface and you may get out. Don't forget to inflate them back to normal soon after, though.

Watch out for frostbite any time the mercury dips to eight degrees—but rarely will frostbite be serious at that temperature unless there's a high wind.

A Milwaukee medico warns against rubbing snow on your ears or nose if they're frostbitten. Much better, he says, to warm ears or nose with your hand or a little water. Snow-rubbing increases risk of skin infection. . . .

Let this be a lesson to the hatless: A university student on a cold morning did away with his millinery. He froze his ears, gangrene set in and both ears had to be amputated.

One gent I know solves the cold weather problem without long underwear. He just wears his pajama bottoms under his suit trousers on the sharpest days.

Girls who go around hatless and barelegged should take a hint from the housemother of a Minnesota sorority. She usually has 35 girls in her care, and among them almost every winter are several cases of frozen legs, earaches and neuritic shoulders. The h.m. feels certain that most of the disorders are due to the no-hat, no-stocking fads of the college girls.

However, girls, don't let the opposite sex chide you about scanty attire as regards your normal winter clothing. You have expert medical opinion on your side. Go ahead, say the docs, and dress in as flimsy a get-up as you can stand, because the closer your skin temperature is to the weather temperature, the less you'll feel the cold. Make you any happier?

Midwinter is when a lot of you will be suffering from niphotyphlosis. It isn't as bad as it sounds. It's highfalutin for snow blindness.

SNOW BITS: Our sightless folk have a tough time as pedestrians in winter. The drifts and snow make their cane-tapping very difficult because the cane is hitting unfamiliar territory. So if you spy a blind person plodding along, slip him a little aid.

My heart really goes out to elderly women when I see them picking their way cautiously over icy streets. One slip and a hip could be nipped, to put them flat on their backs for months while tired bones knit. And usually the grand-mother types look as though they're thinking hard about that very thing.

Shoe stores will be pleased to have you remember this during the winter: When and if your youngsters come in with wet shoes, always dry the shoes at a very low heat, never right up against a fire or radiator.

OFFICE PARTY DEBATE

THIS IS DYNAMITE, I KNOW. It could easily start discussions in hundreds of homes that would last right through the holiday season. There's much to be said on both sides, however, which is not quite coining a phrase. But read the beef and then let your conscience be your guide.

"I hope you publish this," writes P. L. D., "just to see if other wives agree. Maybe it's I who am too quaint or strait-laced. My husband's company, and there must be dozens of other firms and offices that do likewise, has what it calls its annual Christmas party. Actually it amounts to drinks, a dinner, more drinks, mistletoe, exchange of gifts, more drinks, dancing, more mistletoe and more drinks, with the Old Boy rolling in about 3 A.M. very unsteady on his pins and covered with lipstick. The wives or the husbands of the workers are never invited to these office or company shindigs. I have never been able to discover who instigates these parties, whether it's the wolves or the wolverines. But I do know that as far as the wives and husbands on the outside are concerned, the company is not creating any good will.

"I've heard all the old and familiar arguments about it. My Old Man said time after time, 'You don't have anything in common with those people at the office except the source of the pay check. You wouldn't enjoy yourself because you don't know the people.' Or there have been times when he uses this argument, 'I'd like to take you, dear, but none of the other fellows takes his wife, so I can't be the only one. And you don't want them to think of me as henpecked, do you?' I've often thought that it might be a good idea for all the wives to come back at their husbands with something like this. On the night the office entertains, we should stage a little party at our homes for the iceman, the grocery man, the milkman, all the people we wives do business with. We could have some drinks and a dinner and some mistletoe and some more drinks. My milkman is tall, dark and handsome, and single. I just wonder what my husband would think if he came home to a party in his own home of the same caliber as that staged by the firm he works for. I wish the presidents of firms or the board of directors would give the whole matter a little consideration when this year's holiday office parties are being planned. But they won't, so what's the use?"

OUR YULETIDE SYMBOLS

The Danes should have credit for our Christmas seals. It was a Danish postal clerk, Anton Holmboe, who started the custom way back in 1903 as a source of revenue for an anti-tuberculosis society.

The only known copy of the first Christmas card designed by W. M. Egley and published in London in 1842 is now in the British Museum.

Post offices in virtually every town and city in the country have to destroy thousands of Christmas cards annually for want of proper addresses. The postoffice suggests rechecking address lists before mailing.

This is mailbox advice for rural people. Frequent bottlenecks develop that slow down delivery of mail, so a few do's and don'ts from our rural mail carriers may help. The president of a county rural letter carriers association supplies them:

DON'T LEAVE PENNIES or coins in the mailbox with your letters. Buy and affix the stamps yourself. Your carrier has stamps all the time. If you have to leave money in the box, put it in a container, not loose in the box. Don't delay the carrier. He may have 200 stops in addition to yours. Don't allow anything but United States mail to be put in your box. Don't be backward about asking the carrier for postal information. Keep the snow cleared so the carrier can drive up to your box. Keep the flag down unless you have a pickup, and when you have outgoing mail in the box, stand the letters up at the side and front end of the box so the carrier can reach them easily. Print your name on the box on the side from which the carrier approaches.

Christmas is just another day as far as MOST of the people in the world are concerned. Only an estimated 31 per cent of the world's population professes Christianity, which leaves a billion and a half non-Christians who do not celebrate the birth anniversary of Jesus Christ. Mohammedans, who make up 13 per cent of the world's population, skip it, of course. So do the Hindus, who comprise 11 per cent. Buddhists, who comprise 8 per cent, observe another holiday, to name some of the best-known non-Christian groups.

In China the name of Santa Claus is Lau Khoong, which means nice old father. . . . Sounds like home, doesn't it?

The naiveté of kids probably reaches its seasonal peak about Christmastime, and there's no better outcropping of it than is witnessed by department store Santa Claus actors.

An insurance man I know who works frequently as a clown and each December takes the role of Saint Nick jotted down a few conversational bits that he's picked up from youngsters as they make their Christmas requests. The youngsters whom Frank has contacted come from all stations of life. Their wistfulness, their range of desires in some instances, their spirit, their simplicity—all are amazing and amusing. There must be some pretty good stuff in one little girl. Santa Claus asked her what she wanted. This was her reply: "Never mind about me. Just bring Mother a butcher knife." . . .

Santa had a pretty definite problem with one little three-year-old who accosted him. "All I want," the tot whispered, "is a little brother and sister." Another more practical-minded youngster answered with this, "Aw, just gimme some britches." There must be the start of a Home Ec. girl in the little youngster who said, "All I want is an egg beater so I can help my mother." A bit of the scolder was in evidence in another reply. "For two years now I've asked you for a doll buggy and I haven't got one. I'll ask just once more—that's your last chance." . . .

Order of preference in boys is bicycles, trains, doctors' sets and desks. Girls are frequently inquisitive (it starts young apparently) about where Santa lives and what he eats. Children who want clothes are very rare. Scores of kids have their requests all counted out and then reel them off from memory. Fathers could take an object lesson from a store Santa. The patience, the tenderness of these men and their imagination astound me.

Something went wrong. I actually did a little Christmas shopping early one year. Before I'd always been one of those last-minute birds. But I decided to change, bucked the crowds, came home a wreck and still had the three Adams lads to buy for. Found myself a couple of things, though, and I'll bet a buck I get duplicates of them for Christmas. I looked at motion picture machines and electric trains and mechanical contrivances and gadgets till I was blue in the face. While I rested my aching calves that night I skimmed back over the years and thought of some of the simple things that thrilled me as a kid. Let me see if I can revive some memories for you. . . .

Remember the magic lantern? I'll never forget the first one I had. It contained a little kerosene lamp that furnished the light. The top of the magic lantern had a curved chimney which emitted the smoke from the lamp. If you wanted to put on a de luxe performance of your slides you hung a sheet up on the wall. For your own amusement, though, you used the wall as a screen. Sometimes the wallpaper design interfered, but you didn't mind too much. Since then, I've sat through showings of home movies that haven't been half as interesting.

ALL LOCOMOTIVES FOR KIDS USED TO BE RED, IF MEMORY SERVES ME. They had a weighted wheel in them and you got that flywheel going by shoving the engine across the floor three or four times and then letting the engine go. The piano or the library table always had a few marks where your engine was hitting them, and the knees of your pants wore out long before the locomotive. I suppose we have to accept progress, but it seems to me there was almost as much fun in shoving one of those flywheel jobs around the floor as there is today in flicking a switch and watching an electric engine zoom around a confined and established course. And how many fathers remember the electric motors than ran from dry cell batteries? Along about February 1 you had to make the rounds of the garages in town picking up old batteries and using the last remaining juice in them for your train.

It's long since I've seen a play store, too. Remember those? They had three walls, counters, shelves, an imitation cash register, miniature boxes of cereal, canned goods, spices and what not.

Cast-iron fire rigs were popular, too. The ladders on the hook and ladder outfits came off, and the firemen had little pegs coming out of the seat of their pants to hold them in place on the engines. Then there were those little steam engines which developed the steam with a little alcohol burner. The engine rarely ran after the original supply of alcohol was used up because nobody ever took the trouble to bring home a fresh supply of the fluid. . . .

No Christmas ever was complete without a popgun, and what a lark it was to hit your Old Man with a cork from close range. There was always the bachelor uncle, too, who lived in the city and didn't have too clear an idea of what kids should have for Christmas. He'd send a Daisy air rifle or a bow and arrow set with steel-tipped arrows. I didn't see a single Horatio Alger book this year nor any of the Tom Swift or Rover Boys series. Surely "Tom Swift in Caves of Ice" or "Phil the Fiddler" or "Tom the Bootblack" would make just as exciting reading today as they did 30 years ago. There was another game, the spelling of which may be wrong. Remember **crocono?** The manes on hobbyhorses are no longer made out of twine, either. But the shoes on dolls are still that thin imitation patent leather. I didn't see a doll that was sawdust filled. With that wetting arrangement they have now, I suppose, the sawdust would mildew. I guess dipping into our old toy boxes would be pretty dull stuff for the kids of today. But if anybody has a magic lantern and a set of slides that still work, I'll come over any night and bring popcorn and apples for the crowd.

Is there a little poinsettia in your home? If there is, let us repeat a warning—don't neglect that "tia" ending. It isn't poinsetta. The poinsettia, as a Christmas flower, has only had about 100 years of popularity. It was introduced in the United States by J. R. Poinsett, then our minister to Mexico. Pretty as it is, it's rated as a terrible weed in its native land.

Very few people know that the sprightly sprig of mistletoe is, of all things, a parasite. It has been known to choke the trees on which it grows.

The more mistletoe harvested, the better it is for the woods. Despite the romantic connotation, mistletoe is pretty harmful, robbing trees of their sap. And the same goes for you, dearie.

FATHER & SON SOLILOQUY ON THE SPIRIT OF CHRISTMAS

Dear David: there's enough of the Christmas spirit in the air and I guess you're old enough now for Pa to tell you a little bit about what we call Yuletide. Christmas to those of us in the newspaper business is just another laboring day. There's really quite a lot of sense to the holiday, though, and I'd sort of like to have you a little old-fashioned about Christmas. . . .

I used to know a young fellow who had a unique way of celebrating Christmas. The day before he'd load himself up with 200 brand-new silver dollars and then he'd parade up and down the streets of the Loop and drop four or five of these dollars into each of the pots the Salvation Army has at various corners. He could have sent them a check and avoided all that trouble, but he got a curious delight from watching the expressions on the faces of the usually old men and women in charge of the pots as his dollars clinked in. . . .

There's a very wealthy man in St. Paul who spends about $10,000 for others each Christmas. He feeds orphans—they're little boys and girls whose parents are dead—and then he has a full-time shopper for about a month who does nothing but plan and buy and wrap gifts for about 300 men, women and children who otherwise might not have a very happy Christmas. He makes a lot of people happy and himself as well. Then I know of another family who pack up 10 complete Christmas dinners from the turkey right on through. Christmas morning the four members of the family pile into their car and take these baskets two at a time and drive to the poorer sections of town. They find families who haven't much in the house and leave them a basket. When that family of givers sits down to Christmas dinner, they enjoy it more because they know 10 other families are sharing with them! . . . There's one of our nightclub owners in town, too, who closes his place to the public on Christmas and packs it instead with kids off the streets who otherwise wouldn't be eating very much. And he fills them up with turkey and dressing and cranberries and pie. That's the way he has his Christmas fun.

Right now, David, most of your fun at Christmas will and should come from getting things. Santa Claus is a great old guy, but he also likes to have the youngsters he remembers willing to share a little, too. In your own family your two brothers will want things this Christmas, so Santa has to be careful to have enough to go around.

I was in a home just the other day where the father had been taken to the hospital and the mother was left with five children. Three of the little boys didn't even have overcoats so they could go out to play. The oldest boy was 11. He had been out all afternoon with his wagon picking up pieces of coal off the railroad tracks. It isn't likely that those kids will have many toys around Christmastime. And there are a lot of little boys and girls just like them everywhere. That's why when you write your letter to Santa Claus, I think it would be swell to put in a little line telling Santa that if he hasn't quite enough to go around this year, and if he gets to your house first, he can keep out one or two of your toys for those little fellows that Pa saw the other day. . . .

If you get the idea of not wanting everything for yourself, of thinking of those kids without any mothers or fathers, about the youngsters without overcoats or mittens or of little boys who have been sick for a long time—if you get so you'd sort of like to share what you have with them and if all the other more fortunate boys and girls do the same thing—say, what a happy Christmas it would be! Let's try it this year, anyway, and see how it works.

- o -

A precaution worth repeating: The National Fire Protection Association recommends cutting off the base of your Christmas tree at an angle at least an inch above the original cut and then keeping the tree standing in water during the entire period that it's in the house, always maintaining the water level above the cut. It reduces the flammability and also aids in keeping the needles on.

Local librarians in the technical department pass on these directions from the United States department of agriculture for making Yule trees resistant to fire: "Dissolve ammonium sulfate or calcium chloride, one pound for each four feet of tree, in 1½ pints of water per pound of chemical. Saw off one inch from end of tree in an oblique cut and immerse in a narrow-mouthed container holding the solution. Allow the tree to stand in that solution in a cool room until all the liquid is absorbed. The more solution it absorbs, the more resistant to fire your tree will be." The fire department also warns not to hang wreaths anywhere near a fireplace if you're going to have a fire in the fireplace.

Improved snow technique for your Christmas-tree decoration from an electric power company worker. First you mix up a batch of ordinary soap flakes—a small box will take care of an average tree. Put your soap flakes and water in an electric mixer, if you have one, or a hand beater will do. Beat the suds to the consistency of dry egg white. Then with a spatula apply that to the branches of your tree. On top of that you sprinkle your packaged snow. The base mixture holds the artificial snow on the limbs and the whole thing has a very natural effect.

ONE MAN'S CHRISTMAS EVE

(NOTE: Gathered around your tree the night before Christmas with presents and happiness and good cheer in abundance, there's contrast indeed with the thousands whose Christmas Eve is being spent in the prison cells of the nation. The following poem, written by an inmate of the St. Cloud, Minnesota, reformatory, is certainly worthy of a place among our Christmas classics.)

Open the shutters, O Lord, this night
 For a vision I fain would see.
Carry me back on tinseled wings
 To the foot of a Christmas tree.
Banish this cell and all that it holds
 Of heartache, of loneliness and rack;
Replace them, O Lord, just for tonight
 With the treasures of Old Santa's pack.
Tuck me once more in a trundle bed,
 All nervous and awe-filled and free
To dream of joys that await little boys
 At the foot of a Christmas tree.

Muffle the sound of sobs this night,
 And spare me, O Lord, the tears
That dot the road from Might-Have-Been
 That tarnish the wasted years.
Let me mount again those magic stairs,
 Lighted by love in a mother's eye;
Put me to sleep with the soft refrain
 Of a Christmas lullaby.
Let me sneak from bed at crack o' dawn,
 And tiptoe softly as can be,
Till my joy runs o'er, and I drop to the floor
 At the foot of my Christmas tree.

Widen my cell, O Lord, this night,
 Till I feel not stifled by bars;
Give me the world and a reindeer strong—
 Up, Dunder! Up, Blitzen! To the stars!
Deck me with holly and tinsel bright,
 Sprinkle my shoulders with snow!
Lead me o'er valley and hilltops
 Back to that fireplace aglow.
Just for tonight—that's all I ask—
 And tomorrow the brighter will be;
For I'll take my joy as a little boy
 At the foot of his Christmas tree.

Some odds about Christmas that may amaze you, dug up by Leo Guild, the odds expert. Here they are: It's 60 to 1 against snow in Los Angeles for Christmas. Happened once in Weather Bureau history. It's 7 to 1 against a man getting a tie for Christmas. If he does, it's most likely to be red first, blue second and green third. Odds are even that you get three Christmas cards and send out three. (Don't forget, this is based on our entire population.) Odds are 3 to 3 you'll eat turkey for Christmas, chicken second. Odds are 4 to 1 you won't have a Christmas tree. A little girl is most likely to get a doll, a boy blocks for presents. It's 119 to 1 you'll be alive next Christmas and be a little healthier. If you listen to the radio Christmas Day, it's 4 to 1 you'll hear "Silent Night"; 5 to 1, "Jingle Bells," and 6 to 1, "White Christmas." The odds are even you'll arise at 9:27 A.M. on Christmas. Children bring down the time average. Accidents are down a little on Christmas because it's a stay-at-home day. For the child under 6, it's 5 to 1 he or she won't believe in Santa. Odds are 2½ to 1 you'll get a present (adult or child regardless). Every two people will get five presents.

Here's how we gents fare at Christmastime. One of our department stores made a survey among a large number of Christmas shoppers showing that of every 1,000 Christmas gifts bought, 323 are for women, 302 for youngsters, 127 for men and the remainder unclassified. Shirts, ties, sox, slippers came in that order in the gifts for men. . . .

Wouldn't it be a splendid idea if we could all take a sort of national holiday between Christmas and New Year's?

There's one business that's humming the week after Christmas—busiest week in the entire year for the line. You'd never guess, so I'll have to tell you. It's the vacuum cleaner repair trade. Wives, in trying to vacuum the Christmas-tree leavings, tinsel and stuff, discover the machine won't pick them up the way it should. So off it goes for repair, the week after Christmas.

I can see very little change in the new year.

At least 300 noons out of the year you're going to tell a waitress that you drink your coffee black and five seconds later she'll be shoving a cream pitcher at you. . . . Some 26,000 secretaries are going to say "Who's calling, please?" And 26,000 people on the other end of the wire will be annoyed. . . . At least 175 people are going to slap you on the back and say, "You don't remember me, do you?" . . . Roughly speaking, on 42 nights of the year you'll just settle yourself comfortably in bed to discover you left the downstairs hall light on. . . .

When men are introduced to women on countless occasions they're going to offer their hand to shake hands, pull it back, start all over again and fumble once more. . . . Strings in pajamas are going to be pulled out with approximately the same frequency. . . . If parties in homes last until 2 A.M., the ice cubes will continue to run out about 1:15. . . . Conversationalists are going to interject, "To make a long story short" and then go on with 10 minutes of unimportant narrative. . . .

Newly engaged girls will still be at a loss for words when they show you the "rock" for the first time. . . . Insurance salesmen are going to open up their sales talk with, "We're discontinuing this type of insurance at this rate within 30 days and I wanted you to get in before the deadline." . . . Sales personnel in the stores won't forget their pat line: "That DOES something for you." . . .

Guests who should know better will still sit eight feet away from an ash tray and continue to flick ashes on living-room carpets. . . . Magazines are going to arrive as regularly and will be read by as many people from back to front. . . . Fumblers will take fully as long standing in front of the token box on streetcars pawing through their purses for a token. . . . Wives will continue saying to husbands, "John, it's time you took Wilbur aside and told him things." . . . Little Wilbur will have at least another year without such information. . . . It probably will happen every week to men over 40: someone standing over you will glance down at your scalp and remark, "Getting a little thin on top there, pal."

The graphs of the economists may move up or down; the charts of the experts may dip or zoom; indices may change. But basically you and I will remain about the same this new year, so may it be a happy one.

WRITTEN ON JANUARY 1, 1941

Maybe I'm a peculiar sort of duck, but last night I didn't feel like celebrating. The year, 1940, has been a good year to me and mine. The mortgage had been whittled down a little, the washing machine and the icebox payments had been completed, the kids had come through with nothing worse than a chest cold or two; and yet, the urge to go out and hip it up was humming itself in a minor key. Maybe middle age was settling on me. We had made no plans for ringing out the old and ringing in the new. So when I finished with the New Year's Eve broadcast I was without immediate purpose. As a result I did something that I hadn't done for years. On the way home, I drove by a little neighborhood church. There was a sign out in front that was lighted and it said *"Welcome"* on it, a few cars were parked out in front so I stopped in. . . .

It wasn't unlike the very first church I attended down in Magnolia. It had a spire on it. I think every church should have a spire. I remember the church steeple in Magnolia was the first thing you could see as you approached the town from any side. Somehow, the little edifice that I found myself in last night had recaptured a lot of the charm of my home-town church. . . .

The vestibule was about the same. It was chilly and on the floor were rubbers and overshoes. There was never any jumble about the arrangement of them down in Magnolia. Each worshiper, on his way in, removed his and put them in a certain place and knew well that when he came out they'd be in that same place. Well, I opened the door that led into the church proper. There weren't more than 40 people seated when I arrived. It was quiet. I looked down the main aisle. At the far and the near end were huge registers from which warm air billowed out of the furnace. And

I wondered if the Ladies' Aid had put the furnace in this little church as they had in Magnolia. . . .

Nobody met me at the door last night. And I was glad. City churches always have ushers and they've always bothered me. Invariably they haul me to the very front of the church. Maybe they sense that I'm near-sighted, but I always have a hunch that the ushers are saving the choicer seats in the rear for their intimate friends. But I had no such trouble last night. I sat exactly where I wanted to sit. I found that I was a full half hour ahead of the starting time of the service. But I thoroughly enjoyed it. I didn't do anything but think. . . .

I thought of Times Square in New York, of hospital wards and homes in Beverly Hills and bars and automobile accidents and living rooms in apartments and mortuaries and waitresses and actors and cops on the beat and airplane pilots and rich men. I thought of the distinguished and the forgotten. In the enchantment of that little church, I had a fine time for myself. . . .

The service opened with song. It was a classic hymn, "Oh, Come, All Ye Faithful." Deep and solemn. Over on the far side was a quavering voice that lifted above the others. The pastor spoke with power and conviction. At times his rich voice reverberated. He came close to our daily lives. He pictured our struggles. Grave faces became more solemn. The proceedings were straightforward, sincere, without guile. . . .

Midnight came. I was a little worried. I didn't know exactly what would happen then. It seemed to me that in previous years I had kissed the woman next to me. I waited. There were moments of silence. Noise of the whistles and the bells came from outside. We knelt. The pastor asked for God's blessing. And it seemed to me, as never before, we had it in that little neighborhood church. And so began my new year.

- o -

This remembrance stunt should be passed on. The minute a new kitchen calendar comes in at the beginning of the year, one correspondent fills out every important birthday or anniversary date of her intimate friends on the pages of the calendar and follows up each one with a card or note. And she amazes her friends with her memory.

A former North Dakota woman recalls that in her home state, whenever mild and foggy weather prevailed around the holiday season, farmers said it meant good crops the following autumn.

Statistics assembled by an insurance company show that sledding and coasting, among the most popular winter sports for children, kill in a single season approximately 300 American youngsters under 15 years of age. More than half the number die in collisions with automobiles. Thousands of others are injured. Bicycle-car collisions kill only around 150 a year. Among the children who meet death in coasting accidents, boys outnumber girls six to one.

The rest of the nation should know exactly how cold it gets in Minnesota. A Minneapolis barber had to thaw out a customer's hair before he could start cutting it. The high-school lad obviously had plastered his hair down with water and, hatless, had walked or run two blocks in 10 below zero weather to the barbershop. The barber used hot towels before his barbering could begin.

Comes now a fellow who says the annual snowfall over farm areas is worth hundreds of millions of dollars. Snow blows around, he says, because that's what it's made for. The action of its centrifuging through the air deposits on our land four kinds of chemical fertilizer; free ammonia, nitrates, nitrites and albuminoid ammonia. These are equivalent to many pounds of expensive imported chemical fertilizer per acre. For the farmer snow means a lot more than its moisture content. We'd better hope and pray we get enough each winter.

Most abandonment cases come in after dark, gloomy days or immediately following the holidays. Sharpest, then, must be the feeling of loneliness, and the deserted wives figure they'd better be doing something about it.

FOR THE BIRDS

"Please prod the folks," urges a reader, "to toss out some crumbs for the birds and particularly the sparrows." When I got that far in the note I thought he must be crazy. But read what he has to say about these little fellows: "If it were not for our hardy little friends, the sparrows, the bugs would eat us alive in the summertime. Sparrows don't migrate. They stick around the neighborhood where they're hatched. You can always tell by the looks of the sparrows whether the folks in that neighborhood are kind. Then, too, a scrubby, rough-feathered bunch of sparrows will respond quickly to liberal and regular feeding, especially in winter. It's a genuine pleasure to watch them change to lively, plump, cheerful, slick-feathered friends that come at call or sometimes roost and wait for their feeding. Remember, you'll be less buggy next summer if you scatter a few crumbs over the snow regularly now."

When you toss out a crumb or two for the birds, be glad to remember that a few tree swallows will consume 2,000 mosquitoes a day during insect time. The bread cast upon the snowdrifts will be worth it, maybe.

Here's another timely tip for bird lovers. Water is just as important to the birds in the wintertime as in the summer. By heating a brick daily and placing it in the water pan put out for birds, the water stays unfrozen long enough for the little feathered ones to quench their thirst.

Mama's little helper has another midwinter suggestion for you. If you're the type who keeps water in jugs, pans or pots on your radiators, before you refill them empty out all the water and clean the receptacle. Do it daily, because there's nothing like a pail of water sitting around to collect dust, microbes and other baddies. . . .

I'll bet you've forgotten the old trick of saving your eggshells, putting them in a jar of water and then occasionally sprinkling your house plants with that water. It gives your posies and plants a dose of much-needed lime.

HOT STUFF

Heating hints that sound practicable: A housewife writes: "Every morning after breakfast, I open my front and back door, my bedroom and bathroom windows and thoroughly air my house. You really save a lot on your heating bill. Your house heats up faster with fresh air and you feel better. Your house smells clean because all the stale air, musty odors leave. I always do it to the basement, too. And I do it daily no matter where the mercury is. We never have colds. And we don't have to open our windows at night. I have friends who never air their homes and you can tell it. Their clothing always has an odor of smoke or cabbage or pancakes or something. Tell your readers to try it just a week and see the results. But keep working while you're doing the airing."

A heating engineer from the University of Minnesota is the authority for this: Sleep nine months out of the year with your bedrooms windows closed. You'll not only reduce your fuel costs, but you'll cut down the possibilities of colds, sinus infections, and other disorders. And here's why: One window in your bedroom, weather-stripped and with a storm window on and closed, will still infiltrate enough fresh air (provided your bedroom door is left ajar) to make sleeping healthful and comfortable for four adults in that room. He says a house "breathes" just as a human does, and without the doors or windows being open.

Take a cold-weather hint for homes that don't have automatic heat controls: Never open the furnace drafts wide. Leave a safety margin and you'll avert most chimney fires.

Hey. Now you are asleep. Pay no attention to me. I'm just earning my living. I do this regularly. Go on, doze off, I don't care. I'll get my dough whether you read this or not. You'll be sorry, though, that you missed this item. Come the real blasts of winter, you'll be much comfier if you put a couple of blankets underneath the bottom sheet.

Newspapers offer the same kind of insulation but they're noisy every time you roll over.

WEATHER STUNT: One of the principal reasons why mailmen can stand going barehanded in the coldest winter weather is because they always make a point of washing their hands in cold water.

Want to know why you feel pepped up on brisk winter days? Bracing weather contracts the blood vessels near the skin's surface, raising the blood supply to the warmer inner tissues.

INEXPENSIVE FUN: Take a reading or magnifying glass and examine the frost on a windowpane. You'll see a brand-new world. And isn't that what we need? . . .

TAKE THIS OR LEAVE IT

A well-known man-about-town in Minneapolis popped up out of his red flannels long enough to recall this one. The chilly weather brought it out. It was years ago when the late lumberman T. B. Walker was still alive and was the wealthiest man in Minneapolis. He was a bank director then and rarely missed a meeting because, in those days, it was the policy of the bank to pay each director $20 in gold for every meeting he attended. It was the policy, too, of the directors to make a pool of the pay for absent directors, at $20 a shot, and split it among those present. T.B. looked out of his office one wintry morning. The mercury stood at almost 30 below. It was an ugly morning to attend a bank directors' meeting. "Aha," thought T.B., "I'll go. I'll probably be the only one there." So, with a shawl about his ears and bundled in the heaviest of clothing, he made for the meeting. The attendance that morning was 100 per cent. Each of the other directors had figured the same way.

Why wouldn't strips of canvas laid over a sidewalk or a driveway during the winter season make snow removal a lot easier? Comes the snow and you simply jerk back the canvas containing the snow and you have a cleared area.

Must be something wrong with it or it would have been thought of and used before this.

Let's get practical. The suggestion comes from somebody who, for obvious reasons, signed nothing more than "Laura." She writes, "No doubt there are others like myself who have gone through the same experience of waking up during the night cold and discovering that the bed partner who promised to comfort till death do us part has all the covers. You find yourself covered with goose-pimples and shivering while he snores blissfully on, as snug as a bug in a rug. This will stop all that—sew a drapery ring to the top comforter. Take a garter from a discarded garment (I know what she means), tie it to the bedspring or sew it to the mattress. On retiring, fasten the garter to the ring. Then he can squirm, he can even do somersaults, but the blankets stay put."

Next time there's any groping for a simile, I'm going to remember, "Colder than a farmhouse bedroom floor."

One of the vivid wintertime memories of my early life in Magnolia is the hum of the telephone wires that ran past our home. I just found out today what caused that hum. It was the wind vibrating them like the strings of a musical instrument. I thought all along the hum was messages going back and forth.

There's nothing any more peaceful than a small town on a crisp wintry morning after a soft, fresh snowfall. Smoke rising straight up from chimneys, neighbors out shoveling paths and puffing, the tinkling bells of a cutter, the bark of dogs at play, housewives shaking a rug off the back stoop. Sometimes I wish I could say, "Magnolia, here I come."

The bridges spanning the Mississippi River are several inches shorter in winter than during a summer hot spell.

A friend of mine thinks he has winter colds down to a minimum. Understand, we're not recommending the system, merely reporting it. This is what he does: Periodically, two or three times a day, even on the coldest days, he'll go outdoors for a few minutes, up to 10, in his shirt sleeves or without an overcoat, hat or gloves. He's careful not to do it when he's overheated, of course. He thinks it sort of immunizes his system to colds, reduces his danger to drafts, and so far has proved 100 per cent effective. To date, he hasn't had a cold and the average person catches four a year.

Still another man I know has a good trick for overcoming a chill. When the blasts set your teeth to chattering and the rest of your body to shivering, take a deep breath, hold it, and then, while holding your mouth shut, force that air into your mouth, but don't let it out for 30 seconds or so. It's that force that does something to your bloodstream which, in turn, makes the chill vanish. It works, too.

Here's a stunt for elderly people who can't get out now for their walk and exercise. You can beat the weather by walking in the basement carrying a water bucket about three-quarters full. The oldster who suggested it walks five or six minutes two or three times a day swinging the bucket. I quote his last paragraph, "Have your elderly readers try it. It gets all the gas off your stomach."

A furniture dealer out at Willmar, Minn., has a stunt for pedestrian protection when walks get icy. If you sprinkle sand on the slippery spots of your sidewalks, heat it a little first. Heating does away with the sand sticking to your shoes, which means you won't carry it indoors.

SCREAMING OF A WHITE WINTER

The insurance companies are out with a winter warning for those of you who are over 40. Heart trouble, they shout, is 30 per cent deadlier in the wintertime than in the summer. So beware of cranking a stubborn car or shoveling snow. In fact, they continue, watch any overexertion.

Even before you start your snow shoveling, it's a good idea to give your snow shovel, be it wood or steel, a good coat of floor wax. The snow slides off immediately and your work is lightened at least 25 per cent.

If you have louvers or ventilators of any type in the attic section of your home, it's advisable to make an inspection of them or any cracks at the eaves to determine whether driving snow sifts into those openings. Insulated top-floor ceilings usually prevent trouble, but it's still a good plan to take a peek.

Tobogganing is one of the most dangerous of all winter sports for adults and should be done with extreme caution if at all. When adults sit on a toboggan, they sit on the end of the spine with their legs usually wrapped around the person in front. Go over a bump in that position and it frequently results in a spinal fracture or a misplacement. Many of them can't be mended, either. Thought you ought to know while the toboggan season is still with us.

Little things in life: Don't let the late-season snow flurries fool you with regard to the moisture they leave. It takes 10 inches of snow to equal one inch of rain.

Snow and ski enthusiasts among you might adopt this stunt. Rub mentholated oil on your knees before you go outside. It not only keeps the limbs from tiring as rapidly but it also prevents cold from penetrating.

A mild January always throws a scare into me. I hesitate to think what March may hold. At best, though, spring can't be too far away.

A normal heating season is 75.7 per cent over on Feb. 28 and 89.4 per cent through on March 31.

Part Three

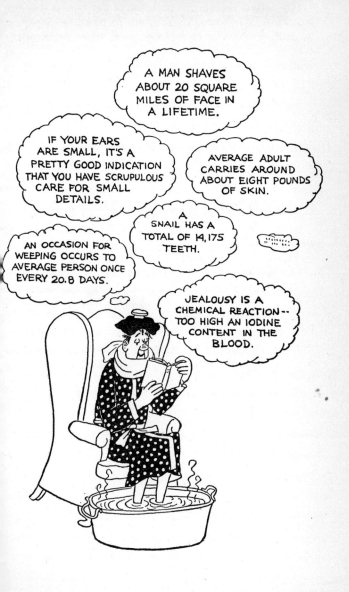

WHAT TO READ TILL THE DOCTOR COMES

MEDICINE—IN GENERAL

Ah, health!

What would we columnists do without it?

To be perfectly frank, the same things that we do with it.

We make daily copy out of health and all its phases, good or bad. The impact of health came to me pretty strongly in going back over columns I had written these past 20 years to pick items for this little collection. It was emphasized when I turned out about a week's worth of copy about my experience in an automobile accident. That got me to reflecting about the state of my health generally—the annual physical examinations; the one time before when I was laid up with an ankle injury as a result of slipping while boarding a boat; the thousands of items I'd gotten from medical gossip, home remedies, chatting with druggists and scanning medical publications.

Now I can report definitely that over the years I've written more about health, in fun or seriousness, than about any other equally broad general topic. You're all interested in your own health or that of your friends, but my interest is even wider because I've got to satisfy an editor every day with some newspaper copy. Since the Old Gent is the nervous ulcer type, he probably thinks every health item I turn in is written expressly for him, so he's more likely to pass it without the usual heavy touch of his big blue pencil.

I enjoy an advantage over the doctors, too. They have to deliver results with their diagnosis and treatment, but Ol' Doc Adams can prescribe all sorts of medical trivia and just let it go with a warning to readers that it is only somebody's gossip. Also, I can make hay with medical jokes, while your physician has to keep up a pretty dignified front for his patients. Which reminds me of the advice a medical dean used to give students at the University of Minnesota.

"Every medical graduate," he'd say, "should do two things: raise a mustache and develop piles. The mustache to make you look mature and the piles to make you look concerned." How many medicos do you know who would try that one on a patient?

Even the more serious medical facts, however, often have their lighter side and lend themselves to being items for a columnist. For instance, from my own writings I've got advice in the line of practically every medical specialty being practiced today, and I didn't know until quite recently that even experienced doctors have to go through intense screening by national boards to qualify as specialists. But a columnist can practice a new specialty every day, writing about flu, flat feet or fat as the spirit moves him. What real doc can make that claim? Now, before we get too involved in specialties, let's look over some of the notes I have on what might be called the general practice of medicine, and I do mean practice:

THE FRUIT OF KNOWLEDGE
OR
LINES TO AN M.D.

From the day, so to speak, of creation
  Mankind has been subject to ills,
Though he waited for civilization
  To learn about powders and pills.
The pains that so often assailed him
  Made our primitive ancestor squirm,
And he never found out that what ailed him
  Was only a germ.

> An ache, under certain conditions,
>   Has been through the ages the same,
> But the efforts of learned physicians
>   Have fitted it out with a name.
> We are told with mellifluous quickness
>   Which no one can quite understand
> That every conceivable sickness
>   Is due to a gland.
>
> Our forefathers suffered acutely
>   From things that afflict us today,
> But we are aware more minutely
>   Of what is the trouble than they.
> The doctors are endlessly clever
>   At telling us habits to shun—
> Being sick is as painful as ever,
>   But vastly more fun.

We're in a nice class—the world's creatures which live longest are whales, elephants, turtles and human beings.

Man's an odd duck when you consider him objectively. Think upon this (all a matter of record) : He can live without sleep for 115 hours; without water for 22 days; without food for 75 days; hold his breath for 20 minutes, five seconds; stay under water for six minutes, 29 seconds; live in a heat of 248 degrees F.; live in a cold of 103 degrees below zero F.; glide for 465 miles; climb without oxygen to 28,200 feet; climb with oxygen to almost 100,000 feet; dive below water to 500 feet; run, in 59 days, 5,625 miles; walk on his hands 16 miles a day for 55 days; hike on stilts 31 miles a day for 58 days; squat on a pole for 10 days; parachute jump from 30,800 feet; have a family of 44 children and live after his heart has stopped for 20 minutes.

Modern Medicine Magazine lists the following tidbits of medical progress in a nutshell: A man can live and breathe with only the two upper lobes of his lungs, according to a surgical report. Women who go without salt during their pregnancies are more likely to have short labors. Treatment of cross-eyes should be started before a child is seven. An emulsion of soy beans is used in place of milk for infants with eczema. The average United States citizen spends between 3½ and 4 per cent of his income annually for medical services of one sort or another.

OWED TO OUR M.D.'S

Yet it's estimated there are $350,000,000 worth of unpaid doctors' bills in the country.

Medicos are pretty well agreed that only 10 per cent of their night calls are urgent.

Help, help, cries a busy hospital worker. What can we do to make people keep track of their own hospital bills for income-tax purposes? As if we at the hospitals don't have more work than we can handle now, without having to take care of all our ex-patients over again! All through the first part of the year we're swamped with requests to look up old bills, information the patients should have when they leave the hospital.

Might be a good idea if you'd check right now on whether you are carrying any identification. City hospitals usually have several "unknowns" a month, and it's very confusing, particularly if some die. Or won't you care then?

It might be well if more of us adopted the philosophy of the man with this formula for a long and happy life: When I walk, I walk slow; when I sit, I sit loose, and when I worry, I sleep.

Maybe you don't want to live to be 100. In case you do, however, here's your best possible chance, according to a doctor who delves in statistics. You must be a woman, keep interested in life and romance, keep busy and plan for the future, have both a hobby and a hubby, never lose your sense of humor. The same rules apply to men, but only about half as many men live to be 100 as women.

Want to know how long you're going to live, roughly? Add the number of years your father and mother and your two grandfathers and your two grandmothers lived, and then divide the total by six for what you may expect.

A French institute computed these figures: If you live to be 70, you've talked an average of 13 years, eaten six years, washed for a year and a half, and amused yourself for 23 years. This leaves 26½ unaccounted for. Well, there's always sleep.

You probably wonder if doctors, because of their superior knowledge of medicine, live longer than the average United States citizen. The answer is no. Life expectancies are about the same. Many more doctors die of diseases of the heart and coronary arteries, probably because of their hard work, than the general population, but fewer doctors die from most infectious diseases and from conditions which surgery can correct. The two balance each other and, as a result, the physician or surgeon has about as long to live as you and I have. . . .

Despite the fact that the life span of Americans has materially and steadily increased since 1776, the life span of presidents of the United States has decreased 13 years since the birth of the nation.

Only time I ever envy a doctor is at the dining-room table when there's a carving job to be done. The dexterity of the average physician and surgeon is always noticeable the minute he puts a carving knife in his paw and goes to work on a bird or a roast. I don't suppose a survey has ever been made, but I'd guess that 95 per cent of the rest of us are in the awkward stage, at least when it comes to carving.

It's fun beating doctors at their own game. I once had occasion to pull a little quiz program on a group of physicians and surgeons. Here are a few of the stumpers the medicos missed; see how you'd fare: If a man fell 15 feet and landed on the bottom of his feet, what would happen to his tarsal cartilage? Not much in all probability, because it's his eyelid. One of the physicians didn't know what he'd do if a patient came in suffering from pendiculation. Another had no idea how to treat sternutation. Pendiculation is laughing loudly and sternutation is sneezing. I asked a half dozen doctors for the name of the little trough or groove that leads from the nose down to the upper lip. In case it ever comes up in your life, call it the philtrum and you'll be correct. It goes without saying, however, that every doctor in the crowd could have stumped me readily with questions about my own business, so I'm not gloating.

I'll bet even the docs who practice it don't know what dichotomy means. It's the highfalutin term for fee-splitting indulged in by some of the profession.

Quick—what does epizootic mean? Assuming you missed, it's when a disease spreads among a group of animals. The same condition among humans, as you know, is an epidemic.

This may be one of those legends that make the rounds, but myth or no, it still carries with it a lesson. It concerns the woman whose child pulled through a critical illness. Came settling up time with the doctor and the woman presented him with a pocketbook she had embroidered.

"You can never be paid fully for what you've done," she told him, "but this is a token."

The doctor told her rather coldly that his fees were payable in cash, not gratitude. The fee is $200, he informed her. Whereupon the woman opened the embroidered pocketbook and extracted five $100 bills. She handed the doctor two of them, picked up the purse with its $300 and walked out.

Then there's the one about the woman who accused her doctor of overcharging, to which he countered, "Don't forget, I made eleven visits when your son had the measles."

"Yes," retorted the mother, "but don't you forget, he infected the whole school."

THE WHOLE MAN

Vague indeed were my ideas on what going through a clinic was like. Until my first trip through the famed Mayo Clinic at Rochester, Minn.

When you hit the 40 mark you start arguing with yourself and you say: "Maybe I should have a complete physical check-up." Along comes something like the cancer campaign and you hear that cancer kills one out of eight. You read the messages of the heart campaign and you discover that heart disease takes one out of three. You shudder a little and you take a good look at yourself in the mirror. You don't have the freshness you had the day you were graduated from high school, but you feel pretty well. You can still turn out a day's work. Then you start searching for symptoms. You picture the details of an examination. An instrument going into your ear, blood coming out of your arm, the awkward positions you have to assume. You weigh the possibility of the shock you'd get if you were told you had a bum ticker against the joy of being pronounced sound. You think of the pretty nurses standing by as spectators. It's a tough decision to make when you finally resolve you'll visit a clinic or have a complete physical check-up by your family physician.

Here's the report on my first eight hours of clinical examination. There was a new experience at every turn and a turn about every three minutes. If I had it to do over again I think I'd go to Rochester in a Gypsy Rose Lee outfit—something you can get in and out of with dispatch. Outside of the constant undressing and dressing, there is little or no confusion in a place where you'd expect confusion to be the keynote. The entire procedure is perfectly established, orderly and simplified. There are waits, of course, but they're comfortable waits, and there's always the surprise element. You have no idea what's coming next. But it comes.

The Mayo Clinic building itself is a series of doctors' offices. The waiting rooms resemble small auditoriums. The doctors' offices are standardized and aren't unlike those of any M.D. in your home town. No splendor, no tinsel, no glamor. Registration comes first, and then you are assigned to a medical fellow who in most cases is a young man taking specialization under the University of Minnesota and working toward another degree. He sits with you in his little office for as long as you like in a very informal session as you give out with your history. That must be a joy to a lot of patients who dote on reciting their ills. It's a perfect opportunity for the hypochondriac. If you think there's something wrong with you, you tell him. He asks you for symptoms. You can tell him that as far as you know there isn't anything wrong, that you simply wanted a routine check-up. He makes very copious notes as he goes along, asks you questions, goes back as far as your measles and mumps days. After he's written what seems like 20,000 words about you, he asks you to peel off. You go behind a little screen for that and he tells you to come out wearing a nightshirt in cape form and carrying a sheet that you may drape over you where the cape doesn't reach. I know I must have looked like an overstuffed version of Mahatma Gandhi. The fellow's examination starts you on your way. He checks your reflexes, takes your blood pressure, counts your pulse beats, taps your back, listens to your breather. He then begins to fill out cards for your appointments in the various sections which you are to visit subsequently. The cards carry the floor location of the desk to which you report and the time you are to be there. Follow those cards and your day is almost as simple as a Sunday at home.

Patients who are on their third or fourth day usually open the conversation with, "How are you getting along?" They really don't care, all they want is an opportunity to open up on you with their own troubles. One man spent 45 minutes telling me the disadvantages of the whirlpool treatment as against deep therapy. He never did get around to naming his exact trouble. He figured I was smart enough to guess. Another man wore a white canvas glove on his left hand. I was dying to know what was under the glove. But he never cracked.

Rochester is not a city of smiles. People everywhere are going sternly about the business of getting well. Canes and bandages and impediments abound in almost every waiting room. There were mothers with tots as young as three. Even early in the morning the mothers looked weary. It must be hard for the little ones to understand why they must be subjected to the strange ordeals of examination. On the evening of my first day, I couldn't help but wonder what the charts and the X-ray film and the blood slides might reveal when tomorrow comes. How dependent we are on health.

If somebody came up to the young fellow doctor who was my guiding light at Rochester for two days and asked, "How're things in Glocca Morra?" he might not be able to answer, but that's the only place he didn't look into. Up the nose, down the throat, through the chest, into the stomach, across the liver and over the skin. Where the hand of man can't set foot, there's some scientific device that will do the job. Surprisingly, there is virtually no pain to any of these processes and very little distress or discomfort.

I quickly discovered a way to tell something about the reports that come back from laboratories and what not. You listen to the doctor as he examines a chart of a laboratory report or an X-ray. All he says is, "Hmmmmm." The inflection he gives it is the tip-off. When he says the Hmmmmm with a rise and a fall, that's cause for concern. When he sort of sighs it out happily, you can relax. If he gives just a little short "Hmmm" that's somewhat mystifying. You don't know whether he's amazed or disappointed.

I want to toss a posy or two to the Mayo personnel at Rochester. I've never seen a more delightful group of men and women than the employees. The girls, whether they're technicians, desk attendants or nurses, are utterly charming. They seem to sense that most of their contacts are with sick people—people who aren't in normal health, anyway—and they extend themselves to take perfect care of everybody. They're alert, courteous, cheerful. Somehow they have been inoculated with a demeanor that is extraordinary. Many of them come from small towns adjacent to Rochester. Some of them have service records that extend beyond 20 years. Whether they're young or old they have developed a relationship toward the public that is phenomenal. The same is true of the men attendants—elevator operators, doormen, guides. They seem to anticipate the needs of the infirm. They're solicitous, eager, understanding. Rochester should be proud of every one of them.

I just discovered that I have ergasiophobia. Medically speaking, it's a dread of work.

Well, that general stuff doesn't include much diagnosis or prescribing, so it should be pretty safe. In some of the specialist material which follows, however, there are frankly a lot of old wives' tales and medical gossip, so you'd better play it safe and see a doctor if you don't feel well. You can take the book along, however, and have fun reading some of the stuff while you're waiting in the physician's office.

PHYSICAL MEDICINE

INCLUDING PHYSICAL FITNESS AND PHYSICAL JERKS

LIFE CAN'T BE BEAUTIFUL, APPARENTLY. Look what a Ph.D. in physical education once put into a bulletin: "Condition of the abdomen is a key sign of physical fitness status. A soft and pendulous abdomen is usually associated with splanchnic pooling and poor circulation of the blood: The blood pressure usually drops in changing from lying to standing and organic endurance is exceedingly poor. Men who are 35 per cent or more above average weight for their age and height have a mortality rate of 1½ times that of the average man. When the abdominal girth is more than two inches greater than the chest girth of full expansion, the extra mortality is 50 per cent above the excess mortality associated with overweight itself. The so-called 'bay windows' are usually high indices of high blood pressure, glypcuria, brain hemorrhages and Bright's disease. Blood from the heart goes to the fat instead of the nerves and vital organs."

A friend of mine who operates a health service comes up with this as the right way to start your day: When you get out of bed in the morning, stand in front of your open window and take 20 deep breaths (he forgot to say what the neighbors are going to think), and then get down on the floor on your back and rise into a sitting position. Start with five times and increase one a day till you're up to 25. Consistently done, says this expert, the exercises will make a new person out of you. He also has some suggestions on how to walk: Square your shoulders, swing your arms easily, arch the chest, breathe deeply, draw in the abdomen, put the weight forward and hold the head erect.

You might apply the theory of football coaches in handling their players so carefully the night before a game to your own exercise. Rest taken before physical exertion is much more valuable than rest taken after one is worn out.

Has your posture been suffering under current burdens? Try this: Walk as if you were carrying a book on your head with your shoulders down and your toes pointing straight ahead. And without holding your breath, contract and relax the abdominal and posterior muscles until they show signs of tiring. Definite posture improvement, the experts say, will be in evidence in three weeks.

And here's a hint that will help improve posture while you're driving. Most of us slump our worst while at the wheel. So simply sit up perfectly straight and adjust the rear-view mirror for that position. Then, every time you glance in the mirror, it brings you to perfect sitting posture once more.

FALLING DOESN'T HELP

If you're fearful of office bulge, try a little skating. Skating elongates the muscles, particularly in the arms and legs, it strengthens back muscles and thins down the waist. And here's something I didn't know about skating: when ankles ache, it doesn't necessarily mean they're too weak for skating. It simply indicates that the lower leg muscles are getting the kind of exercise they need.

This is a heck of a subject to bring up, but when the average adult (a he or a she) sits down, from three to six inches are added to the spread of the body.

Tests show that climbing ordinary household stairs consumes about 15 times as much energy as just walking across a level floor.

LEGS CAN BE BEAUTIFUL

Check your own pins with these measurements for a perfect leg: Ankle, eight inches; calf, 11½ inches; knee, 12; upper leg, 19½. How did you come out?

LOOK NOW IF YOU WANT TO: Only two out of every five people have legs that are the same length. Chances are the right pin also is more developed than the left.

A pretty fair bone specialist tells me that women should never sit with one of their legs curled up underneath them. It was this custom among Japanese women, for instance, that developed unshapely pins among the Nipponese.

One of the common injuries of parachutists is called "silent fracture." It's a break on the outer bone of the leg, has very few symptoms. The soldier frequently doesn't report for several days, and then has just a little pain.

They're telling about the two men who saw a tree surgeon hobbling along the street with his leg in a cast. "Wonder what happened to him?" inquires the first gent. "Probably fell out of a patient," replied the other.

HOW ARE YOUR TOOTSIES

Let's pause in the day's occupation to devote a little thought to the faithful appendages that function so well in getting us from place to place. The chiropodists have worked out a few very simple home exercises that'll do a world of good in relaxing you and strengthening your feet. The next spare moment or two you have, run through this routine in your bare feet. Sit down and move the toes vigorously back and forth and go through the motions of grasping something with your toes. Then give your feet a rotary movement first to the right, then to the left. Raise and lower the body while standing on tiptoe, also walk around the room for a minute or two on your tiptoes. Then alternately walk on the inner and outer borders of the feet. Be sure to lift the bottoms of the feet clear of the floor. Rub the feet vigorously with a towel a few minutes after your bath or shower. Aches and other signs of foot discomfort will often disappear if we regularly remove our shoes, relax and stretch out the legs and feet. Nerve irritation is often reduced that way.

Back in the first century, the same practitioners used to care for the teeth, hair, and corns. Odd combination of duties, wasn't it?

Don't spend the day breaking your neck trying this little stunt. Instead use a ruler. Either way, though, you can prove it. The length of your foot is the same as the distance from the crook of your elbow to your wrist line.

Big feet are an organist's best asset, according to a music expert, and next comes independence of motion.

Football players and drummers suffer alike. The rhythm section often becomes afflicted with Charley horses in the enlarged muscles that develop just below the elbows. . . .

A LOAD OFF YOUR FEET

Department-store workers and others who have to be on their feet a lot during the day will find it helpful, counsels one of them, if they switch shoes about midday. Use a pair with a slightly higher heel for afternoons. It does something beneficial to the spinal column, she says.

You girls who spend many hours a day on your feet without a chance for rest can build reserve strength in your pins by that old-fashioned wall-climbing exercise. Lie flat on your back with your hips about two feet from the wall.

Then literally climb the wall with your feet, raising your hips from the floor as you work your feet upward and lowering them as you come down. It isn't as hard as it sounds and it makes your hip and leg muscles capable of carrying on longer.

WE LIVE AND LEARN: I've been told by a physician and surgeon that one of the first places we humans show our age is right behind the knee. Line up the members of your family and you'll be able to note the difference.

Another simple method for discovering whether a gent is fudging on his age is this: Look closely at his ears. For some curious reason, advancing years take their first toll on the male ear. The ear begins to sag a mite, the skin in the region around the ear begins to look on the tired side.

ODD STATISTIC: During the Civil War, four left legs were lost in battle to every right leg, whereas in the matter of arms, four right arms were lost for every left.

Added to housemaid's knee and writer's cramp is a malady bank clerks get. It's called bill-counter's thumb, which comes from the manual counting of paper currency.

If you want to see how your hand compares with the average mitt, measure it by your third finger. The average third finger is as long as the hand is wide.

Now it comes out that people grow up a trifle lopsided. A Michigan State College survey indicates that the majority of adults develop a right arm that is a trifle longer than the left. . . .

LET'S GET THIS STRAIGHT: The funny bone isn't a bone; it's a nerve which, when struck, gives you that funny feeling. . . .

NOGGIN NOTES

There are more than 125,000 skulls fractured in the United States annually.

At birth, the widest part of a baby's body is its head.

Relative to the respective heights, short people have larger heads and brains than the tall folk.

Strange thing, your noggin doesn't get much bigger with increased weight. For instance, take on 15 pounds and you need but an eighth size larger lid at most.

No matter how big your head is, if you take a piece of string, start at the middle of your forehead, and wrap the string around your bean three times, it'll always equal your height.

You can also get a quick approximation of anybody's height by measuring the length of the individual's middle finger and multiplying that by 19. The figure is the height of the finger's owner.

If your height is bothering you, shorty, take your measurements in the morning. A medical authority says most men are up to an inch taller in the morning than they are at night. It has something to do with the discs of cartilage between vertebrae of the spine flattening out after you've been on your feet all day.

There may be exceptions, but these two yardsticks sounded unusual to me: A grown man is always at least as tall as his mother. And when a boy is 12, his weight is half his adult weight and he's two-thirds as tall as he'll be when he reaches his full height.

Johns Hopkins University once ran a study of 2,332 dead men and the research revealed that body height has nothing to do with the length of life. Talls and shorts were among the long-lived and the short-lived in virtually an equal degree.

One of the nation's leading geneticists has just found that if one parent has a prominent nose, large ears or the like, while those features are normal in the other parent, a child born to that couple will very likely inherit the features of the more extreme type, which is certainly the kid's tough luck. But there's nothing, I guess, that he can do about it.

Not that anyone will ever ask you, but a man can be perfect physically and mentally and yet be rejected for enlist-

ment in the United States Army if his mug is characterized by extreme ugliness.

PLASTIC SURGERY is one of the oldest branches of medical science. The Aryuveda, a sacred journal of the Hindus, reveals that marked skill in plastic surgery was attained in India more than 2,500 years ago.

The upper part of the average human face ceases to grow after the fifteenth year, while the lower part keeps right on growing on and on and on, which probably accounts for your double chin, and mine.

Don't change your disposition when you hear this, but the experts are now saying that wrinkles do not generally come from worry. Instead, most of them originate from laughing.

Does your chin recede? Take heart, my little pet. That alleged handicap does not necessarily indicate a weakness of character. A historical survey of chins shows that some of the most forceful characters of all time were people with Andy Gumpish chins.

Watch your collar for tightness. A collar that's too pinchy will bring on attacks of dizziness in people who have an irritable reflex at the forking of the carotid artery in the neck.

If you think you're going into epilepsy, a Mayo Clinic expert advises, first of all check the tightness of your collar. A tight collar pressing against the sensitive carotid arteries may occasionally cause unconsciousness.

From a nurse comes this handy bit of information: If you ever feel a faint coming on, simply bend over as though you were about to tie your shoelace. In fact, actually untie and tie it again. It shoots the blood to your head and counteracts the tendency to faint.

Because the average person will faint in less than 30 minutes if held motionlessly upright, army recruits sometimes feel dizzy when they stand stiffly for long periods of inspection. They soon learn, though, to bear the ordeal by doing inconspicuous toe wiggling and muscle contracting.

Ever noticed that when you're hurt you'll often, perhaps subconsciously, try to inflict pain to some other part of your body? For instance, sock your finger with a hammer and you may bite your lip or pound your head. Medical research on the subject has revealed that one pain serves to deaden another, which is really why you do it. . . .

Out of every 1,000 risks you take, like standing on a wobbly chair, 330 of them will give you a scare; and of the 330 endangering ones 29 will result in minor injuries; and —this is the bugaboo—one will end in a major injury.

Met a gent a while ago who was seriously injured in an automobile accident. And here's a tip he gave me: Every man at 45 should plan to spend six months in bed. The rest, at that age, is the greatest revivifier one can imagine.

This shocker from a faculty member of the University of Minnesota medical school: "No one has ever proved that a clean man is more healthy than a dirty one." Put that in your bathtub and smoke it.

Britain may have its faults, but this isn't one of them: **Britishers refer to setting-up exercises as "physical jerks."**

YOUR INNER SELF

The average adult takes about 12 breaths a minute. Better check up to see if you're getting your share.
The usual resident of an American industrial city inhales a teaspoonful of dust, dirt and soot each weekday.
BREATH CONTROL can be useful. Some day you may be in a hospital with a fresh incision and some gagster will come in with a fast joke. To prevent ripping a stitch or excessive abdominal pain, remember this stunt: Simply gasp through your mouth as though you were short of breath. It works for eliminating an approaching laugh and also can forestall a sneeze.

You are a mass of muscle, if you must know. Your body muscles constitute about 43 per cent of your total weight.

Assuming that you're normal, your brain is only 2.37 per cent of your total weight. Even at that, it's six times heavier than your kidneys.

If you're an average human being your skeleton weighs 32 pounds.

EVER HEAR OF A XYSTER? Well, it's what the doc uses on you when he scrapes your bones.

YOUR BODY TEMPERATURE reaches its height around 6 p.m. and is lowest about 2 in the morning.

"Passing out cold," according to the medicos, really occurs in some cases. There are records of alcoholic intoxication where a man's temperature has fallen to 75 degrees and he has still recovered.

Next to city editors, birds have the highest body temperatures of any creatures.

It won't do your mate's back any good, but you might as well know that if you regularly have cold feet, you're suffering from what is known in medical circles as Raynaud's disease.

CONSIDER YOUR HEART

That busy little organ, weighing about a half a pound, generates enough energy in 12 hours to lift a tank car of 65 tons a foot off the ground.

That heart of yours (with the possible exceptions of bankers and credit managers) pumps six and a half tons a day.

One of the nation's greatest heart authorities contends that unless you do manual labor all day long, three meals a day are extremely bad for the heart, let alone the stomach.

Ma, get this one: Despite all the torchy and sugary songs the lyric writers have been penning to you dames, a woman's heart is about 20 per cent smaller than a man's.

Hey, you cardiac guys, back away from that card table! The medicos are saying now that card playing, not boozing, is the chief social enemy of the heart. Excitement of the playing is what does the damage.

Ninety-five out of every 100 applications for life insurance are put through, but heart trouble and high blood pressure are the main reasons why the other five per cent fail to qualify. Overweight is high on the list of "failures in qualifying." Fewer than one-half of one per cent are turned down because of excessive drinking.

WARNING NOTE FROM A MEDICO: Anyone with high blood pressure has a race going on in his body to see whether it'll be apoplexy, kidney disease, or heart failure that will take him. And it's usually heart failure.

Got any more cute stories, Doc?

NOW HAVE A LIFT: Contrary to what many people believe, high blood pressure is not a disease but a symptom. Bad heart, arteries or kidneys can bring it about. Overweight persons, those who work continually under mental strain and individuals who obtain improper diet or rest, frequently develop it. The condition cannot be inherited but a susceptibility often exists in families.

MORE COURAGE TO YOU PUFFERS: Medical records list victims of high blood pressure who lived to be 100 years old.

Pleasant week-end thought: The blood vessels of an adult have a combined length of about 100,000 miles.

If the family doc gives you some of that high-powered stuff about what your blood contains, pay some attention. Here's what it means: If you have a lot of iron you're intellectual and artistic; when your calcium content is high, you're quiet and plodding; those with too much carbon are dull, lazy and plump; if you've an excess of oxygen you're too optimistic and friendly, and if sulphur is what you have too much of, you're unstable and emotional.

I hate to be persnickety, but if you must refer to me that way, call me a white-blooded he-man instead of a red-blooded individual. It's the white corpuscles that attack poison microbes in your blood and destroy them. And those same white cells die by the thousands in conducting their onslaught.

Women faint more readily than men because their blood contains more water and fewer red cells than that of males

and, in a burst of emotion, women's blood lacks the energy and oxygen of a gent's blood.

To be a professional blood donor, you should live on liver —and spinach.

WATCH YOUR HAIR. It's a good reflection of whether you have a disease that affects the bloodstream. In other words, one afflicted with poor circulation or anemia will have lusterless tresses.

You don't happen to have one of those black moles on your face, do you? A medico told me that they're very bad little fellows once they become irritated. And once they turn malignant, they spread into the bloodstream and you're apt to wind up with most anything. But they're easily treated or even removed if taken early.

Can't remember a childhood illness that was any worse than a green-apple bellyache. Oh, boy!

The docs are calling it "match bellyache." It's a reaction some people get when they light a cigaret too quickly after striking the match. The burning sulphur settles in the abdominal regions somehow and creates the discomfort. CURE: Let the match burn for an instant first.

Let me ask you, are you a eupeptic? It's a person who digests food easily—just the opposite of a dyspeptic.

TO SQUELCH THE BELCH

I've waited now for weeks trying to catch myself a batch of hiccoughs so I could try this alleged cure, but so far it's no go. Rather than wait it out, I figured it was better to pass on the trick untested: Next time the ailment overtakes you, a reader suggests, simply lie down flat on your stomach and relax. It beats that hand-in-ear, breathing-in-a-bag or drinking from the opposite side of a tumbler technique all to pieces. Just don't get the hiccoughs in church and you'll be all right.

If you're seized with a severe attack of hiccoughs while in the kitchen, try placing a couple of drops of vinegar on your tongue.

Many a lasting case, or even a shorter attack, of hiccoughs surrenders to a small teaspoon of peanut butter. A
second spoonful is rarely necessary. . . .

MY FAVORITE ORGAN

Don't let them twit you about the size of your stomach.
At capacity it only swells to about the size of a football.
That pear-shaped stomach of yours will hold two quarts
when it's full.

Clinical tests have recently shown that there's a pronounced rise in stomach acidity both during and after
smoking.

One thing I learned from a surgeon: Hyperacidity indicates ulcer; hypo-acidity indicates cancer. And how are
all your folks?

The medicos don't know why, but ulcers attack hardest
during the fall and spring, so if you're susceptible, watch
out at those times.

Worry and overwork are far more important factors than
going off the reservation in a dietary way in kicking up
an abdominal fuss such as ulcers, say the experts. So skip
both of them.

It's probably because we males fret more than women,
anyway, ulcers in the upper part of the digestive tract
occur four times as often in men as in women.

**No wonder so many people suffer from ulcers—the
stomach contains 35,000,000 glands.**

According to experiments explained in *Modern Medicine,*
cold applied externally to the abdomen increases both the
motor activity in the gastro-intestinal tract and the secretion of acids. Cold internally diminishes the secretion of
gastric acid. Hence, it appears that cold drinks and hot
packs are appropriate for the patient with stomach ulcers.

If you have to have something wrong with you, you might
as well go fancy, and the fanciest handle for an anatomical
difficulty I've heard lately is "a turbulent colon." That's
really drawing-room conversation.

I don't want to scare you, but life insurance statistics show that only 15 per cent of all persons dying from gall-bladder trouble have shown any evidence of that condition during their lifetime.

Don't let your gallstones get you down. For some curious reason, Chinese purchasers have been known to pay from $125 to $175 a pound for the little nuggets. Most of them come from cattle, though.

The august United States Supreme Court had this dilly: A woman was suing a steamship company for $50,000 because the vibration of one of its liners had dislodged her kidney stone and subsequently, she alleged, damaged her health. In the event you may be planning similar action, delay it. She lost.

It's the fourth most fatal disease in the United States, and yet, I'll wager, if I shouted it at you, you wouldn't know what "nephritis" is. It's the disease of the kidneys. While we're at it, you may as well have the complete list. No. 1 is heart disease, next is cancer, cerebral hemorrhage follows. The fifth in our land is accidents. In the world as a whole, however, malaria kills more people than any other disease.

Check yourself thoroughly, and you're probably suffering from some form of "itis." A standard medical dictionary contains 796 words that end with the suffix "itis." It means inflammation of some part or tissue of the body. Tonsilitis is a good example. Some are funny, though. You can get attic-itis. That sounds as though it might mean bats in the belfry. It isn't. It's an inflammation of the attic of your ear. If your girl friend has "Cheil-itis," however, she's okay. That means hot lips.

Why, I don't know, but men, say the medicos, are more susceptible to appendicitis than women.

About fifty per cent of those operated on for appendicitis want a gander at their appendix after it has been removed. And that's probably one reason why hospitals always keep them "on file." If you've had yours out, and comes along a dull moment at a house party, you can bundle up your guests, drive down to the hospital where you had the appendix removed, and there, stored permanently in a vial, you'll find it.

So far as your appendix is (or is it are?) concerned, the doc could snip it off without making you wince a bit because it's insensitive to pain. It's the getting at it that gives you the twinge.

SOUNDS LIKE A LOT OF GUFF to me, but a friend told me that her doctor told her it was strictly legit. Here's the gag: To test yourself for the condition of your appendix, take the curved end of a hairpin and draw it down over your right side with a little pressure, going from your waist down. If you wince, the friend said (and the doctor, too) you may have an appendectomy coming on. I tried it and winced like all get-out. And strangely enough, nothing happened when I did it on the left side. Anyway, it'll give you a little diversion when you get into bed tonight.

This writer has always felt more or less a personal interest in the health of his readers. So take this warning from the Nutritional Review: This organization advises against eating polar bear livers. "They have too much vitamin A," the group points out, "and the man who partakes may find his skin peeling off from head to foot." I know you'd all get pretty chilly going around without your skin. Besides, a lot of people who haven't been eating polar bear livers would probably stare at you. *You WILL watch yourselves, won't you?*

A SHORT BEER, DOC

Nearly all of us have watched while a physician has struck the wall of our chests with sharp blows with his fingers. Or he may lay one finger on the chest, nail outward, and strike the nail of that finger with the nail of a finger from the other hand. All the while he listens intently. This is called, in case you hadn't heard, "percussion."

But I wonder how many know that it dates back to the eighteenth century. A young Austrian lad noticed that his father, an innkeeper, could determine how much wine was in a cask by tapping on the outside of it and listening for

he peculiar sound produced at various levels of the fluid
within. The lad subsequently became a physician and simply
ransferred his father's technique to tapping the human rib
o determine, by sound, the conditions of the parts within.

If you've ever had sunstroke, you'll not only find heat
hard to bear, but you also will have an abnormal susceptibility to the action of stimulants.

**Water's the last thing you'd think would put you on a
binge. But word from the Harvard Medical school is that
it's an easy matter to become water-intoxicated. The water
jag also results in nausea, dizziness, weakness.**

An eminent medico advises that if distillers added half
a milligram of vitamin B_1 to a pint of whisky, it would
eliminate staggering and other aftereffects ordinarily produced by drinking the pint. Deficiency in vitamin B_1 also
is a big factor in producing delirium tremens.

If the boss pops off at you, here's the reason: During a
day's work when a person is active, calcium and potassium
are drained from the nerves and muscles through the
bloodstream and later restored during sleep. The Old Boy
probably hasn't been getting his required rest, his nerves
and muscles are exhausted and he nettles easily.

**The human body, unfortunately, doesn't retain proteins,
which is the reason why you have to keep stuffing them in
daily.**

Whenever you have what you call a "splitting headache,"
be aware of the fact that the brain itself is incapable of
any pain sensations.

Bacteria experts will tell you that as a germ spreader a
telephone mouthpiece isn't any worse than a doorknob, a
brass rail or any other object that comes into frequent contact with the human hand.

On a cut of most any kind, even those considered serious,
simply apply black table pepper freely. It not only stops
the bleeding, but also seems to eliminate the soreness and
stiffness that usually follow a wound. There's no sensation
in the application. In fact, our youngsters should welcome it.

Few of you, I'll bet, knew that "ptomaine" is pronounced in three syllables.

Red Crossers get a laugh now and then. A lecture on rabies and hydrophobia had just been completed. The speaker asked his listeners if they had any questions. He asked the first one himself. "What would you do," he inquired, "if you had rabies?" "I'd ask for a piece of paper and a pencil," came the reply. "To make out your will?" presumed the speaker. "No," commented the listener, "to make a list of people I'd want to bite."

Science got the idea of the hypodermic needle from the stinging apparatus on a bee.

WARNING FROM A NURSE: Don't send your youngsters back to school after a measles attack until the nasal discharge is completely gone. The disease can be easily transmitted from 10 to 14 days after the rash has disappeared, so the patient should be isolated for at least that length of time.

DERMATOLOGY

INCLUDING
THE HAIR, NAILS, AND ITCHES

YOUR OUTER SELF

Amazing to me is the fact that an average adult carries around about eight pounds of skin.

Now, don't go peeling yourself to prove it, but a person of average size has about two square yards of skin.

AN INSULATION EXPERT SAYS: "You know that when you change temperatures suddenly, your flesh breaks out in goose-pimples. Know what those goose-pimples are? They're nature's way of insulating you. Those little goose-pimples are actually air pockets to ward off the sudden heat or cold."

I read some place the other day that the average number of obvious body scars according to a survey made, was five. What in the world would anybody want that information for?

If your precious body bruises easily and you keep turning up with black-and-blue marks, it's probably due to a shortage of vitamin-C in your system. Let your physician check, anyway. Or do you like black-and-blue marks?

LITTLE THINGS IN LIFE: No wonder we occasionally grab hold of a mitt that feels as clammy as a piece of oilcloth. Each square inch of a man's palm has 3,000 sweat glands. . . .

"Sweat of your brow" is right—perspiration on your forehead can be more profuse than on any other part of your body. . . .

Bet you didn't know that if you take a brisk rub-down after your sun bath you lose a good part of the vitamins you've been acquiring. *Explanation:* Secretions from the skin contain precursors of vitamin-D which, after irradiation, are due to be reabsorbed by the body. Removing them tends to produce a dearth of vitamin-D unless it's applied in some other form. So don't go hard on the turkish towel after you take your sun.

Even the experts have been feuding over the merits of sunshine. One group is shouting phooey to the ultraviolet rays we all try to snatch from an hour or two in the sun at the proper time. And those who are convinced that sunshine's not too important point to the Eskimos of Greenland who are healthy without ever getting a flock of Old Sol's best rays on their skins.

IF YOU FRECKLE easily, pat yourself on the back. Exhaustive experiments reveal that if you have freckles, you have not only vibrant health but also buoyant spirits far greater than your unfreckled pals. Freckles are no longer considered as imperfect pigmentation, instead they're deeper than the skin. The same scientists allege now that freckles actually spell sex appeal, that they should serve as facial decoration to attract attention. The experts wind up with this, *"Wear your freckles with pride."*

A prominent physician speaks: "Skin cancer is becoming more common, and, in many cases, has been traced to sun bathing. The consequences in many cases may be delayed for years. I've had cases where skin cancer has developed 10 years after a bad sunburn."

A medical student forwarded these rather interesting "medical oddities." For instance, says he, beware of a boil or boils on the upper lip. They have a 50 per cent mortality. The blood from the upper lip drains upward toward the inner corner of the eye and thence inward to the brain. Even a simple pimple on the upper lip should be watched carefully.

HAIR

Do you know what your hair consists of, if you have any? Well, it's 49 to 50 per cent carbon, 21 per cent oxygen, 17.93 per cent nitrogen, 6.66 per cent hydrogen and from 3 to 5 per cent sulphur. . . .

Have a few items from a hair authority. Each square inch of scalp contains about 1,000 hair follicles. Normally, a blonde will have up to 180,000 hairs, a brunette 120,000 and a redhead only 50,000. The normal adult has about 120 square inches of scalp that in 70 years will grow about 240 ounces (15 pounds) of hair. If the scissors were kept off and the hair permitted to grow normally, it could reach a length of about 35 feet. Average woman spends $50 a year on permanents, shampoos, waves, dyes and tonics. Normal fall is about 80 hairs a day that are replaced by new hairs. When hair begins to appear on a young man's chest, it's often a sign his scalp hair is beginning to fall out. As the scalp weakens, the hair growth on other parts of the body is increased. Hair can be stretched about one-fifth to one-third its original length. Males have rounder hairs than females. Hair color darkens with age prior to the time it turns white. Hair flattens out and expands in size as it grows.

If you live a normal span of life and never become bald,

you'll grow about 15 heads of hair or about 1,650,850 hairs. A hair, incidentally, grows to maturity in about four years.

This may sound like a defense mechanism, but it is really true: Hair on the chest is no indication of strength. The growth of bodily hair is due to glandular development and not muscular power. So there, you old Beach Strutters, you.

When your pal tells you you're getting in his hair, he's actually calling you arsenic, and the expression has a basis in scientific fact. Your hair is a popular storage place for arsenic which finds its way into the body as a common constituent of foods. The body deposits that chemical around the roots of the hair, where it's introduced into the hair shafts.

SHAVES WHILE THINKING

NO WONDER SHAVING IS SUCH A DAILY JOB: The average man has about 24,000 hairs on his face and neck, and each of them protrudes .006 of an inch from the skin surface at the beginning of the daily shave.

The barber makes a grand total of more than 900 individual strokes during an average shave.

Wonder if a guy saved the whiskers he shaved off how big a stack it'd make in a full year? Might be good for stuffing a pillow.

A man shaves about 20 square miles of face in a lifetime.

Give your eyelashes a gander. If your lashes are gracefully curved, without much doubt you're a calm person. Short, straight lashes indicate nervously inclined people. Now take a good look at them out toward the ends. If they're getting thin at the outer ends, it denotes laziness. . . .

Athletic persons, as a rule, possess the longest and most beautiful eyelashes.

If your eyelashes keep hitting the lenses of your glasses, you can halt the annoyance by curling them up out of the way on an eyelash curler. This does for men, too, says a beauty expert, but men had better do the trick behind locked doors. . . .

SO WHAT?

Thomas Jefferson was actually a redhead. Those Revolutionary wigs, of course, kept most of the people from knowing it. You might as well know, too, that Queen Elizabeth and Sarah Bernhardt were also auburned.

Does hair grow gray or turn gray? If it turns gray, some day I'd like to catch one in the process. . . . Just a thought.

Actually, there's no such thing as true gray hair. That's what it says in a book on Alopecia Areata—whatever that is. Hair is either the color you had in your youth or it's white. The admixture of the whites with the pristine hairs is what makes hair look gray. The book even suggests this novel stunt: Next time you accost a dignified matron, pluck out a handful from her coiffure, tabulate the colors of the strands. You'll find no gray ones. Science marches on.

It'd be hard to tell which was the worse, the cure or the malady. Anyway, scientists have discovered that by feeding dried liver to rats, they can restore the blackness of the rodents' hair. I like the way the experts phrase it. Author of the treatise called it, *"The Effect of Pantothenic Acid on Achromotrichia in Rats."*

MAN'S TOP WORRY

Just for fun, wives, ask your old gent this, "Tell me, dear, how is your alopecia today?" It'll probably stump him. It's another name for baldness.

Constant wearing of hats has often been blamed for men's loss of hair, and one school has urged going without a hat at all times to prevent baldness. Those theories have been exploded now by a well-known trichologist. Overexposure to the hot summer sun, says he, is one of the most common causes of conditions leading to baldness. And he states further that it never has been really proved that the wearing of a hat had the slightest effect on the loss of hair.

You handsome males who want to avoid baldness should never let the spray of a shower nozzle come into contact with your scalps.

TO FIGHT BALDNESS (you'd better get a load of this your-self, Adams), bend your head downward when you brush your hair and brush it with downward strokes so the blood can flow from your body to the roots of your hair. But really bend. . . .

If you guys just beyond the 35 mark keep rubbing the tops of your beans, it'll forestall the period of your bald-ness. Circulation's most sluggish up there, and a little daily massaging will help.

You get bald because you get tense on top, says one member of the American Association of Anatomists. The top of the head where baldness comes with age doesn't have as rich a blood supply as the muscular sides of the scalp where the hair usually hangs on the longest. Tension zones in the scalp cut down the blood supply to the top. Tension zones, says the expert, result from contraction of the muscles, growth of the skull or from external pressure. A tight hat or the explosion of an atomic bomb may set up a tension zone. So, be careful of both.

A barber in Ladysmith, Wis., offered perhaps the most startling hair restorer ever to come to my attention. This fellow went to the village blacksmith shop as his source of treatment.

You remember the tub into which the blacksmith dips the red-hot horseshoes as they come from the blazing forge? Well, it's the water from that tub, he claimed, when applied to the human scalp, that prevents and eliminates falling hair. A squirt or two of that kind of water rubbed into the scalp periodically or applied on a brush and then into the hair, he said, is sufficient to turn the trick.

That small-town barber should bottle the forge water and send it to the city.

Statistics show that city slickers suffer five times as much from scalp diseases and subsequent baldness as rural-ities.

Bald spots are curious things. Some of them are per-fectly round. Others swoop down in a sort of V-shape. A few come out almost triangular.

Redheads are the least likely to lose their hair and blondes are more susceptible to baldness. . . .

One thing you can say about baldness: IT'S NEAT.

Curiously enough, the following information comes from a man: An anemic woman can't keep a permanent wave in her hair. If it's a bad case, the wave comes out with the first washing.

The chin and upper lip are, for women, the most common places for superfluous hair, but inverted eyelashes that curl under and scratch the eyeball are the most bothersome. When the electrologists are working on a woman's mustache, they work in checkerboard fashion. Ten to 15 treatments of half an hour each will remove the most abundant mustache.

Men with ingrown hair or infected hair follicles or with hair on their noses are frequent customers, too. Shaving nose hair off can be a bad practice because the shaving also gets the fine hair, or down, and turns that into bristly growth.

Electrologists advise against plucking, since it enlarges the hair root. Hairline raising and eyebrow shaping or arching are common tasks for electrologists. Once an eyebrow is arched by electrolysis, it's done forever. Some women have widow's peaks made. Waxing or multiple plucking is not advised because it eventually makes the fine hair coarse. The electrolysis needle goes directly to the hair follicles, extracts the hydrogen from them, and the hair decomposes. A man's whole beard could be taken off, but it would take too much time.

ON THE OTHER HAND—AND FOOT

Hair and fingernails don't grow continuously at the same rate from hour to hour. Fingernails grow fastest between 11 A.M. and noon, while hair grows fastest from 9 to 10 A.M. But who do you suppose ever took time to figure it out, and what prompted such research?

Nobody knows just why, but your fingernails grow faster than your toenails and the nails on your right hand grow faster than those on your left. . . .

Fingernails grow at the rate of about an eighth of an inch a month, or twice as fast as toenails.

In the course of a year all your fingernails and toenails grow about 11 yards in the aggregate. Maybe that's why we're tired of caring for them now and then.

QUICK, GIVE YOUR MITT A LOOK: A group of manicurists, reporting their co-operative observations over a period of time, say a woman with triangular fingernails is not to be trusted.

Look now to see if you have a blemish on the white part of a fingernail. In the character-reading trade it indicates a shortened life.

On a more scientific basis, short oval fingernails without moons and with a slightly bluish color may signify you have an organic defect of the heart.

Tip to stenographers: Any time you happen to have a hangnail, a scratch or any kind of open wound on your hands, be extremely careful about handling carbon paper. A young girl I once heard about burned herself on the hand. The burn was open, she infected it from carbon paper and for two weeks, until doctors licked the trouble, she was threatened with the possible loss of the hand. . . .

Oh, Girruls, here's something just for you. And particularly you housewives and stenogs who have trouble with breaking, cracking fingernails. Soak your nails nightly in a warm solution of Epsom salts and water. Put about two tablespoons of Epsom salts to a half pint of water. Do this daily for 10 days, advises a hotel manicurist, and your nails will stay hard and almost unbreakable for weeks.

For better fingernails see to it that your daily diet includes milk, buttermilk, fish or cottage cheese. The calcium improves nails. . . .

WOE IN THE TOE

Have you a little athlete's foot in your home? News comes now that more than 70 per cent of the athlete's foot in this country has nothing at all to do with running around barefooted in shower rooms or bath compartments.

Medical research indicates that in hundreds and hundreds

of cases the disease is due to nervous exhaustion an
inability to relax properly. People of the restless, high
strung type who "never get tired" are very apt victims. An
proper rest and relaxation are the simplest cures in thes
cases. When the skin infection is of this type, it isn't con
tagious. Only the fungus type (shower-room bug) is catch
ing.

**A medico friend says he has cured many a bad case o
athlete's foot simply by keeping cotton between the toes t
keep the spaces dry.**

This is one housewife's corn cure: She simply pastes
small strip of adhesive over her corn, keeps it there da
and night for two or three weeks. By that time the corr
has softened up and comes right off. It all seems fai
enough, doesn't it?

Some years ago I thought I had a swell item for m
column when a woman in Owatonna, Minn., wrote abou
her home-tested corn cure: Said she, simply wrap an onio
around the corn overnight, and in the morning you'll hav
a vastly improved corn. In just a few days (this was doubt
ful to me) no corn at all. She may be in the onion business
I thought at the time.

A few days later the same Owatonna woman wrote bacl
by special delivery with a correction, apologizing all ove
the place, stating that she should have said a piece o
lemon instead of an onion. So any readers who had beer
going to bed with a Bermuda on their little toe were advisec
to switch immediately to a slice of lemon. None reported il
effects from either treatment, fortunately.

Don't let yourself be fooled on poison ivy. It isn't onl
the leaves that can do the business. The stem, the roots
the unripened fruits can land plenty of damage on tha
beautiful skin of yours.

Poison ivy will hit a number of you sometime this sum
mer, so it might not be a bad idea to copy this paragraph
for handy reference. An attorney at Montevideo, Min
nesota, says he learned about the treatment from the Indian
80 years ago, which is a source acceptable to me. All you
have to do is go to the lumberyard and get a little slaked

lime, the old-fashioned kind. Make a whitewash out of it and bathe the affected parts. The irritation will vanish immediately, the lawyer promised. The lime should be fairly fresh, though. Let the whitewash dry and later brush off the powder that remains. The barrister also has a simple recommendation for another skin irritant, wood ticks for both humans and pooches. A wood tick will not touch a dog nor a person who drinks buttermilk. A pint a day will do the trick, he says. Let me emphasize this on the lime treatment for poison ivy. Be sure to use only slaked or air-slaked or hydrated lime. Unslaked lime will prove more irritating than the ivy infection itself. If you mix the slaked lime the night before, you'll get the "heat" out of it, too.

We're lucky, though, that only one person in 18 is likely to be discommoded by contact with poison ivy.

To be pricked by a pin is no more dangerous to your skin than to get a jab with a needle. Germs can be passed through the skin by either one, and the kind of metal makes no difference.

EYE, EAR, NOSE, & THROAT

EYESIGHT CONSERVATION WEEK early in June deserves our attention. One out of every 47 people in the United States loses useful sight at some time during life, and authorities are now agreed that at least two-thirds of all cases of blindness are preventable. Eighty-three per cent of the cases are due to neglect, abuse, infection and disease. Apparently it's quite a chore for our eyes to keep up with our modern pace—long hours under artificial light, speed in motor cars, flickering movies, and television, numerous magazines. Tips from the specialists: When reading or doing close work, spare one-third of a second occasionally to wink the eyelids or take a trifle longer to switch

to a more distant focus and back. After a hard day, a ho
cloth placed on the eyes to draw up refreshing blood is fa
less a nuisance than to have to feel your way around later or
in life. Only about 16 per cent of those fitted with glasse
are fitted properly, so pick your eye specialist with care
Apply reasonable thought to lighting your home, your office
your factory. And don't think it can't happen to you. I
can. In at least 60 per cent of all cases of serious ey
trouble there is no painful warning.

In that pretty little head of yours there's a "boss eye."
One of your eyes does most of the work of seeing. Usually
in right-handed people it's the right eye, and vice versa fo
lefties.

**When you read a novel of average length your eyes ho
along for a half mile in sixteenth-of-an-inch skips. Th
average adult reads 250 words a minute.**

THAT QUICK-AS-A-WINK business isn't so quick after all
Every time you wink you create a complete black-out o
vision for as long as three-tenths of a second. If you'r
normal you blink every 2.8 seconds—that's for men. Girl
wink less often.

Bum break: It's harder for a man to see a blonde out o
the corner of his eye than it is to see a brunette, especiall
if the blonde is wearing a red dress and the brunette
black and white gown. Sounds silly, but there's scienc
back of it. The difference in visibility is explained by th
Better Vision Institute. Colors are perceived best whe
focused by the eye at the center of the retina. Colore
objects far to the side are less easily distinguished than ar
black and white objects. . . .

Nothing will ever be done about it because of the uni
versal acceptance of the combination, but vision expert
contend that use of red for danger and green for safet
is precisely the wrong way around. Green is perceived b
the human eye more quickly than red, they say. Whe
a highway or street is noisy, it's still more difficult to dis
tinguish the colors used in traffic signals. Loud noises ten
to make green appear brighter and red dimmer to th

average person. But can't you just imagine a traffic judge's guffaw if you alibied with, "You know, Judge, it was so noisy coming to work this morning, I didn't see that red light"?

To test your eyesight, step into your back yard on the next starry night and gaze up at the Big Dipper. Look for the double star in the handle. If you can see it, you and the oculist may remain strangers. Here's the catch, though. These "double" stars are only three trillion miles apart and—get this—the little star you see is really made up of two and the big one is made up of four or maybe eight stars. Perhaps you're not seeing so well after all.

Want to see how important vision in both eyes is? Hold the index finger of your left hand out in front of you at about half an arm's length, point the finger upward. Now bring the same finger of your other hand swooping down in front of your face and try to make the two fingers meet one on top of the other. You hit them all right, didn't you? Now close one eye and go through the same process. Then try it with the other eye closed and the first one open.

"Seeing double" is, as you know, usually associated with drunkenness, but prolonged wakefulness will produce the same result, even if you're stone sober.

For a little family fun today, examine one another's eyes. People whose eyes slant up are capable of keeping secrets. Eyes that slant down indicate honesty and forthrightness. Small eyes denote originality. Medium-sized eyes show a balance of wisdom and temper. Large eyes give evidence of an easily impressionable and observant nature. Breadth between the eyes indicates a strong will and determination. Eyes set close together are indicative of a practical observer of details.

Men with blue eyes are said to be better shots with a rifle or shotgun than men with eyes of other colors.

Incidentally, blue eyes and black eyes contain exactly the same coloring pigment, known as melanin. The apparent difference is the result of the way in which light is reflected from the surfaces of the fibers which make up the iris.

Scientists must have a gay time at their work. Here's a finding recently reported: The human eye as a light sensitive device far exceeds any other known system of light detection. The smallest amount of light capable of stimulating the eye has been found to be between 5 and 14 quanta. Here's where the research boys went to town. A quantum is two to six trillionths of the energy required for a flea to jump about four inches.

Nobody should ever look directly into the sun, we know that, so come an eclipse, be sure to protect your eyes when giving it the look. The experts say that an old hunk of glass held over a candle flame for a second or two still functions as a screen for eclipse gazing. Funny how, through the years, the technique hasn't been altered a bit. The same eye specialists also have a warning for sun bathers. We shouldn't lie for even a few minutes with our faces toward the sun without some kind of eye protection. Even small exposures of the eyes to the sun may result in serious and permanent damage to our optics.

If an acquaintance passes you unseeingly on the street, he may not actually be snubbing you. Hundreds of persons have what is known as gun-barrel sight—straight ahead they see perfectly, but their vision to the side is extremely faulty. The affliction's dangerous, too. Such affliction not infrequently causes people to step smack into the path of an automobile.

If there's a heavy reader in your home, pay attention to this: A youngster in grade school should never read for more than an hour at a sitting, and even adults should never go for more than two hours at a stretch. It's a smart trick to look across the room occasionally while you're reading to give the eyes a temporary rest.

So you think life begins at 40, huh? Well, the focusing range of your eyes at 40 is about one-fourth what it was when you were 10. Stiffening tissues is what you have.

Psychological Item: Medical science has now determined that even the pupils in the eyes of a sightless person tend to contract when they think of a sunny day. . . .

Monday is the biggest day in the week for the eyeglasses people. More specs are brought in for repair on that day than any other. It's the week-end revelry that does it, the opticians explain. The first business day after New Year's hits an annual high. And you'll have no trouble in understanding that one.

If you have eyesight difficulty in driving your car at night, it's because you're deficient in a purple liquid that enables humans to see better after dark.

If you wear specs and the sun drives you crazy while you're motoring, put a drop or two of bluing on each lens. It dries quickly and the color takes the glare out of the sun's rays. One wipe will bring your glasses back to normal.

The experts are now saying that women who hang clothes out on the line on sunny days should wear colored glasses to be on the safe side. Eyestrain may result from the sun rays reflected by the white clothes that go on the line.

Here are some of the common causes for smashed specs given to one eyeglass firm: Sitting on them. Grandchildren grabbing at them. Putting frosted glasses in hot water after coming indoors on icy days. Cows swishing their tails. Chickens flapping their wings. Horses suddenly shaking their heads. Store salespeople have their specs broken frequently by women flailing their arms while trying on dresses. Fast-moving elbows on streetcars or buses often break specs. All opticians assume that fisticuffs account for many a broken pair of glasses. Seldom, however, does the owner of the glasses confess that angle. . . .

Just in case you ever get stuck without your glasses and can't read, here's a little stopgap that may work. Punch a pinhole in a piece of paper, then look at that exasperating fine print through the pinhole. You'll find that you can bring the print up to within a couple of inches of your eye, where it'll look nice and big and black. The idea is that the pinhole acts as a sort of lens. The same wrinkle has been tried out with success in pinhole cameras.

Too bad the first inclination is to rub an eye the instant a dust particle gets into it. If we could but close the lid for a few seconds, the tear ducts would function and the foreign particle would often be washed out. But we never wait for that. Have to set up increased irritation.

If you absolutely have to rub your eyes, use the lower or fatty part of your palm instead of your fingers. The pressure exerted in the eyeball is much more even, the palm is usually cleaner and there's less danger of injury to the eyeball.

It's okay to let your tear ducts flow all they want to at a sad movie or play. The psychologists say that crying over film or stage plots is pretty good evidence of imagination, which is an important phase of intelligence. Other doctors say it's the best eyewash.

The United States public health service says you'd do much better to eat a piece of beefsteak rather than apply it to a blackened optic. A cold compress is much better for a shiner. Anything moist and cool serves just as well as the beefsteak, the service says. They're puzzled, too, how the beefsteak remedy got started. Very much overrated, in their opinion. . . . Probably more expensive, too, than the services of an eye doctor, with the price of meat where it is these days.

EAR, EAR

Nature did a wonderful job in designing the human ear. No matter from what angle the shower water comes down at it, no water runs into the ear.

It seems to me, however, that the upper section of the ear might have been designed a little differently to make it more accessible for effective washing. . . .

You may run to the mirror right now to prove it if you like—there isn't a human being who has a perfectly matched pair of ears.

If your ears are small, it's a pretty good indication that you have scrupulous care for small details.

About 50,000 school children in my home county were reported to have impaired hearing. So the American Society for the Hard of Hearing urges parents to make an attempt to detect ear trouble in their youngsters. Children who for no apparent reason have the following difficulties, they say, should be given ear tests without delay: Inattention and frequent mistakes in carrying out instructions, faulty articulation, mispronunciation of words, habitual failure to respond when questioned, and a wearied expression before the school day is half over.

The specialists will tell you that deafness among children is definitely on the increase in this country and, as yet, they haven't discovered why.

Daytime noise on the average busy American street is loud enough to make a normal person one-fourth to one-third deaf. But there is no dependable evidence that life or work in noisy places decreases acuteness of hearing except during the first few minutes after the noise stops.

Your spines, shoulders and facial muscles are all a part of the listening apparatus.

An expert gave me this the other day: If you want to hear better, have your head X-rayed. Even people who have been unable to detect the slightest hearing deficiency have noted a vast improvement after treatment. Recent research has explained this effect, he said, as being due to a decrease in the density and viscosity of the fluids in the inner ear, brought about by the action of the X rays on the pituitary gland.

It's neither habit nor the position of the telephone that makes the majority of people use the left ear for the telephone receiver. Most individuals hear better with the left ear.

If you listen to telephone conversation with your right ear, you're abnormal—to the odds of one out of a thousand.

An eminent Harvard professor discovered that you do a lot of damage to your ears by blowing your nose too hard.

NOSE

The sense of smell is the first of the five senses to develop in the human being.

If you can't see, you're blind. If you can't hear, you're deaf. If you can't speak, you're mute. But what if you lost the sense of smell? Well, you're suffering from anosmia, which ought to silence the wiseacres who'd like to say "he doesn't smell so good."

And while we're talking about what you haven't got, if you're minus a sense of taste, the situation is ageusia.

FROM THE MOUTH DOWN

The Minnesota Writers' Project of WPA days unearthed this early "remedy" for lockjaw: Apply a poultice of crushed beet pulp to the wound which led to it. Sadly enough, newspapers of that day insisted that the remedy was reliable and offered substantiating testimonials from persons who had tried it.

Ask your favorite cornettist how his buccinator is. It's a muscle of the cheek called the "trumpeters' muscle" developed excessively from tooting the horn.

In the good old days the very best of barbers stuck a thumb in his customer's mouth to push out the cheek and make the skin taut for easier shaving. Folks apparently weren't so particular about sanitary practices then.

ROOT, ROOT, ROOT for the home team is all right in song, but you should watch your cheering at baseball or football games because of what might easily happen to your voice department. Medical authorities say there are three imminent dangers in excessive cheering. First, you may readily start a chronic case of laryngitis, you may strain the laryngeal muscle, or worse, you may cause a tumor of the vocal cords from rupture of a blood vessel. . . .

GOODY GOODY ITEM: Fatheads make the best singers. A noted oto-laryngologist, says so, anyway. The beautiful tones of a great singer, he explains, are not generated in the larynx, but in the temporal area of the brain, and on release set in motion the muscles of the larynx. A singer's success, then, depends on the number of lipoid or fatty cells in the brain tissue. Such things as nervousness and indigestion tend very strongly to impair the functions of the larynx, too.

If you're an ambitious young vocalist you don't have to worry about having your tonsils yanked. The removal often results in a fuller, more resonant voice.

FAREWELL TO TONSILS
A FATHER'S LETTER TO HIS SON

Dear David: Your mother has just written me that you're going to have your tonsils out tomorrow. That's why I'm writing you. I want to tell you a little bit about tonsils and operations and hospitals so you'll be a brave boy and not mind the hurt too much. Pa is pretty nervous himself because of you and he'll be thinking of you all day long. . . .

Those tonsils are funny things. They're shaped like those almonds you had last Christmas, remember? They're down there in your throat. Some little boys and girls don't have any trouble with theirs, but you happened to get a pair of big ones. And in addition to that, nature played you a pretty dirty trick. Every time you catch a little cold, it settles in your tonsils, and that's what has made your throat sore each time. That will all be different soon.

Really, about the only thing tonsils are good for is to make jokes about them. There's the one about getting your tonsils sunburned from looking at the tall buildings the first time you go to a big city. Then there's the host who, after mixing some terrible concoction, says, "Here, try this on your tonsils." Well, after you've had your tonsils out, the minute anybody tries to pull one about tonsils, you can snap back with, "Skip it, because mine are in a bottle up in Virginia, Minn., and I'm not interested."

Now when you get to the hospital you'll see some men in white and some women in white. They're the doctors and nurses. They've studied for years and they know all about tonsils and just how to take them out almost without hurting you. The doctor on your case, of course, is your grandfather. And if he does hurt you a little, I want you to forgive him right away because he didn't really mean to. He's a swell fellow, and after your throat has healed it'll never get sore again and you'll like Grandpa just that much more.

They'll put you to sleep while they're taking the tonsils out. The stuff they use to make you take your nap might not smell any too good at first, but after you take a couple of deep breaths you won't mind it. And it's much easier to be napping while Grandpa is working. Otherwise you might bob around and bother him. Once you're asleep, though, you won't feel anything and you'll have the best dreams. When you wake up your throat will feel pretty bad for a while. You might even think your brother's buggy is in it, but in just a day or two it'll start to feel fine and you won't even remember when it was sore. . . .

Right after you wake up you'll probably be pretty thirsty. It isn't a very good idea to drink any water too soon, so you just remember that Pa asked you to get along without any water for two or three hours and you'll feel a lot better. Oh, yes, there's one swell thing about having your tonsils out—for three or four days you can have all the ice cream you want. You may have it for breakfast, lunch and dinner. Another thing, it was a throat operation that made Bing Crosby a crooner and Libby Holman a torch singer. The same thing also improved Nelson Eddy's range. So maybe Grandpa will make a great yodeler out of you. I'll see all your chums today—Hoozie and Tommy and Davey and Lou Ann—and tell them what a brave little guy you're going to be; and when you come back you can be just like your mother and talk about your operation.

In her letter your mother said that Pa was really pretty lucky because he didn't have to be around on such occasions. You tell her that I guess she's right, too. Mothers do get in on more of the unpleasant things; but you tell her, too, that mothers are endowed with a greater capacity for those things than fathers are. Nevertheless, all day long tomorrow Pa will be a jittery fellow. He'll be hoping mighty hard that everything will be okay. And even though he hasn't been doing much of it lately, he'll probably pray a little for his boy.

UNCOMMON IS THE
COMMON COLD

When we repeatedly speak of a bad cold or a bad backache, do you ever stop to realize that there is no counterword—a good cold or a good backache? Why, then, not play safe and call it a serious cold or a severe backache?

To cut down on the family's colds sprinkle a little chlorine (your druggist will tell you how much) in your dishwater. In tests, chlorine, used properly, reduced the number

of bacteria on a spoon from 100,000 to as low as two or
even none. Call me Doc, dearies.

For a cold remedy some people now take two aspirin
tablets in a glass of warm milk, and effective results have
been reported.

**Or you might try this home recipe for curing a cold: Sim-
ply go to bed with your hat on. . . .**

AN OLD SOUTHERN HAT TRICK: When an attack of *la
grippe* was approaching victims used to hang a hat on the
bedpost, hop into bed and then drink whisky till they could
see two hats.

This variation sounds like a breeze from the Middle
Ages, but it's from the dear old American Medical Association Journal. Here's the advice given: Immerse one hand
in water chilled to a temperature of 50 degrees Fahrenheit,
one or two minutes a day for two or three weeks. The Association reports that it worked as a remedy for colds with 16
out of 22 persons affected.

*A woman who claims she hasn't had a cold for 20 years
gives this as her secret:* The instant she discovers any cold
symptoms, she stands erect and then stoops to touch the
floor with her fingertips five times. On the fifth stoop, she
holds her head down about the length of time it would take
to tie her shoe. It's getting the symptoms early, she says,
that does the trick. Many a time while shopping she's noticed a cold coming on, darted into a ladies' rest room for
her trick and gone home in fine fettle.

OCCUPATIONAL REMEDY: Get yourself a job with the gas
company or a manufacturer of salt and you'll probably go
through life without a cold. Workers in those two branches
of industry are less susceptible than any other classes.

After you're 50, you're less apt to have a cold than a
younger person, which is one compensation for growing
old, anyway.

**Also more immune from common colds than most are
the chorus girls. It's attributed to their constant exercise
and to the scanty apparel they wear most of the time.**

Eight glasses of water a day are a swell thing to aid in
combating a cold.

There's compensation, in life, it seems. Medicos are saying that some women who catch the all too common June colds are better off for them. And here's their reasoning: Coughing will give you a fine start on firming the muscles of your diaphragm for the non-girdle summer days ahead.

If you happen to be trying to cure a summer cold, decrease your daily quota of sugar.

Summer colds, believe it or not, often hit our populace hard. The following "cure" was sent to a Jamaican cook by another West Indian friend. Sounds like something we should paste in our medicine cabinets. Here it is exactly as it came in: "Buy five cents black castor oil, half of five cent good nutmeg, one teaspoon of salt, mix altogether good. Buy 10 cents tobacco leaves divide it in three and you will use on each night but you must mix just enough to serve you for three nights. Don't make none left the last night you will use it. Warm it before using it but use it more cold than hot. Part your hair very small and tight and in the night before you go to bed rub it good in the head. Cool and skim and take the tobacco leaves, pass it over the fire and put it on the head properly and tie your head way down to your face. In the night if you feel it sweat take a dry cloth and wipe it and tie it with another cloth so the next day when you wake up you can take out leaves. But don't untie your head or go in rain or wash clothes and you must keep your head tie for two weeks after using this." The West Indian added this line so it may be the world has its long-awaited cold cure. "This remedy did get my own cold better."

When you're at the peak of your wheezing with a cold, your germs are not a serious threat to others. It's before you realize you have a cold yourself that you begin spreading the active virus among your pals. . . .

When chronic colds come into their own in the fall, some experimenting done by medicos at the University of Illinois should interest you. They devised a treatment of alternating hot and cold shower baths, which serve to massage the capillaries nearest the mucous membranes of the nose and throat, and a diet which boosts the consumption of fruits, vegetables and milk and cuts down on pastry. Favorable results up to 65 per cent were reported.

Best treatment for a sore throat, according to one specialist, is a regular hourly dowsing of the oral cavity with plain hot water, about the temperature of your morning coffee. The dowsing may be administered with a fountain syringe attached to a hot water bottle. A few years back this simple treatment reduced lost class time at the University of Minnesota more than 82 per cent. Students were taken into the health service, kept for a day while the water was administered, and in most cases were sent out completely well.

Even if it goes against your own early childhood training, you'll find youngsters' sore throats and head colds improving much more rapidly if you have them sleep in bedrooms with the windows closed.

One thing I have to thank my boss for—there's hardly a dull moment in my office. An energetic fellow of 77 came puffing in one day with what he claimed was a sock preventative for the flu. "All you have to do," he counseled, "is eat amber vaseline three times, eight hours apart." Can you think of anything yummier on a restaurant menu than a vaseline sandwich?

The very same day I talked with a woman who positively had the flu licked. "All you have to do is onionate," she urged. "Flu germs can't stand the lowly onion," she went on. "I eat them in every conceivable form. Boil them in milk. Make poultices out of them. Permeate the house with their odor. Onions have completely immunized me."

It must have been medicine day because my next caller had his flu remedy. "It's a cinch," he began. "Just add two or three dashes of table salt to your drinking water and drink 30 glasses a day." . . . The stretcher, Watson!

The Northwestern National Life Insurance Company's experts say one of the very best means of hitting back at winter flu is to go to bed at 7 o'clock for a few evenings. It'll give a lift to your vitality. Americans, they point out, are chronically behind on their sleep.

From a medical journal: Coughing serves a useful purpose and should not be checked unless it is harassing or exhausting.

You singers keep this in mind: A tenor of my acquaintance never had the whooping cough until after he was married, but not long after that happy event he whooped so hard he broke a rib. Because he's a singer, his chest muscles had been exceptionally developed and the violence of his cough was accentuated to the point of the rib breakage.

Funny thing about whooping cough: Parents who've had it in childhood are immune, but grandparents often contract it a second time from children.

Ozark mountaineers have a curious treatment for sinus infections. They dig up fresh earth and then kneel down and sniff it for nine days in succession. It's probably the kneeling that does the trick.

Take an old "cure" for chilblains: Soak your feet for 15 minutes in warm water, put on a pair of rubbers, without stockings, and go to bed.

Unskilled workers are three and one-half times more susceptible to pneumonia than are professional men.

No wonder that type of pain is so severe—there are from 20 to 30 sinuses inside that noggin of yours.

A great percentage of sinus infection, according to a Minnesota specialist, is self-imposed. Wrong technique in blowing one's nose is responsible for much of it, says he. Too many nose-blowers toot one nostril at a time, which increases the disorder. A schnozzola should always be blown with both nostrils wide open. . . .

D.D.S.

My dentist supplied me with these notes from his profession. Only one in 10,000 babies is born with a tooth showing in its mouth. Richard the Lionhearted and Caesar were born each with a tooth in his mouth. Seventy per cent of the lower back molars in children are decayed by the time the child reaches 3½ years of age, and those teeth don't make an appearance in the mouth until the youngster is at least 2½. The only third sets of teeth on record are those made by a dentist. The so-called third sets are supernumerary, impacted and unerupted teeth of the first permanent set. Of the 160 surfaces in the normal set of teeth, 36 are more susceptible to decay than others.

Rich children have better baby teeth than poor children, but after the permanent teeth take their place the tables are reversed—the poor kids have better teeth. Dentists, by the way, have a slogan they should make more of: *"Be True to Your Teeth or They'll Be False to You."*

When junior yelps for that fourth or fifth piece of candy, quiet him with this: Studies made at the University of California show that of the 5,000 American wild animals, only bears have toothaches. Researchers found that 8 per cent of 350 bears checked had tooth decay, and he blames it on their traditional love of sweets. Only polar bears, who seldom get sweets, had perfect teeth.

A dentist would have a field day if he ever got into the yap of a snail: He'd find 135 rows of teeth, each row containing 105 grinders and a total of 14,175 teeth.

Let's talk about our mouths for a bit. Certain medicos are now advancing the idea that there isn't a better morning mouthwash or gargle than the juices of fresh fruit. Another oral hygienist says we should have two toothbrushes always. One, says he, should be kept soaking in an antiseptic solution for a day while the second one is in use, and alternate. A bacteria-laden toothbrush can leave your gums with more germs than if they hadn't been brushed.

SAD SIDE STATISTICS: At least half the inhabitants of the United States do not own a toothbrush, census takers say.

There ought to be a better way to hang a toothbrush than right out in the open the way they are in most bathrooms.

Any time you gag, it means you've stopped breathing. So, if you suffer from that little circumstance when you brush your teeth in the morning, simply accentuate your breathing and your gagging will stop.

If you're a "gagger" when you get into the dentist's chair, you're suffering from gagodontia. . . .

You women can do your dentist a great big fat favor by leaving lipstick off your mouth at the next appointment. Lipstick leaves a terrible mess in any dentist's office. It dirties the towels, the water glass, the instruments and the dentist's fingers. The dentist who brought this up says he's had women patients who slap on a new coat of lipstick just before stepping into the chair. The average dentist much prefers his women in the natural around the mouth.

Redheads are livelier, if you want to take the word and work of a London dentist. His studies proved that blondes go under anesthesia the most readily—average, 52 seconds. Dark-haired people take 62 seconds. But the dear little redheads resisted for 68 seconds. And .13 per cent of the titians had to be held down while being put under gas as against .5 per cent of the fair-haired and .04 of the brunettes.

HINT TO DENTAL HYGIENISTS: Just before your boss starts that gosh-awful drilling, stick a small wad of cotton in the patient's ears and the noise of the drill (which is half the annoyance) won't be nearly as bothersome.

If you know in advance your dentist is going to do some yanking, there's a simple diet for reducing the afterpain. For 24 hours before and 48 hours after the extraction, you're supposed to eat plenty of citrus fruits and drink plenty of fruit juices, drink a quart of milk daily, add lots of leafy vegetables to your diet. Those foods alkalinize the blood and make for ideal healing conditions in body tissue. Acid-producing foods such as meat, fish, fowl, fats, cheese, grain, sweets, rhubarb, alcohol, coffee and tea should be avoided. The dentist who told the American Dental Association these findings also warned against exercise before extraction. Patients about to have teeth pulled should drink large quantities of water before the extraction.

A dentist in the little town of Mahnomen, Minn., saved all the teeth he's pulled. Had about 30,000 at a recent count.

CHECK YOUR MOUTH: If you're average, 20 of your original 32 teeth will be bad, missing or filled by the time you're 30; 25 will be bad, repaired or gone by the time you're 65. **It requires 60 pounds of pressure between the jaws to bite into a rare steak.** With modern plastic bases and improved artificial teeth, the average dentist now has available materials and methods for building dentures which are as great an improvement over the old type "plates" as this year's car is over a 1915 model. In fact, teeth can be constructed to afford as much as 60 or 65 pounds of bite pressure. The average pressure possible between the jaws with natural teeth, however, is around 150 pounds. There are available to the dentist between 10,000 and 12,000 different molds and shades of teeth from which to select the correct type, shade and form for one individual set of dentures.

Heard about the dentist who made a set of artificial dentures for a patient and waited a long time without getting any payment? One day the impatient dentist met the patient on the street.

"Let me have a look at those teeth," he requested. The fellow obligingly took them out and handed them over. The dentist threw the dentures violently to the sidewalk, smashing them in a hundred pieces, and then walked calmly down the street.

A raspberry seed must feel like a hunk of coal when it gets under a false teeth plate.

If picking one's teeth were made more acceptable socially, we'd all have better teeth. And very few actions are much more fun. . . .
Personally I'd rather see a toothpick user do it out in the open than try to hide the indulgence behind a curved hand.

PSYCHOLOGY FOR ANYONE

How you solve your problems tells what kind of personality you have, and the psychologists are out now with a method of sizing up yourself and your friends. Everybody at one time or another, the experts say, uses all these ways of tackling problems. You might want to pick your favorite:

Direct attack. The person who goes straight at the trouble, working all the harder or improving his technique when the problem is difficult.

Going around. This person dodges obstacles and tries a new approach when one method doesn't seem to work.

Escape. He ignores problems or stalls for time until something happens to relieve him of the problem.

Diversion. He throws up a smoke screen in the form of a temper tantrum to distract attention from the main issue.

Sour grapes. This man pretends to himself and others that the question wasn't very important, anyway—that he really never wanted to solve it. . . .

Basking. He hangs around with successful people so he'll get credit for their bright ideas.

Passing the buck. He blames failures on other people or circumstances.

Spotlight seeking. When he can't succeed, he tries to get attention even though it's unfavorable because that's better than being ignored.

Giving up. He acts childish or plays sick so that people will not expect him to solve the problem.

Daydreaming. He ignores real problems while he dreams of imaginary successes.

Did you find yourself?

Hysteroids, manics, depressives, autistics, paranoids, epileptoids—that's what we all are, and in business the problem is to get each one of us with his dominating trait into the right job. An individual with a marked hysteroid, for example, is dangerous to have around money; yet if an individual is devoid of this tendency, he may be a softy in dealing with other people. Sociable and responsive people are called manic types, and these make the best employes generally. But guess what trait is common to all bill collectors? It's none other than the paranoid, which is generally associated with a persecution complex and a tendency toward a fixed idea. Persistency, in other words.

To decide, if you don't already know, whether you're an extrovert or an introvert, check your color likes and dislikes. Introverts and conservatives prefer blue colors. The others red.

Are you touchy, easily insulted or grieved? Do you carry your resentments long? Reason is, say the physiologists, that you go through life with your jaws set, your face strained, your muscles tense. This causes you to jump at the slightest noise or the slightest insult to your ego. You may say your nerves are on edge, but really it's your muscles from your eyelids to your toes. When all your muscles are relaxed and at ease, your nerves and your ego will be, too.

Wonder how many of us could take this kind of treatment? "Get in touch with as many people who know me as you can," instructed a man to his friend. "Ask them to write down what they consider my worst faults. Tell them not to sign their names and promise them I won't make any attempt to find out who they are. Nor will I ask you anything about whom you contacted. I want to study the things I'll find out about myself to see if I can't find a simple way toward self-improvement."

We should quit calling it that because a nervous breakdown isn't a breakown and has virtually nothing to do with your nerves.

The very fact that you think you might be losing your mind is definite evidence that you aren't.

One out of every 140 Americans is perfect, but the 1,000,000-plus perfect people in our midst have no anxiety, no fears, no prejudices, no attractive vices, no weaknesses. They'll live long, however. The experts describe the perfect people this way: They are like the few completely insane: not very interesting.

A prominent psychiatrist is out with the suggestion that when anxiety, fear, sleeplessness or excessive perspiration hit us, the thing to do is chew a lump of sugar. Frequently those distresses, he says, come from low sugar levels.

Jealousy, according to the psychiatrists, is a chemical reaction—due largely to too high an iodine content in the blood.

Maybe you've already noticed this. An eminent psychologist says that when we're elated we think of our assets and otherwise of our debts.

Next time you find yourself thoroughly angered, depressed or elated, give your fingertips a little feel. You'll find them chilled as a result of your mental state. But I'll bet you'll forget to do it.

Check yourself on this one: Psychologists have discovered that when a normal individual tells a lie, the flow of saliva in the mouth ceases.

PICK YOUR PHOBIA, PARDNER

If you're afraid of women then you're suffering from gynephobia. . . .
Do you have a terrific fear of public speaking? If you have, you're suffering from lalophobia.

You'd think that if you were a victim of sitophobia you'd

be scared to sit. 'Tain't that at all. Instead you'd have a repugnance for food.

Are you a victim of taphephobia? If you are it means that you live in constant fear of being buried prematurely.

Are you afraid of being afraid? Then you're suffering from phobophobia. . . .

A feeling of hopefulness of eventual recovery is felt so frequently by patients suffering with tuberculosis that there's a special word for the feeling—spesphthisica.

Not that your old lady couldn't drive you nuts at times, but the largest proportion of persons admitted to American asylums are unwed, with divorced and widowed people following in that order.

A PSYCHOANALYST AT WORK: Single women who fall in love after they're 30 should be extremely careful, this expert warns, lest this love which you experience, coming comparatively late in life, be motivated, without your suspecting it, by gratitude, by economic or other necessity, by fear of being left a spinster or by ego, so that you may prove to your friends that you, too, are wanted. The psychoanalyst winds up his little treatise with this gem: Love is tricky.

I've never noticed it, but a doc who's supposed to be skilled in the psychology of color says women who wear polka-dot dresses usually are happy women. So, he continues, put on a polka-dot scarf when you visit a sick friend, or wear a polka-dot dress when you have to call on a tough business executive.

Baffling indeed was that statement I read awhile ago that the human mind is capable of entertaining 3,155,760,000 ideas. How in the world would they ever figure that out? Busier men than I, Gunga Din.

If you really want to compliment somebody on his intellectual ability, don't refer to his abundance of "gray matter." The dumb bunnies' brains contain as much gray matter as the smart gees'. It's the white matter or connecting nerve cells that constitute the big difference.

Here's a little statement from a top man of New York's Bellevue Hospital psychiatry department: Smoking is in the same class as thumb sucking, and a baby's pacifier will accomplish the same purpose as a cigaret.

There's a spot about the size of a nickel in your noodle that contains the meaning and pronunciation of every word you know. And no matter how smart or stupid you are, your brain has the same number of units as the next guy's.

Next time you're stumped in trying to remember somebody's name or anything, for that matter, try whiffing in a few deep breaths and then relaxing completely. The wanted word should come to you, the psychologists say, because memory depends a great deal on your nervous condition.

Women dream oftener than men and unmarried women outdream the married ones, a psychological survey shows. What bothers me is how they took the survey.

You might check this one on yourself: An eminent psychologist from the University of Illinois has discovered that an occasion for weeping occurs to the average person an average of once every 20.8 days.

You're not always aware of it, but during an eight-hour working day your brain steals about an hour and 15 minutes of catnaps. With stenographers and managing editors it runs a little higher.

If you were told (and it's true) that one of the four most common methods of suicide in the United States is defenestration, would you know what the method is? You'll get some pretty wild guesses, if you pass the thing around. What it actually means is jumping out of a window. The word stems, apparently, from the French "fenêtre," meaning window. . . .

Sunday is the favorite day for suicide by men, while Wednesday is most frequently picked by women.

JR. DEPT.

Next time you have a group of young fathers and mothers gathered around and you really want the words to fly, get them started on this: Should the male parent be actually present during the birth of an heir? There are two schools of thought on the issue and you'll find some very definite ideas that both fathers and mothers are willing to express.

Now it comes out that a "planned-for" child is not necessarily happy or secure. Psychologists have realized that an unwanted child starts life under a handicap, but planned-for children have their problems, too. Many planned-for children are brought into the world in the hope of saving the wreck of an unhappy marriage. If it doesn't work and the baby fails to bring peace to the parents, they don't want the child any more.

One reason you don't get too far in trying to reason with an infant, most pediatricians and child psychiatrists agree, is that up to two years a child has no sense of the ego. That means that the child has not yet learned to think of himself as a separate being, distinct from his environment. After the age of 2, the conception of himself as an entity, divorced from everything else about him, begins to sink in. (The ultimate of that is seen, of course, in the child's mother.)

And child psychologists are now saying that if a child isn't spanked by his parents and the other kids in the neighborhood are, the unspanked one often resents the fact that it never happens to him. He feels he's missing out on a common experience.

DON'T TAKE IT AS GOSPEL, but, to me, it had a cute twist. A mother consulting a psychiatrist about her small son's refusal to eat, was urged to let the child eat whatever he wanted. So the mother went home and asked the child what he'd like to have.

"A worm," said the lad. The mother winced, but decided to follow the instructions of the mental expert. The boy added he wanted the worm fried in butter. Mama even did that.

"Now what shall I do?" she inquired of the lad.

"Cut it in half," he replied, "and you eat half and I'll eat half."

The mother gulped but obeyed, then told her son to eat his half. "Naw," cried the youngster, "you ate my half."

EAT, SLEEP, & UNHEALTHY

I eat too much and sleep too little, which may be good for my purse but bad for my middle.

In that little rhyme you have the key to most of my health problems and probably to those of a good many other people. That's why this little department of sleep and fat is given a spot along with other health items in this volume.

Sure, I've written reams of copy over the years about this Rotund Reporter's personal battle with his bulge. Sure, I've written more copy that sounded as if it came out of pure dreams. But I figure if food and sleep have been so important to me, they probably create problems for thousands of others.

Some of my efforts have been a lot of fun because so many of you have willingly shared my misery. Probably tops in that line was our mass dieting experiment during the food-saving days of World War II. During two weeks, 22,765 of you bothered to keep actual records and we were able to shed 159,355 pounds. How many more pounds were shed by how many more participants in that grand effort I'll never know because people didn't bother to send in their report cards, but it was a lot of fun that time.

Other diets have been pretty grim business with me, however, and the constant effort for girth control has caused me so much worry that I've lost lots of sleep over it. Fortunately, being up long hours that way has been profitable, because by staying awake worrying about my weight I've found extra hours for productive work that pays well.

It's a vicious circle, I suppose, but here are some of the notes that have resulted from that phase of my life.

NOTES ON SLEEP

Another myth goes overboard. An authority on the subject says counting sheep, reading in bed or any other mental gymnastics requiring concentration are merely tricks for the repression of unpleasant ideas and actually lead a person away from sleep rather than toward it.

An eminent expert on sleep advises a substitute for counting sheep. Try holding your breath, he says. Inhale a big batch of air and hold it while it fills your system with carbon dioxide and also serves to take your mind off active things. Four or five long-held breaths should do the trick. And, says the same authority, not enough of us are sleeping on our bellies. It reduces the possibility of snoring.

Another substitute for counting sheep: Try just barely

letting the fingertips of one hand touch the fingertips of the other.

If the finger trick fails, a man I know says you can get to sleep by bending your toes and straightening them repeatedly in bed. You'll rarely get up to 500 times before you fall asleep. Besides, it's excellent for your arches.

To end insomnia, nibble on lettuce leaves just before retiring, according to old-time advice.

If getting to sleep is a major problem, you might try remembering the position you're in when you wake up in the morning. Since it's likely to be the most comfortable one for you, it may be a good idea to start the night in that position.

Don't let your insomnia worry you, however. The experts say that even though you stay awake for hours during the night, you're still getting your rest just by lying in bed. But the one thing you must do during your insomnia is to stop worrying about your inability to drop off to sleep.

Experiments show that lying down requires the least bodily energy but that sitting up requires only four per cent more. Standing up takes 12 per cent more energy than lying down.

An authority on sleeplessness points out that invariably insomnia afflicts brainworkers by giving them cold feet despite the fact that their blood circulation may be okay. It seems an active brain draws the blood out of your tootsies, hence the chill. The expert suggests a hot drink just before going to bed. . . .

A husband I know cannot go to sleep unless the open end of the pillowcase is to his left. His wife has tried changing it in the dark, but he never fails to feel for that open end and reverse it before he goes to sleep.

Wish I could remember to have a bedside pad. Thoughts while suffering insomnia might make a terrific story sometime.

When you yawn, you might as well know that you're usually suffering from one of these: boredom, hunger, fatigue or poor ventilation. But science hasn't yet discovered why yawns are contagious.

Take this moment right now and think hard about yawning. Really concentrate! If you were perfectly fair about it, you probably found yourself in the middle of a big one. *Fun, huh?*

Cover a yawn, but don't suppress it. Gulping that surplus air into your lungs is exceedingly good for you, which is why you get that satisfied feeling.

Ever notice how a person's eyes sparkle right after a yawn?

Want to know how to sleep the best? Here it is: Lie flat on your back, your feet about two feet apart, spine perfectly straight, hands at the sides, palms up and no pillow. If you simply have to have your head up a little, it's better to raise the mattress slightly. Authority for it is a physical culture expert who takes care of some of the most famous movie stars.

Ever wonder what actually happens at the moment that you drop off into slumber? Well, at the exact instant that you yield to unconsciousness, those tiny electrical charges called "brain waves" do a switch on you—moving from the back part of the head to the front. Now don't spend the night worrying about a "short circuit," because all that shift does is to keep the blood right there in the brain at the same time that it lets your blood pressure fall, your heart rate decrease and your temperature drop a bit.

There's a "sleep-control" center in the brain stem—a little stalk extending from the top of the neck where it connects with the spinal cord all the way up to the two hemispheres of the brain.

Is it Ma who sleeps right through and Pa who wakens every time the refrigerator starts up or stops at your house? There may be a reason for it. Women seem to be able to use up to half the evening just preparing for bed—washing, creaming their faces, brushing their hair, doing small chores—and, if it doesn't do anything else for them, it is relaxing. But you and I, old man, may be sliding under the covers without any pre-bedtime routine for unkinking.

Don't let anyone tell you, either, that sleeping doesn't use up energy. In fact, if you change position between 30 and 40 times a night, as some folks do, you might be wise to spend a few extra hours each day resting up for it. Average folk probably expend 0.43 calories per pound while sleeping. And I'm not telling how many calories that totals for me, so don't inquire.

CHECK THIS WHEN YOUR SLUMBER BEGINS: In going to sleep, power over muscles is lost first, the ability to detect sound fades last. In the morning it's the reverse—sounds are detected before the drowsy one can move an arm or leg.

Most comforting note in a long time is from a Cornell University psychologist who made a study on sleep. **Five to** five and a half hours a night is plenty, he says. The first hour of sleep is just a sort of adjustment. The next three and a half to four is when the body really does all of its recouping, and any amount of sleep you get after that is just so much gravy, but not at all a necessity for most adults.

SUGGESTION TO BURGLARS: The most difficult time to arouse the average adult is one hour after he's gone to sleep.

Watch your youngsters in bed some night and you'll find their deepest slumber occurs between the third and fourth hour and again between the seventh and eighth.

If you have an aversion for cold sheets, girls, jump into bed, hang on to the covers and then kick your feet, wave your arms, go through all the movements possible for 30 seconds. It's not very ladylike, but it takes the body jar out of sliding into a cold bed. And that's something on winter nights.

Some experts are urging those who must sleep on a side to sleep on our right sides. Sleep is more beneficial on that side, they say, because the food in the stomach moves over into the intestines more readily.

The medicos are now agreed, however, that it's so much poppycock that sleeping on your left side is bad for the heart.

Scientists are now out with the theory that we sleep better in beds pointing north and south than in those pointing east and west. And I'll bet you had to stop to think about the direction of your own bed. They doped it out that it takes 19 more energy units to sleep east and west than the other way.

One of the nation's best slumber authorities tells us that alcoholic beverages cause a person to change positions fewer times during normal sleep, yet leave one stiffer in the morning—and by "stiffer" he means, of course, muscularly.

I don't know who conducted the survey, but recent research indicates that more men than women sleep on their stomachs, which is said to be much better for resting the spinal column.

If you sleep on your stomach, the experts also say, you're the calm, placid type emotionally.

A mattress company discovered in a survey that 1,250,-000 New Yorkers sleep in the nude.

I'll bet you don't know what you really mean when you say "I slept like a top." So here's the background. Top is a corruption of "taupe," which is French for mole. The French phrase, "Il dort comme une taupe," means, "He sleeps like a mole."

THE SNORE

Hey, guys, show this to your little squawker: One person in every eight snores.

Only one in eight people snores, but only one out of 10 realizes the affliction without being told about it. Many a snorer, though, does it with such gusto that he wakes himself up.

A sporting-goods dealer once told me he got a call in midwinter for some earplugs for swimmers. "I don't want to use them for swimming," explained the woman caller, "but my husband snores so loud every night that I can't sleep."

Goody, goody—people who snore have a clear conscience.

Remedies for snoring have bounced in frequently to my column, but some are so vicious, it seems. Pepper strewn under the nostrils of the offender, one caller said, was a certain stopper. A clamp-style clothespin pinched over a big toe will halt the most sonorous of snorers, another claimed. Golf balls sewn in the back of a pajama coat never fail, according to another. The little lumps, it seems, keep the sleeper off his back, the downdraft is stopped and, consequently, no snoring. . . .

Take a dreamland safety hint: If you ever get a cramp in your foot or leg in the middle of the night, leap out of bed, if there's a leap left in you, point your toe up and your heel down with as much force as you can muster and the cramp will leave instantly.

Ever wake up in the middle of the night with your head hanging over the side of the bed? The sleep experts say that's because the nervous strain you've been under has been so great that you were too tired to pull your head back into its proper position on the pillow.

Or did you ever wake up with a curious feeling of excessive warmth? A sleep expert says all you have to do to overcome it is to shift to the other side of the bed, toss off covers till the body cools and you're all set. Ben Franklin was a victim of this type of body heat and maintained four beds that he used alternately.

More than 40 per cent of us wake up feeling tired in the morning after what we consider a good night's sleep. The trouble with most is that we use too many covers, experts explain.

More reasons why you wake up tired now and then: In the process of breathing, the average person lifts the blankets 16 times a minute. If the blanket weighs a mere five pounds, that means an 80-pound heave every minute, or more than two tons an hour. The poor guy who actually sleeps eight hours has tossed around 16 tons while he's supposedly relaxing.

Comes now some really good news: We should never bounce out of bed, the medics announce. The brain's still a little anemic from the action of sleep and therefore it's better to loll in bed for a few minutes after waking. Leap out as soon as the alarm clock rings, and you're apt to develop a headache or suffer dizziness.

Try this for a week: Take a five-minute period of yawning and stretching before you get out of bed. You'll be amazed at what it does for you.

NOT A BAD CRACK: The older generation thought nothing of getting up at 5 o'clock in the morning. The younger generation doesn't think much of it either.

See to it that your pooch gets plenty of slumber: He can survive much more readily without food than without sleep. A dog will die after four or five days and nights of sleeplessness.

THE SUET AROUND US

The old saw that everybody loves a fat man has one notable exception, and that's the doctor. Surgeons dislike to operate on the rotund ones because it's extremely difficult to sew human fat, and the stitches tend to pull out unless the most exacting care is taken.

THERE'S A GREAT DAY COMING: Scientists are concentrating on tests to find out why fat people eat. Understanding of the fat person's motives for eating, the experts figure, will aid immeasurably in treating the condition.

No wonder some of us are expansive around the middle: Fats, more than any other food, have the ability to satisfy hunger.

A prominent medical writer calls the United States a "nation of food drunkards," while another attributes our intensified desire for food to such causes as nervousness, monotony, occupation, organic diseases and environment.

Scientists are generally agreed that the offspring of parents tend to be of the same sex as the better-nourished parent. I have three boys, remember that. What they did was to take a group of female rodents, give them a low protein diet, then mate them with amply fed males. The 64 resulting litters produced 327 males and 226 females. Then the diets were reversed and that turned the sex ratio to 237 females and 218 males.

Want to find out whether you're fat? Here's a little test used in the air force. Multiply the inches of your height over five feet by 5½, then add 110. If you weigh more than the total, according to air force medical authorities, you're fat. I'm a roly-poly by those standards. And don't go muttering that I'm a roly-poly by any standards.

LIFE, DEATH AND WEIGHT—DO THOSE THINGS INTEREST YOU? Recent records show definite correlation between body weight and longevity. Get ready to sigh, here come the figures: Among short men, five feet seven and below, aged 40 to 44, an excess of 20 per cent in weight involves mortality of 30 per cent above normal. An excess of 40 per cent in weight involves an 80 per cent increase in mortality. How you doin', Fat Stuff? Among tall men, five feet 10 and above, 40 to 44, an excess of 20 per cent in weight carries a 40 per cent increase in mortality. A 40 per cent weight excess doubles mortality. In early adult life, being underweight is a disadvantage. In tall men, those 20 per cent below average weight showed increased mortality of 30 per cent. Those 30 per cent below average weight have 50 per cent excess mortality. An excess of 10 pounds above the average is most favorable between the ages of 20 and 24. At 50 years it's much better to be 30 or 40 pounds below the weight-age average.

EXERCISE—THIS I DISLIKE

Every time I see a man or a woman with a big abdomen, I always obey the impulse to pull mine in. Too bad the impulse isn't more lasting.

Good news for those of us handicapped by big middles, and experts say the scheme can take inches off the tummy line in less than a month. Stand erect and work your abdomen with a snappy pull-in-let-out movement. Do it 50 times a day regularly for the reduction.

You hikers are reducing the hard way. Health authorities assert that it takes a 36-mile walk to take off one pound of fat. . . .

Here's another doctor's prescription for people who dream of a streamlined figure (not necessarily indorsed by this writer but passed along for those who are inclined): Get up a little earlier in the morning. Instead of driving all the way into town and then fuming and fretting about the shortage of a parking place, park your car in an unrestricted zone at least a mile from where you work. Then walk the rest of the way. Says the doc: You'll keep your blood pressure down and arrive at work with a chestful of fresh air. The walk back to your car in the afternoon will refresh you after a day indoors. Streetcar and bus riders could do the same, he suggests, and avoid congestion caused by pellmell piling on of passengers downtown. Best of all, he concludes, more of those excess pounds would melt off.

GIRTH CONTROL

Laugh, Ladies, you're entitled to this one. It used to be the man who worried most about his waistline. In the past men artifically constricted their waists by wearing tight broad belts of metal.

While on the topic of girth control, unless I told you, you'd probably never have the following valuable information on girdles and foundation garments:

It just goes to show how we try to cover all the various news fronts. For instance, some foundation garments for summer weigh no more then seven ounces. Stout women, strangely enough, are easier to help with their figure problems than their slimmer sisters. It's the lack of false illusions in the fair, fat and forties that does it.

Women should spend at least an hour in selecting their girdles. Subdebs with posture difficulties are going in for foundation garments as figure "guidance," which means they start early to do something about that "dowager's hump." Once a week isn't too often to wash a good corset. . . . A correctly fitted foundation garment will take away as much as three inches of unwanted girth by scientific shifting of flesh. Girdles, like electric refrigerators or radios, need service, and professional corsetières make regular "service" calls at homes. A corset having a slightly shorter skirt line in front allows more freedom for walking.

Measurements for a girdle should be taken both standing and sitting down. The body has a spread of three inches when in a sitting position. Girdles, like toothbrushes, should be bought two at a time. "Resting" a garment adds to its life. I guess that'll hold you.

TO EAT OR NOT TO EAT

Medical authorities agree that the best way to start a diet is to shrink your stomach right off the bat. A really good stomach shrinking will take the old fellow down to about the size of your index finger. When you think of your stomach, don't confuse it with your abdomen. What a joy it

196 Poor Cedric's Almanac

would be to get your abdomen down to about the size of
your index finger—or even your middle finger.

**Drink a glass of orange, grapefruit, or grape juice after
every meal for a month to shrink the stomach.**

Stewardesses on some of our leading airlines also use
what they call the orange routine if they notice their weight
increasing. They maintain normal eating both in quantity
and quality. But on the first control day they eat one
orange, the second two oranges, the third three and so on.
The oranges may be eaten any time of the day and in as
rapid succession as desired. By the time the girls get up to
around 12 or 14 oranges a day, weight reduction has become obvious. The citrus juice is responsible. But as the
quantity of oranges increases, the intake of other food
diminishes some, too. Stewardesses swear by it.

How does this sound to you for a pretty sensible way of
dieting? It comes from a leading medico. Eat all you want,
with just this one little restriction. You can do that every
other day. On the "between" day you can have tomato
juice, one hardboiled egg and half a head of lettuce. You
can go as heavy as you want and as often as you want on
the tomato juice each dieting day. This doctor says it'll take
20 pounds off a fat man or woman in a month.

**Here's a diet note from a man in the corn belt: Sweet
corn eaten within 24 hours after it's picked is not fattening
because the starch hasn't had a chance to form. . . .**

After faithfully sticking through a diet and watching
eight pounds drop off ounce by ounce, and realizing the
magnitude of my inward struggle to get rid of that weight, I
went to a physician for advice on maintaining the slimmer
shape. Here's about what he said:

Starting a diet and then abandoning it entirely not only
causes a return to the previous weight level, but also results
sometimes in an upsurge beyond all previous highs. After
the initial rapid loss, an established reduction of a pound a
week is enough from any diet. Fats can be sacrificed. Vitamins must be considered. Vitamin C is usually taken care
of by fruits, but A, B and D must be supplemented. There
is no high road to correcting obesity. It's toil and sweat and
diet.

Part Four

CHILDREN

WHERE WOULD THE REST OF US BE WITHOUT THEM?

I've never had a thrill like the first kiss I gave my first-born.

And ever since then I've been especially interested in children. First in my own children, then in yours, then children in general.

Maybe I'm just a softie, the kind of guy who isn't supposed to exist in this news-gathering business. Maybe it's the lure of copy rather than a personal feeling. But I can't help marveling at the wonders of growth and the pains, problems and pleasures the little ones bring unto themselves and the grown-up world.

For instance, even after all these years I still can't keep a lump from my throat whenever I read, write or broadcast about a tot's being smothered in its crib. And each year brings so many such tragedies. I suppose in families where that's happened the mother may never quite get over feeling a certain amount of responsibility.

On the other hand fun and happiness from children come early and stay long. But it takes a lot of patience to bridge the gap between children and adults. If you can calmly dissuade a little girl from the mess of jamming a three-pound mud pie into a two-pound bag, you'll probably be doing some future husband a favor by teaching his wife-to-be that she can't keep up a $10,000 existence on a $5,000 income.

The quality of patience has to be doubled and redoubled for children who are hard of hearing, short of sight or otherwise limited. That's why handicapped children have always elicited a great deal of sympathy from me.

Consider the training of a deaf child. You probably know that a child born deaf, although he may be perfectly normal otherwise, cannot learn to talk because he cannot hear. Sharp though he may be mentally, and with healthy active vocal cords, if he doesn't hear speech and has no chance to imitate a spoken word, he has no names for the things he sees. Amazing to me was a visit to the Minneapolis school set aside for children whose hearing loss is great enough to cause difficulty in regular classes. Youngsters start there at a nursery school for those about four years old. Understanding comes first. The children learn that everything has a name and that by watching lips, thoughts can be conveyed. When a child begins to read lips, a one-way communication at least has been established. . . . The child places his fingers to the teacher's face to feel vibrations and rhythm of speech as various objects are identified. So slow is the process that an average child will need a year to build up a lip-reading vocabulary of 75 words: 30 nouns, 25 verbs, 9 colors and some parts of the body. It may take months of a teacher's effort to bring out the lone first word. It is only after many movements of the lips are tied up with objects like "ball," or "shoe," or "mama" that the real education of these tots begins. But it does begin and in the wonderful magic of childhood development the afflicted youngsters somehow catch up.

Those are what we call handicaps, and many are overcome. In addition, as every parent knows, youngsters can find or invent so many hazards for themselves that it is a wonder enough ever grow beyond childhood to people the earth with adults.

I want to wish good luck and good health to all youngsters, for where would any of us be if it weren't for children?

PRENATAL

You can make practically as much money as the operator of an honest roulette wheel by betting even money with all prospective parents that it will be a boy. A roulette operator has 19 chances in 37 of winning a red and black bet, while the chances are 21 in 41 that an unborn baby will be a boy. At least the U.S. sex ratio has for many years been fairly constant at 1,057 boys for every 1,000 girls.

Three months before it's born, X rays have established, a baby begins to suck its thumb and thus educate itself for nursing after birth.

For the bouncingest babies, have them arrive in the fall, says a pediatrician. Prospective mothers, he points out, get a more varied diet in the spring and summer, more vegetables and more sunshine, too. For those reasons, the autumn arrivals are stronger in bone structure and mineral content.

SIMILE: "Troubles, like babies, grow larger by nursing." . . .

NOTE TO EXPECTANT FATHERS: Research by the University of Nebraska indicates that Robert and Richard are favorite names for men, with both men and women expressing their choices. Charles, Jack, John and William follow in that order. Jean is the best-liked name for a girl. Jane, Dorothy and Virginia come next.

William or one of its variants, however, is the first name of more men and boys than any other in the land. Some 5,000,000 bear the monicker or its derivations.

And what would you guess is the most common boy's name in the world as a whole? Two to one you're wrong. It's Mohammed.

Actually they're as sensible as many other monickers, so let's not laugh too scoffingly. Birth records in Louisiana show that children down there have been given these names: Castor Oil, Pickle, Sausage, Evil, Huddle, Louse, Rascal, Delirious and Rat.

BIRTH OF ELATION

The first 15 minutes after a baby's birth make up the most dangerous quarter hour of the tot's lifetime. The three principal causes of death during that brief interval are prematurity, cerebral hemorrhage and asphyxia.

Twins have been known to be born as long as a week apart.

And identical twins very frequently utter the same words at the same time when conversing in separate groups.

The chance of death in infancy is 37 per cent greater if babies in a family are born only a year apart than if they are two years apart and 50 per cent greater than with a three-year split.

Mothers of newborn babes might want to check their own infants with the national average: Boy babies have an average weight of seven pounds and ten ounces while girl babies weigh on the average of seven pounds and two and a half ounces.

I never gaze through a hospital nursery window at a baby without recalling the fact that two-thirds of its weight is accounted for in its head and liver, with the liver just about equaling the head in weight.

You wonder why all the fuss when a newborn baby is 74.6 per cent water.

WORD COMES NOW that the newborn infant is bilateral, with neither right- nor left-handedness pronounced. Which means we have a 50-50 chance to become either right- or left-handed and learn to favor one or the other. Preference for either side is a cultural and social convention. Left-handed parents are frequently imitated by their offspring, but the young do not inherit such tendencies.

A blue-eyed child is quite likely to grow up to be a gray-eyed adult.

CRYBABY

The average newborn baby cries 113 minutes a day, and that's more than should be necessary for the normal use of the cry as a signal of need. Must have been quite a job to check the bawling, but doctors at the Mayo Clinic did it.

Mother's little helper passes on this advice from a wise

woman: If your little bundle from heaven persists in crying himself to sleep, plug in your vacuum cleaner and place it near baby's crib. The high-pitched hum of the vacuum cleaner will magically shut off the tot's wails and lull him into a peaceful slumber. What it'll do to the old man's nerves, the mother didn't say.

Wonder if tiny babies ever get that "needles and pins" feeling that results from having a hand or an arm or a leg go to sleep? I'll bet if they do, that's what makes a lot of them cry when they first wake up.

Now it comes out that babies often cry when they're perfectly comfortable. One medical authority states that they do it just to keep in practice.

Don't crack down too hard on your thumb-sucking off-spring—once in the lifetime of every human being the habit has to be overcome.

There isn't a much more pleasant sensation than that of having a baby grab one of your fingers and hold on.

Next time you do a little adjusting on the baby's diap, you might shed a tear for the gent who invented the safety pin. He sold out for $400 when he might have made millions.

Take a look at that baby of yours tonight. If it has dimples just below the anklebone, it's an indication of flat feet later on in life unless some kind of correction is made.

LOOK, MA, IT GROWS

After your baby has reached the six-month stage, it should recognize its name when spoken to and should turn its head in response. One that fails to react thus should have its ears examined.

A child learns to say, "No, no," before it learns to say, "Yes, yes," and infants *understand* the meaning of "bad boy," or "bad girl," long before they know the actual meaning of the words. . . .

Until your tot is nine months old, you're wasting breath by giving him or her anything in language form. They don't catch onto words until after that age.

Babies in Samoa often learn to swim before they learn to walk.

STATE OF THE NATION AMONG BABIES: A noted pediatrician tells me that he has seen almost no babies in his long career who did not like beer. It seems that the usual baby just loves the stuff, which might prove that the liking for beer is not an acquired taste. . . .

Never feed a baby candy bars that contain nuts. . . .

You mothers will promptly forget about it, but the New York State College of Home Economics urges this: Buttons on young children's clothes should be large enough for the child to grasp easily and to push or pull through the buttonholes. Buttons about an inch in diameter are satisfactory. Cases of severe stammering, they say, have come from children being thwarted in buttoning a button. . . .

Stuttering, incidentally, is most likely to develop in youngsters when they're around 11 years old.

But watch your youngsters carefully between the ages of three and eight. That's when many speech defects develop and you should spot them early.

If the shoe fits: The oldest child in a family tends to be more jealous, more selfish and neater. The younger brother or sister is likely to be happier, more generous and more punished. . . .

Ask your nearest neighbor what they call that gadget in which a papoose is carried and chances are slim you'll get the proper answer. It's a "deekanogan," in case it ever comes up again.

A FATHER & SON SOLILOQUY
ABOUT ACCIDENTS

Climb up here on my knee a minute, David, I want to talk to you. You see this picture in today's paper. That's a little boy four years old. He's just your age. That picture was taken in a hospital. Down below the picture it says, "Critically hurt by car." Those words mean a lot. Down there at the hospital when the nurses, all dressed up in their white uniforms, come quietly out of a room and say, "The patient's condition is critical," that's just another way of saying, "He's been hurt pretty badly and right now we don't know whether he'll pull through or not." The little boy's eyes are closed. He looks like he's sleeping. Maybe he is. And maybe he'll never wake up. But if he does, it's a pretty sure thing that his little body'll hurt all over because over here in the story it says that one of his legs was broken and that his head was injured. Injured means hurt. . . .

It's pretty hard to understand just how some little boys never get hurt and others dart unfortunately into the path of a car. Whoever it is that's running the world doesn't let us in on that. But it's a good thing to do all we can to prevent accidents like the one that happened to this little fellow. There are all kinds of ways that accidents can happen.

And even little boys like you or little girls like Joan or Hoozie or Betty Lloyd can do quite a bit toward keeping yourselves out of the hospital. There aren't very many drivers who'll chase you right up on the sidewalk to hit you. If you keep out of the street, you're fairly safe. Even if your ball rolls out there, don't chase it. Pa would rather buy you a new ball than have to go down while the doctors set your leg or sewed up a big gash on your forehead. Lots of times drivers don't mean to hit anyone, but kids sometimes run right out in front of their cars.

Next time you sort of get an idea that it'd be more fun to ride your trike or your scooter in the street, remember the night you sat on Pa's knee and we looked at the picture of the little boy in the hospital. Remember how his eyes were closed and how there was a bandage on his head, and how when he woke up he was going to feel like somebody had hit him with a hammer. So I'll make a deal with you, Son. You remember those things, and Pa'll remember, every time he drives, that cars and little boys smash pretty easily.

- o -

Why do some adults cling fiercely to the leash of their pups yet allow their kiddies to scramble unaided across busy and dangerous thoroughfares?

Experts say that between the ages of two and five years a child forms mental habits of concentration, self-control and self-reliance or their opposites. These habits, good or bad, are little likely to be changed in later years.

What's better than to have a little son crawl in bed with you on Sunday morning?

Can you think of anything sweeter than to have one of your youngsters give you a "Thank you" for something? They get a pleasant, sincere quality into those words that adults should emulate.

This seemed to me to be the best ruse used on landlords who objected to tenants with children in the wartime house pinch. A woman with half a dozen kids, the story goes, was having the usual trouble finding a house to rent. One day she went out house hunting and put her children in the cemetery to play. When a prospective landlord asked her if she had any children, she replied, "I have six in the cemetery." The landlord replied, "Well, in that case, I think I can let you have the place."

Interesting quote from a young mother: "I don't think you should ever spank a child unless you have a definite end in view."

Do you have a stumbling child in your home—one who stumbles over a piece of paper or trips on a shadow? Mustn't scold him for being clumsy. That tripping and stumbling, if he does it constantly, may be a sign that he doesn't see as well as he should. The expert advice now is to trot him off to an eye doctor, your family physician or a baby specialist. A frowning child or one who rubs his eyes a lot as if trying to brush away a blur is another type who needs eye attention pronto.

FATHER & SON SOLILOQUY
ON GOING INTO THE FIRST GRADE

Well, David, day after tomorrow you start school again. This year you'll be in the first grade. That's a pretty big step for a boy to take. Kindergarten has been sort of play for you. I mean you went just half days and you learned how to cut out things and paste and make little doodads. But now you're going to learn to read and to write and to add things up. So next Tuesday is a pretty big day for you. It's just the beginning of a long string of "firsts" that you'll have.

Pa remembers a lot of his firsts. I remember the first time I ever smoked. It was a piece of horsewhip. And then I graduated to corn silk. You're a normal boy, so I suppose you'll go through the same thing, only a piece of horsewhip will be hard to find these days. So if I were you I'd wait a long time till I tried that first smoke. . . .

I remember the first girl I ever had. Unfortunately, it wasn't your mother. She wasn't around then. But judging from some of Mother's girlhood pictures, I guess it wouldn't have made much difference if she had been—I still wouldn't have picked her out of the field then. But I'll tell you something about that first girl you get. Some day she's going to jilt you. And the minute she does you'll think that the whole world is crumbling, that life just isn't worth it any more. But remember, if you can, that Pa said a long time ago recovery from that first jilt is rapid. . . .

After a while you're going to have another first that you'll think is mighty important. Some day you'll look in the mirror and you'll see that fuzz on your face and you'll think that maybe it should come off. And you'll probably sneak into the bathroom and use Pa's razor. Well, let me tell you right now that the longer you can tolerate the fuzz the better off you'll be. Shaving every day is quite a chore.

The first dollar you ever earn will be an important thing, too. Of course, you've already had some dimes and quarters for chores and errands; but some day, maybe, you'll have a paper route or work in a grocery store and you'll come home with the first real money that you can call your salary. From then on, I can tell you, that will be the thing that you'll always spend a little more of than you get. A little later there'll be your first salary raise. Those raises are funny things. Nine times out of ten you and the boss will disagree as to the frequency and amounts. And you'll be nervous when you go in to ask for them. Pa wishes he could give you the technique for asking for a pay increase, but the years haven't been long enough to learn a sure way of doing it. If I were certain hard work would get me a raise, I might give that a try. But you can't always count on that approach. . . .

You and I might as well face all the facts while we're sitting here. Some day (and I hope this is a long way off) you'll have to go to your first funeral. A funeral's where people that you know or love die, and all their friends gather to pay their last respects. The sad part of it is that you never know just when it will come. It may be one of your little friends who ran out in the street too suddenly and was hit by a car. Or it may be one of the neighbors or a relative. You see, David, funerals are sad. And that's why Pa hopes your first one will be a long time off. . . .

Then there'll be your first long pants, where you'll feel all legs, and your first dance and the first time you flunk in something, and oh, there'll be all kinds of firsts after next Tuesday. So when you slide into your little first-grade seat with your face shining and your neck and ears clean (I hope) and your hair combed and your eyes bright, Pa won't be there in person to help start you off, but he'll certainly be there beside you in spirit. And when that first bell rings you can sort of plan on a little supplication from Pa—a little hope and a little prayer that everything comes out all right from then on.

- o -

ANY SIXTH GRADERS IN YOUR HOME? If so, this survey will interest you. Typical reasons boys and girls have for picking their best friends are these: "He can tell good jokes." "He never hurts people's feelings." "She saves me a seat so I won't have to sit with the boys at lunch." In other words, psychologists have discovered that even in the sixth grade, personality is the important thing among friends. Cheerfulness, kindness, honesty, and generosity are the most important qualities to youngsters when it comes to picking friends. These were some of the reasons the kids interviewed gave for dropping a friend: "She has not been wanting to be friends." "He thinks he's hot." "He stole my girl friend away." "She is always treating me mean." Parents should be sure to maintain contacts with other children for their youngsters, too.

Greatest number of absences from school in America occur on Mondays.

From a schoolteacher speaking at a parents' meeting: "When your child brings home his version of what happens at school, please be as generous in your thinking of us as we are of you when he brings his interpretation of what goes on in your home. Please do not make derogatory remarks about the school or the teacher in the presence of your child, no matter what your opinion might be."

Tip for elevator operators: When mothers get in your car holding babes in their arms, suggest they squeeze the infants tightly during the ride. It eliminates that sinking inside sensation which tots cry for.

You can also ease the child's belly bouncing by having the tot look up instead of down regardless of the direction of the car.

Adults, too, can avoid that sinking sensation in a descending elevator, I'm told, by rising up on tiptoes, while in the car.

21 VARIETIES

No wonder our kids sometimes fail in their ugly chore of getting themselves cleaned up for dinner. Scientists have discovered that there are 21 kinds of "dirt" for a youngster to wash off his hands and face in an average semi-industrial community. And several of those kinds do not respond to ordinary toilet soaps.

A family we know has two lads, both under 10, and took some clever steps to solve their bathroom troubles about towels, etc. They tacked signs up all over the bathroom. Over the towels, for instance, the legend is: "This Is the Private Property of, etc.—Hands Off." And it works. The most functional sign in the whole place, though, is one that reads, "In It, Not at It."

Children and feeble-minded adults are the toughest for magicians to fool—they're actually too simple to get sucked in.

Children conceived in the first half of the year are more likely to be geniuses or criminally insane later on than those conceived in the last half. I'll bet you're checking up on yourself right now.

THOUGHTS WHILE SHAVING: It makes me gulp every time I think about that eight-year-old Iowa girl who accidentally swallowed the stopper from a hot water bottle.

Have you a little genius in your home? If you have, he's one out of 200. Here are some of the ways you can tell: If a child is unusual by comparison with children of his own age, if he uses language advanced for his years, if he answers questions beyond the average comprehension or if

THE CUBE ROOT OF
357,911 IS 71.

he asks questions that amaze you, you have clues he may be
unusually gifted.

Contrary to popular notion, "gifted" children, those with
an I.Q. of more than 135, are on the average large for their
age, well developed and excel in many personality traits
with potentialities for distinguished achievement in life.

FATHER & SON SOLILOQUY
ON USING A BICYCLE

Well, David, get up here on Pa's knee. We've really got
something to talk about tonight. Out in the garage there's
a little surprise for you. . . . But before I give it to you,
you and Pa have to make a few promises to each
other. . . . In the garage there's a brand-new bike for you.
This one has big wheels and a coaster brake and a horn
and lights.

Your mother and I talked this over for a long time. You'll
be 7 pretty soon and that's a little young for a big-sized
bike. But I told your mother that you're the kind of boy

who listens to what Pa tells you. So you've got to come through for me now.

You know when boys get big enough to ride big bikes that's pretty near like driving an automobile, because from now on you'll be riding in the street along with cars and trucks. Your being out there in the street on your bike is going to have quite an effect on Pa. When auto drivers haven't got boys on bikes, they're sort of apt to grow a little careless. I can remember lots of times when I'd be driving downtown on my way to the office and some boy or girl would be just ahead of me on his or her bike, often doing tricks. Well, many times Pa has felt like hollering to that kid, "Hey, you, why don't you look where you're going? Do you want to get yourself killed?" There you have one attitude. But I also have another now. There have been quite a few times when some youngster might have hollered at Pa about the way I was driving. For instance, I might have been rushing to work and thinking of something entirely different from my driving. And that youngster on his bike might well have shouted something like this, "Hey, you big fat stiff, do you want all the road? Why don't you look where you're going or go where you're looking?" In other words, it's largely a point of view.

Remember the time you and I were out on the beach when that little boy drowned? And we saw the father bending over him while the pulmotor squad worked over him? And the father was asking God to spare the life of his little boy? Well, that same thing could happen to almost any father if some motorist came along and carelessly or otherwise struck a lad on a bike. So starting today, Pa's going to promise you and all other youngsters that they have practically the right of way when they're ahead of me on their bikes. And maybe other fathers and drivers will join you and Pa. And that brings us to a couple or three things that I'm going to expect of you. . . .

I think for the most part you can ride your bike on the sidewalk, but there's one thing I know you'll never do. When there's someone ahead of you walking on the sidewalk, don't scoot up silently from behind, then whiz past them. That scares the daylights out of people. Either give them that "beep-peep" that you can do with your mouth or else blow your bicycle horn to let them know you're coming. Don't ride anybody on your bike because the bike's too hard to control with two boys on it. And don't be a smart aleck on your bike. Showing off can get you in some awful jams and even into some of our very best hospitals.

Always signal when you're going to turn left on your bike. Do it for every turn even when you don't see a car in back of you. That'll get you in a good habit. Switching in and out and around cars when the traffic's heavy is a bad thing to do on a bike. Your bike wheels, you know, are sort of slippery. The wheel might slide right from under you if you don't make a turn properly, and wham! a car socks you! When you're in traffic and you come to a busy intersection, take lots of time getting across. It's that old hurrying that causes a lot of grief.

You can make this bike bring you a lot of pleasure, David, or it could mean a lot of misery. If ever anything happens to you when you're on your bike, Mother's going to say, "See, I told you he was too young. But oh, no, you had to get that big bike for him." So you and Pa had better stick together and we'll have a little laugh on her. And another thing, your mother's going to have to get along without a new vacuum cleaner for a while on account of your bike. So keep that in mind, too. Now go try out the bike, and happy pedaling to you, Son.

MINDS IN THE MAKING

English teachers must get some pretty loud laughs out of the efforts of their pupils now and then. When the Flax Institute conducted an essay contest in which some 3,500 high-school students competed, these were a few bits on the guffaw side: "Flax is an excellent nurse crop. As it approaches maternity, its leaves begin to fall!" "Our land is very fertile because father rotates the soil each year." "The flax straw bailing outfit serves employment to many of my townspeople. Some haul the flax straw, others stack it.

Then they spend their money in the municipal liquor store and everyone benefits."

BONERS IN EXAM PAPERS have always been a source of laughs. Take the following: The plural of child is twins. . . . The equator is a menagerie lion that runs

around the earth. . . . An angle is a triangle with only two sides. . . . Gravitation is something which if we had none we would all fly away. . . . Louis XV was gelatined during the French revolution. . . .

Gross ignorance is 144 times as bad as ordinary ignorance.

DEAR FOLKS:

Somebody should make a collection of letters from kids in camp to their parents and publish them in book form. There's nothing more refreshing than the literary style of youngsters from 7 to 13. At times you want to lose faith in the American system of education, but actually the blunders and writing errors give their letters true charm. . . .

We've had some darbs from our own vacationing kids, literary efforts that make you think maybe they're spending too much time with athletics or recess. One of our news writers brought the following masterpiece down for inspection. We won't use the lad's name because his dad needs that much protection.

"I have won two medals in rifle shooting and I am a member of the National Rifle association. They send my targets to Washington, D.C. I lost my toothbrush some place and I can't find it. The tore in my blanket has got bigger but I think I can last through it. I was forced to write this letter or they wouldn't let me out of the cabin.— Love, Mike.

P.S. Please send a toothbrush."

FATHER & SON SOLILOQUY: A LETTER TO THE BOYS IN CAMP

Dear Boys: You may not remember me, you've been away so long. This is Pa, the fellow with so much stomach. Remember? Things have been a lot different around home since you fellows left for summer camp. For the first two days your mother kept me slamming the screen doors and pounding on an old dishpan so the silence wouldn't drive her crazy. And the next time you go away, Pa doesn't want you to take all the toothpaste. We didn't have any old tubes to turn in so I've been using salt for three weeks.

You boys won't recognize Pa when you get back, I'm so much thinner. Remember that old duffel bag of mine you borrowed. Well, I went to use it the other day, and when I emptied it, 3,789 marbles fell all over the floor. Your mother has been making me pick them up one by one, so now I'm but a shadow of my former self. I suppose first I'd better give you some of the neighborhood news. Suttons have sold their house and are moving. They probably picked this time to sell. With you guys away a prospect

would think this a quiet neighborhood. The new buyer will
probably cancel the deal about the time you fellows get a
baseball game started on his front lawn. I went to the Hill-
top Laboratories where our turkeys are kept to watch the
vet vaccinate them. It's done on the leg and the turkeys
don't like it any better than you did. The birds are almost
as tall as Stevie. The one that looks like Tommy Dorsey
will be hard to kill, come Thanksgiving. It'll be like doing
away with a friend.

**Pa wants to compliment you boys for being so good
about writing.** At first I was inclined to hop on you about
your spelling. But the other day the pastor of one of our
leading churches sent me this letter he received from his
son, John, who is one of your fellow campers:

"Dear folks, I'm feeling fine. We had the first camp fire
and we all felt sick after because we burnt the old falfe.
We are going to make a raft and make a dok. We had meet
baal and pototoes and spinict tonight we are going to have
a real show mind reader will come and lots of other fans.
I wash you could be hear. We had seryel for brickfist that
tasted ofal. We are resting now. Your loving son, John."

Don't get feeling too superior, though. Here's one of
David's letters. You fellows pick out the mistakes. "Dear
Mom: I got the chemistry outfit and I love it. I can't do
many asparamnts with it at camp. I jest made a stink bome
and it smalled like the dickens. Please send me some glow
to make planes. Ric can't go swimming because he has got
blisters on his tows from his shows. His side ake has gon
now. To Nite he is going to see the doter about his tows.
Don't forget the glow and also send some onvolops. For
akettivity we are going to take a robote trip. We had ciken
for lunch. Love Dave."

I don't blame you boys entirely because the guy who
thought up our spelling didn't do a very good job of it. In
summer it's hard to think about spelling, too. Maybe if you
and the minister's son get together, you can work out a
whole new system based on the way you spell. At least
there's some sense to your method. Pa got a lump in his
throat the day the bus pulled out with the three of you going away from home for the first time. I couldn't help

think of the thousands of parents who have said goodby to their boys as they pulled out for a different kind of camp —an army training camp. That's why I hope you appreciate fully these summers of fun and swimming and boating and hikes through the woods. Lots of parents' sons are in still another kind of camp—a prison camp. Their fathers can't write to them like I can to you. And those young men don't get cereal or chicken, either. We have to remember, too, that it's the fellows who went off to army training camps and the men who were put into prison camps who probably kept the rest of us from being put in still another kind of camp—a concentration camp.

Things haven't been altogether fun since you left. Your dog called on a skunk the other night and now can't understand why she hasn't the social acceptance she used to have in the neighborhood. She met me on the front lawn the same night (Blondie, not the skunk) so I've been having similar trouble. Your mother told me the other night there was a snake down in the areaway of the basement window. She said she has seen it with her own eyes. I investigated but found no trace of it. After all, it could be her age. Your mother put up 20 quarts of raspberry jam the other day. I don't know why she didn't put up currants. They match the breakfast-nook wallpaper so much better. Well, Pa is anxiously awaiting your return. Remember what I told you about coming back on the bus. Just whisper to the driver and he'll be glad to stop.

Love, Pa.

CLOTHES MAKE THE MAN

INTO EACH LIFE A LITTLE RAIN MUST FALL: I still remember the day I took a close look at my three sons and said, "Look, it's about time you were developing a little clothes consciousness." In unison they came back with, "What's that?" I tried to explain to them that maybe instead of the corduroy pants and flannel shirts they were wearing, it might be a good idea if they'd switch to suits and shirts with neckties and shoes that would take some polish. Inasmuch as we had a Father and Son banquet coming up, I sort of wanted them to look presentable. I broached the idea of a little shopping trip by the four of us downtown of an afternoon. Now, I am fully convinced that if a father wants to spend some time with his offspring, he should select some activity other than a shopping trip. . . .

Our first stop was in the shoe department. The shoe man was a cordial fellow and fortunately so. The three boys sat in the customers' chairs and the shoe seller sat on his little stool in front of them. As he squatted to take foot measurement of my youngest, the 11-year-old, who should have known better, reached down and rubbed the salesman's bald head with the inquiry, "How did your head get so shiny?" It was probably the first time the lad had looked down on a bald head. After the boys had all put on new shoes, the man took them, in turn, to some kind of gadget where you put your feet in an opening, push a button and then peer down through a peeper arrangement for an X-ray view of the bones of your feet right through the shoe. I'm sure it was the first such revelation to any of the three boys. They manifested their delight with more noise than should occur in any first-class shoe department. As I waited at the wrapping desk, the oldest came running with distress clearly on his countenance. "Come quick," he said, "Ric is caught in the machine." Their interest in watching the bones of their toes wiggle had switched to a desire to see what went on inside their heads. Ric had stuck his head in the opening designed for feet only. It looked like it would have to be an ax job to extricate his head. There have been many occasions during their youth when I thought they all should have had their heads examined, but this wasn't exactly the routine I had figured on. We finally sprung him, with both Ric and the machine intact. I'm sure the whole shoe department was pleased when we left.

In the coat and pants department next, a saleswoman helped us select sports jackets and trousers. She told me to have the boys step into the dressing rooms and she would call a tailor from the alteration department. I took a comfortable seat out on the main aisle to wait. In a moment I felt the youngest touching my arm. "Dad," he began, "see if you can get this zipper started." I looked. There he stood in his sports jacket and underwear. The department was crowded with people. We must have been pathetic yet comical figures as we walked down that main aisle back toward the dressing room. Steve in his sports jacket and underpants. Father leaning over ushering him to cover and trying to explain that a department store isn't quite like one's home, that it's polite to put on your pants if you're going to walk around where there are other people. He apologized by saying he thought he had on his old trousers.

A few afternoons after the shopping tour I hurried home with much anticipation. The purchases we'd made had been delivered. I was going to see the boys in their brand-new outfits—dressed as their father wanted them dressed. To me they looked sharp. The coats fit, the pants had a perfect hang, the shirts were snug at the neck, the three ties neatly knotted. It was their mother who spoke first.

"Do you know how long those clothes will fit? Did you ever stop to realize those boys are growing? It's your money. If you want to spend it for stuff that will last about a month it's all right with me. Do you know where those sleeves will be by the end of three or four months? Those pants will be halfway up to their knees before the snow leaves." . . .

As I said, I think fathers should spend more time with their sons, but that once we shopped together was the last time for me.

- o -

Traveler's Aid Society women in our depots tell me that a runaway girl can lie much more fluently and convincingly than a runaway boy. Their theory is that the girls think up their story far in advance and stick to it.

A BOY GONE WRONG

My own sons finally got a little too big to climb up on my knee for a Father & Son Soliloquy. Or maybe it's because my lap is getting too small. But I bumped into something not long ago that would make good material for a

Father & Son Soliloquy. Supposing a boy had just been released from what we used to call the reform school, and he telephoned the school and said, "Come and get me again. I just hit my mother in the jaw and knocked her downstairs. She was drunk again." Pretty serious business, wouldn't you think? Take the case of a 9-year-old, cutest little tyke you ever saw. He'd been in twice. This last time he was caught stealing fur coats through an open window on a fire escape. Gave the coppers a terrific chase. He was finally brought into juvenile court for the third time. The judge found him guilty. The procedure has been changed considerably in recent years. The judge no longer looks down from his bench and says in ponderous tones, "I sentence you to six months in the reform school." It's more informal now and the reform school in our county is called the home school for boys. The judge told the 9-year-old that he wanted him to live out at the home school for boys for six months. . . .

"I don't want to go back there," the lad sobbed.

"You were treated all right out there, weren't you?" the judge asked. "You had good meals and a warm place to sleep and you went to school and you played games, didn't you?" the judge went on. The lad admitted that all that was true. "Why then," the judge pressed, "don't you want to go back?"

And this reply actually came from the 9-year-old, "Cuz it ain't home to me."

The boy was sentenced anyway. A probation officer led him out of the courtroom. And as this 9-year-old was being led out of juvenile court, his mother stood on the sidelines. When the boy passed her, she hauled off and struck him a full, hard blow right across the mouth. . . .

Smugly we parents sit back, perhaps, and say, "Sure that kind of stuff happens, but it couldn't happen to me or to my kids." Get this: NO PARENT IS EXEMPT FROM HAVING A CHILD WHO COULD BE DELINQUENT. In a way, I've always been a little sorry that the term "juvenile delinquent" ever got into the language. It's too soft a term. Furthermore, in about 99 cases out of 100, it's the parent who's delinquent.

Just to see what it's like at the boys' school, let's follow a 14-year-old recently committed. He'd taken binoculars, a camera, a blanket and a flashlight from a car. He'd been doing purse snatching and slugging on the side. He'd been at his racket for more than a year. He'd been chased, shot at twice by police. A probation officer took him from the courtroom. He wasn't handcuffed. He was driven to the home school in an ordinary passenger car. There he was met by the boy mayor or one of the boy commissioners (elected at the school).

The commissioner takes the incoming lad down for a shower bath, clean clothes, a toothbrush and toilet articles. The commissioner then becomes a buddy to that lad till he's adjusted to his new surroundings. In the old days, the reform school didn't really reform. It was more interested in punishment. It's easy to see now, though, where rehabilitation takes hold. The buddy gets all needed information about the new lad—his hobbies, his personal interests, what athletic events he likes. The new boy also is wised up on the few things he isn't supposed to do.

The boys are up at 6 A.M., start the day by making their beds, and then go to the basement to wash up and get dressed. Early chores are done before breakfast, which starts at 8 A.M. Other job details last till around 9 A.M. Then school starts. The boys follow the same grade, take the same subjects, do approximately the same work they did in their regular school. They stay in classes till noon, return after a lunch hour and stay till 4 P.M. One big difference is the holiday schedule. Christmas, Thanksgiving and Fourth of July are the only big ones observed. From 4 to 5 in the afternoon on other days is free activity time, usually devoted to sports. One afternoon a week they get religious instruction, each in his own faith. The lads have no homework unless they're being disciplined for poor conduct. Their longer school day and year-around schedule make that difference. The big athletic program starts after supper. Boxing is one of the most popular sports.

The boys sleep in dormitories and turn in at 9 P.M. . . .

Kids gain as much as 20 pounds in six months out there. It isn't uncommon for some to put away as many as six or seven bowls of cereal at breakfast. The 100 boys frequently eat 150 pounds of spuds at a meal. Dinners and suppers feature a lot of meat that's raised right on the farm by the boys.

One thing the boys are asked not to do is sit around in small groups. There's no smoking. They have to keep busy. School authorities don't want them talking over their past experiences or having an opportunity to plan new escapades. Good conduct wins trips for them to luncheons and entertainments in town. The whole caboodle packs up for a week in the summertime for a camping trip to a northern lake.

There's something in this for childless couples, too. Let me tell you about one 13-year-old from a family of eight children. He was taken into custody the first time when he was 9. A personality kid he was, too. He knew every trick from apple polishing to crocodile tears. After the mother's death, the father took to drink. The boy, a short little punk, used to walk into filling stations, sidle to the cash register, and rifle the currency till while the attendant was out servicing cars. He'd made hauls up to $60, never knew what his total take was. The third time he was caught, his home had been completely broken up and the father finally consented to placement of the boy in a free foster home. They love the kid on the farm where he is; he's getting along famously, never even thinks of his old racket. Kids who need that kind of chance are available for placement.

Could you use some counsel on keeping your own youngster out of trouble? The county home school superintendent tossed these little tidbits our way: "It isn't the hour your kids come in that's important, it's what they have been doing. Parents should know where their youngsters are, with whom they've been. Your boy is always a different boy when he's with a gang. He does things he wouldn't do alone or if with the right crowd. Parents always blame 'the other boy.' Associate with your own boy. Get down honestly to his level in interests, conversation, problems. Develop home ties—picnics, outings, hobbies. Let them have chums at home. Spare-time activities are important—keep a boy gainfully occupied, watch his spare-time indulgences."

YESTERDAY'S CHILDREN

Maybe we're not doing right by our kids. They're growing up without the soothing influence of the tick-tock, tick-tock of a mantel clock. Electric clocks have robbed them of that.

Wonder how many kids would recognize a buttonhook today if they saw one? A household item it was, not too many years ago. . . .

Kids with their modern schools have missed out on one thrill, anyway. What a treat it was to pull the rope that rang the school bell. Once in a while somebody'd yank it so hard the bell would do a flip-flop and it took a trip to the belfry to get it back in order. I could go for a little bell ringing right now. . . .

Been ages since I've seen an itinerant photographer making the rounds with his mule or goat to take pictures of children astride the animal. A lost profession, perhaps.

Wonder whatever happened to hoop rolling as a sport for youngsters. I haven't seen a kid batting a hoop down the street in years, and what joy and relaxation there was in that pastime. Maybe we parents should revive it for our kids. I'd certainly put it above the yo-yo as a sport.

At least one person, however, principal of a school in St. Paul, keeps the sport alive by selling hoops as a sideline during her summer vacation. She sent me a hoop and a guide stick, both made by the Hoopalong Co. of Mason City, Iowa. The guide stick has one improvement over the ones we made years ago. Down the middle is a little groove into which the hoop fits. You roll the hoop down the groove for a start. The crossbar down at the bottom of the guide stick, I thought, was much too short. It was only about four inches. We used half a barrel hoop as a guider. My kids scoffed at the idea of rolling a hoop when I first explained it to them, but soon it completely fascinated them.

Wonder if the kids down in Magnolia still test the toughness of the bare feet by seeing who can walk best in the stubble fields at threshing time. And what fun it was to wade around barefooted in a load of wheat.

Haven't seen a youngster make an angel in the snow for years. Could that be a forgotten pastime?

THOUGHTS WHILE SHAVING: Apparently what used to be a very important milestone in the life of a young man has vanished from our scene today. I can remember that jump from short to long pants and what a step it was and how awkward I felt in those first longies and what a razzing I got from chums for a day or two. Kids are missing something today. . . .

OUT OF THE MOUTHS OF BABES

Bright sayings of children can be dynamite for a columnist. That's why I've made a practice of trying to avoid them. It was a pretty strict rule during the years when my own boys were in the smart talk set, and naturally the children of my friends were just as clever. If I so much as printed one crack, every parent in our crowd came around with a dozen more cute remarks and I'd be stuck. But now and then some youngster's remark has tickled me and I've let down the bars. Here are a few:

Bus business: The little lad got so restless on a bus ride from one Iowa town to another that his mother finally got up and whispered something to the driver. The bus pulled to a stop out in the country and the driver and the little boy got out and disappeared, hand in hand. Soon they returned. The little boy rejoined his mother and the bus resumed its journey. In a moment the other passengers heard the lad talking to his mother.

"Mommy," he began, "It's a good thing you spoke to the driver because he had to stop, too."

During the peak of Christmas shopping in one of our department stores, a patronizing gentleman in his 60's encountered a couple of children in a crowded elevator. "I suppose," said the elderly gentleman placing a friendly hand on the head of one boy, "You're going up to see Santa Claus." "Oh, no," piped back the juvenile in a loud and clear voice, "We're taking grandma to the bathroom."

A small-town family drove down to our state fair and

traipsed over the entire layout, all the while dragging their two-year-old daughter with them. When the family finally returned to the car in typical state fair exhaustion, the two-year-old sighed this query: "Mommie, what were we looking for?"

A 5-year-old girl had been sent to the grocery store by her mother and was very slow in returning. When she finally got back, her mother asked, "What took you so long at the store?"

"On the way home," the little girl replied, "I stopped to watch the funeral of the devil."

Her mother was completely baffled by that one. "What do you mean, dear?" asked the parent.

"Well, as I was watching the cars of the funeral go by, one man who was standing next to me said, 'And just think, the poor devil was sick only five days.'"

Whenever a girl becomes a Girl Scout she must fill out a national organization form which gets her address, parents' names and occupation, church, and so on. One Minneapolis miss was filling hers out and did it this way: "Church: St Paul's. Denomination: 5 cents."

THE COLLEGE INFLUENCE: A Fargo woman reports this one. A grandmother was studying her Bible very intently. Her grandson had watched her on several occasions. Finally he piped up with "What are you doing, Grandma, studying for your finals?"

Maybe it's as old as the hills, but it amused me recently, the story of the mother who was entertaining her bridge luncheon club. All her guests were seated at their tables when a lusty yell came from the upstairs bathroom where an 8-year-old son was taking a bath. "What'll I do, Mom?" the kid shouted, "there's nothing but clean towels up here."

Managing editor to new office boy who strolled in at 9:20: "You should have been here at 8 o'clock."

"Why?" inquired the office boy, "what happened?"

Part Five

ANIMALS

NOTES AND ESSAYS
ABOUT CREATURES OF THE
SOIL, THE SKY, & THE SEA

The animals and I have been friends for a long time.
More than friends, in fact. In many ways I suppose they've
almost been my partners in the column-writing business
with which I've made my living. Friendships are pretty important in this trade, and some of my most faithful sup-
porters have been the little things dressed in fur, fins or
feathers.

There has been love and beauty in our friendships, too,
and one of my regrets has always been that I usually gave
less than I took from the animals. A psychiatrist would
probably say my guilt feelings about that are the reason
I'm dedicating a whole chapter in this book to the animals.

Over the years, however, I've tried to repay my obliga-
tion to the animals with continuing little favors. My best
effort has been the *Give Away Department* which makes a
concluding paragraph for most of my daily columns. In this
paragraph I list names of people who for one reason or another want to give away various pets and animals. And
proud I am of our results in finding homes for many little
creatures who otherwise might have been abandoned in the
cruel world dominated by quarreling humans. Give Aways
have found homes since 1935 for between 175,000 and
200,000 individuals of all species. Impressive total, that,
even though it includes 50,000 minnows, a colony of perhaps 70,000 bees, a real Hungarian countess, several bachelor farmers and a few other lonely hearts on two feet as
well as four.

There's even more in this book for my animal friends,
too. The S-E-X chapter is largely for them, although the
titles and subtitles may be misleading.

Before we plunge into reading this animal section, there are a few matters to be explained. Animals, like weather, have been carefully classified by scientists. For a newspaper columnist, and most of his readers, however, the scientific approach is pretty difficult. So I've established my own classification, which is really as simple as A B C—a list of animals in alphabetical order after an introduction which includes some notes about animals in general.

There are, of course, some exceptions to the classification. All of them, though, have been made on a basis of pure logic. Those of you who've already read the chapter on WEATHER will recall that the SUMMER section had some mention of mosquitoes. Well, just ask yourself where you'd look for mosquitoes if not in SUMMER. You certainly wouldn't expect to find any in winter. By the same reasoning, or shall we say seasoning, "pheasants" are discussed in both the ANIMAL chapter and the FOOD department. Or take "fleas," which you will find in their normal alphabetical sequence as well as in the DOG section. What better place to find fleas, I ask, than in dogs? And speaking of fleas, I wonder if Noah counted them like the other animals two by two, male and female, or just accepted all those on the backs of dogs or camels as they entered the Ark?

One last reminder. The official Be-Kind-to-Animals week in this country starts April 7. I hope you get this section read by then.

WE'RE OUTNUMBERED, MEN

We humans better not get too cocky about the part we play in this universe of ours. Numerically, the world is really dominated by insects. It's estimated that there are more than five million insects in the air above each square mile. The total weight of the world's insect population is greater than that of all the other land animals combined or all the people who inhabit the earth.

A thimbleful of ordinary water contains more living creatures than the human population of the earth.

FABLES

Now our Animal Husbandry Department, under the direction of a University of Minnesota professor, disputes a few time-honored fables for you: The elephant has a memory no longer than his tail. Hummingbirds have an appetite that rivals the greediest pig in the sty. . . . Jungle beasts are not cruel. A house cat, for instance, is more cruel in playing with a helpless mouse before eating it than the most feared jungle cat. It will do away with its prey in short order. The speed king of nonflying bugs is the spider. One species can travel 50 times its length in a second.

FACTS

George Luxton, a newspaper photographer who takes an unusual interest in animals, pointed out something that was new to me. Predatory animals, those which pillage and plunder and live on the flesh of other animals, have their eyes straight ahead. The animals that are victims of man or beast, as a rule, have their eyes set on the sides of their heads.

Nature did a pretty good job in "pupiling" the eyes of animals. For instance, eyes of horses have horizontal pupils. Such an arrangement aids them in "keeping their eyes on the ground," and to see out of the corners of their eyes. Better for grazing. The lower part of a horse's retina (the part that sees the sky) is practically nonfunctioning. The pupil of a cat's eye is vertical, which aids in hunting. The pupil of a whale's eye is kidney-shaped. But don't ask me why. . . . Seeing a movie is a pretty good test of whether your eyes need attention. . . .

You may not like the classification, but monkeys, apes and men are the only mammals that have the ability to see and distinguish colors.

You have 24 bones in your spinal column, a giraffe has seven, a python 400—if that makes you any happier.

Unpleasant thought: Man is the only animal with a jutting chin.

GREATEST SHOW

Here are a few animal facts from the circus that might interest you: Tusks of a walrus are really its eyeteeth. A baby kangaroo at birth frequently measures no longer than an inch, but no matter how small the babe is, it manages to climb from the ground to the pouch unassisted. . . . Male giraffes average 16 feet in height and females are usually about three feet shorter. . . . A camel has four stomachs and can "eat" its own hump, which is made up largely of fat. . . . There are 50,000 separate muscles in an elephant's trunk, which has strength enough to toss logs around and a touch delicate enough to pick up a pin. . . . An elephant's heart weighs in the neighborhood of 45 pounds and fills a bushel basket. . . . Instead of having a lot of brains, a sperm whale carries tons of oil in the back of its head. They call them columnists in a newspaper office. More Circus Notes: Giraffes often die of fright when captured wild, so delicate are their hearts and so brittle their necks and legs. They can't be trapped. They must be stalked and surrounded with infinite patience. . . . Seals, although natives of salt water, thrive best on fresh-water herring. . . . Monkeys are the star boarders. Each monkey gets apples, bananas, cabbage, spinach, boiled rice and potatoes. . . . Chimpanzees occasionally get sherry and eggs. . . . Seals eat about six pounds of herring a day. . . . Emus and ostriches get salads and dessert and kangaroos like rye bread. . . . Giraffes like their drinking water warmed.

Some day, maybe you'll want to get technical, so this might help: It's a covey of quail, a goggle or a skein of geese, a plump of waterfowl, a stand of plover, a sleuth of bear, a nest of rabbits, a fall of woodcock, a gang or rafter of turkeys, a pack of wolves and a herd of deer. . . .

Elk, in the plural, make up a "gang." Sparrows gathered together should be called a "tribe" or "host." The American eagle in association with his fellows is in a "convocation." In general fish go around in "schools" or "shoals," but a get-together of trout in particular is a "hover." An assembly of perch is a "pack," but for smelts it's a "quantity." Grasshoppers travel in a "cloud"; and you'd be correct in referring to a flock of sheep, goats, geese or even camels. . . .

Now add to that little compilation of group words. It's a bevy of girls, a fleet of ships, a gang of thieves, a host of angels, a shoal of porpoises, a troop of children, a drove of oxen, a mob of blackguards, a troupe of actors, a swarm of insects, a muster of peacocks, a skulk of foxes, a drove of horses, a flight of doves, a clutch of eggs, an army of locusts and a brood of chicks. And oceans of love to the bunch of friends who supplied the list.

LIVING CREATURES FROM A TO Z

ANTS

I'm going to talk about ants now. They could inherit your home. That's how important they are. Once when ants got control in the home of a reader, I published that woman's request for help. We got dozens of suggestions, but we also had many more requests for information. A professional exterminator and a professor helped supply the following information:

Grease ants are tough customers. Do you know what a topochemical smell is? It's the ability to recall smells as round, square, elongated, hard or soft and having a certain height or being in a certain direction. That's the ability ants have because of their antennae. Remove that antenna from an ant and it's the same as a blind, deaf and mute human. Ants eat virtually everything humans do. The worker ants, those that do all the labor, and warriors toil for the colony. They're sterile females.

But let's go back and start with ant eggs. One egg contains a female that will be able to reproduce; the other egg contains a fertile male. Sex has been predetermined according to needs of the colony. When these eggs hatch, a helpless, maggotlike young emerges. The young need considerable care from the queen ant or the workers before going through the cocoon stage and becoming ants as we know them. . . .

After the cocoon stage the fertile male and the female develop wings and, on a favorable day, these winged creatures swarm from their nest and fly on what is called the marriage flight. It's on this flight that the females are fertilized and fly as far as possible from the parent colony to establish their own nests. When a female lands, she immediately tears off her wings and digs herself into the ground or under a rock. She stays there without food until her eggs hatch with new young. All of the first batch are sterile females or workers. When they're large enough they take over the work of tending eggs, feeding the young, guarding the colony, enlarging the excavation. Individual worker ants can't exist alone. They are produced for the sole purpose of providing for the queens, who never come out of the nest and do nothing but lay eggs for as long as seventeen years. That's why many chemicals don't work against ants. They kill only the outside workers. To get the queen ant, a slow-killing poison is needed. A SWEET BAIT will kill the grease ants, but if it contains the common arsenicals, it kills too quickly to be carried back to the source nest.

As troublesome as ants are, they do have beneficial aspects. Observations have been made of ants carrying 100,000 insects a day into their nests. They act as a sort of pest-control operator in keeping down the population of other insects. Ants have been used to rid clothing of lice. Naturalists use ants to clean skeletons of birds. Cocoons of certain ants are gathered as food for goldfish. Ants also aerate the soil.

Harvester ants will attack human beings. When their nest is disturbed they not only give defensive battle but also run around in circles searching for the intruder in a positive attack. Once they set their powerful little jaws in your skin, the only way to remove them is by tearing the ant's body

away from the head and then pulling the dead head out of
the skin. They also eject an acidlike poison which is highly
irritating to all animals. Species of army and legionary ants
are carnivorous. They travel in long columns sometimes a
foot wide, devouring all animals they come across, including those as large and tough-skinned as cattle. These ants,
in traveling over a territory, will even cross streams or go
through a fire area. . . .

The average householder bothered by ants should purchase ant poison that contains thallium sulphate. This is
one of the few slow-killing poisons that is effective on most
varieties of ants.

Ants, like rats, soon find out what's poisoning them and
leave the stuff alone. That's why grease ants are more readily eliminated by the slow killers. If it's at all possible, try
to trace the ant trails back to the nest. Then raise the stone
or board that usually covers and douse the nest with kerosene. Kerosene squirted into the hole where the ants come
in or out will suffice sometimes. Incidentally, the best way
to control aphids or mealybugs on flowers and trees is to
get rid of the ants. Ants actually carry the aphids up the
trunk or stem of a plant and place them in the proper position to suck the plant juices. When the aphid or mealybug
is full, the ant carries it back to the ant nest and hangs it
on the ceiling, where it services the colony in much the
same manner as a dairy cow.

*Easy to understand why King Solomon said, "Go to the
ant, thou sluggard; consider her ways and be wise."*

THE BAT

You mothers who groan about walking the floor at night
with your offspring don't know how lucky you are. Consider the mother BAT. A baby bat usually weighs about a
fourth as much as his mother. Until the baby bat can travel
under his own power, he clings to his mammy as she goes
about on her hunting jaunts. Thus a mother bat may be
carrying a pretty heavy load on her nightly flights that fre-

quently are miles long. You human mothers, though, might think Mrs. Bat a fortunate one. When the baby bat becomes too obstreperous, his Ma simply hangs him up on the wall and goes off without him.

Blind as a bat is strictly a phony phrase. Cover a bat's eyes and it has no effect on the accuracy of its flight. But cover his ears or mouth and he'll collide with a wall. In other words, they fly by sound. One more batty item: In normal flight a bat lets out 25 cries a second, but the human ear isn't tuned to catch them—the sounds, I mean. . . .

Things we hate sometimes have a purpose. For instance, a single bat will consume as many as 3,750 pests or insects in a single night's feeding, and mosquitoes are a favorite on their menu.

Next time a bat scoots into your home, it isn't necessary to get a broom or a dustless mop and start a swinging campaign. Turn on all the lights in the rooms to which he has access, then open the front door. He'll make for that dark spot and fly right back into the great outdoors.

Little things to worry about: A bedbug doesn't reach maturity until it has taken at least five bites out of a human being.

Felt mighty sorry for a friend of mine recently who got a bedbug bite on her chest, scratched it and infected it and had to go to the hospital for lancing treatment. You hate like the devil to have something you can't discuss freely with your friends. And a bedbug bite isn't exactly what you like to go around talking about.

It takes 5,000 **bees** to weigh a pound.

You should know, though, that the stinger of a honeybee continues to bore deeper into the human skin even after the bee itself has been pulled away and the stinger is no longer attached to it. What would you do without me? . . .

Nothing gives me the creeps like one of those big bluegreen **bottleflies** buzzing around. Well, maybe a bat does.

Ever wonder why we call them **butterflies?**

Originally they were known as "flutter-bys." Somebody got twisted, called them butterflies and the name stuck.

No wonder a **camel** lasts a long time between drinks. One good filling and 14 or 15 gallons of water are trickling down its gullet.

When a camel gets a stone hole in its foot, its driver puts on a leather patch, sewing it firmly to the animal's tough sole. . . .

CANARY ROW

They're telling this about a stenographer who ordered a canary from a pet shop. The bird came out all right, but when the steno examined it, she discovered the little yellow fellow had a crippled leg. She called up the pet shop. "What's the idea of sending me a canary with a crippled leg?" she inquired. "Listen, lady," the gent at the pet shop responded, "what the h—— kind of bird do you want, a singer or a dancer?"

If your canary has quit his whistling, try putting the bird next to a running water faucet.

Is that canary of yours a bit jittery? Here's perhaps the reason. His little heart ticks off 1,000 beats a minute while yours is doing a normal 72.

If your old gent's voice had the same power in proportion to his weight as that of a canary, his ordinary conversation could be heard 800 miles away.

Next time your canary gets away from you, don't bother the fire department. Squirt a little water from your garden hose on the bird and the weight of the water on its wings will bring the bird down for immediate and easy retrieving. And the water won't hurt the bird a bit.

You'd never guess it, would you? Bumblefoot is something your canary can get. It's inflammation of the ball of the foot of a fowl. Now isn't your day more complete?

C—A—T

Throw away your watches and clocks if you want, provided you have a cat in your household. A close observer discovered that you can tell time by a cat's eyes. As noon approaches, the vertical pupil of the feline's eye becomes just a fine, hairlike line. From noon till midnight it starts widening, and on the stroke of midnight becomes almost a round ball. . . .

That was a funny stunt that Grandma Colvin used to get a foster-mother cat to care for strange baby kittens. I remember she used to let the mother cat keep one kitten from her own litter and then grandma would smear each of the little strangers with butter. After the foster-mother cat would lick the butter off the babies, she'd adopt them. But what ever brought that to mind now? . . .

Learn something new each day department: A reader from Biwabik, Minnesota, informed me that a female cat is called a "chessie." And up in Canada they call the opposite of Tom a Tib.

By rights, you owners of Persian cats should no longer refer to them as such. Should be Iranians. And the Siamese twins should be rechristened the "Thailand Twins."

Did you know that white cats with blue eyes tend to become deaf? Or don't you give a hoot?

If you spot your cat nibbling the leaves of house plants, it indicates that the cat's system lacks something. Give it a little celery now and then.

Watch your cat when you let it out especially in the spring. When the young birds are first left to their own resources, they make ready prey for cats on the loose.

Best way to teach a cat to leave birds alone is to fasten a dead bird around its neck for a while.

If you get a young kitten treed sometime and want to save the fire department a call, send the mama cat up the tree. She'll inspire confidence in the young kitten and the offspring will follow its mother down the tree.

If you've been casting about for this explanation, here it is: A cat always lands butter side up through the angular acceleration of a rigid body under the action of a resultant torque. Kind of nice to know those things.

Nature is a great old girl. The reason, scientists have figured out, that she put hair on the **caterpillar** was to make it distasteful to other animals. But then comes along an old smarty, the skunk, and defeats that very fine set-up. Mr. Skunk has developed a little technique of rolling the caterpillar on the ground till all the hair is worn off, and then devouring it.

KNOCK BEFORE YOU ENTER

Chickens are something like chorus girls—you should knock before entering their dressing rooms. You don't have to say to the chicks, "Are you decent?" as you do with the chorines. But breaking in without a knock on a flock of chickens in their house flusters them sufficiently so that egg production may be affected. Every farmer invariably uses the knock system.

Hens don't lay many eggs while they're on exhibition. The excitement shuts off the production, according to the experts.

Settin' any hens these days? In case you are, 13 eggs is the ideal number to offer an average-sized hen in the hatching mood. The nest should be lined with an odd number of eggs so they can be formed into a real circle. Fewer than 13 limits production and more create a hazard for Biddy, since she may shove some out.

Most accommodating, this hen: A Lyons, Wis., woman who has been raising chickens for years finally got a hen in her flock with some real sense. Every morning the hen came to the back door and cackled a little. The woman of the house let her in. The biddy walked immediately to a special basket made for her and laid her egg. The task over, the hen got up, walked out and resumed her life with the chickens.

And here's a topper from a farm family near St. Peter,

Minnesota. They had a New Hampshire Red hen that cackled every morning at the back door, was let in and jumped into its special cardboard box. Before long, there was the egg. She cackled to be let out, too. But a woman's work is never done, the farmer reported. As the hen left the back door, 11 goslings which she had hatched were always waiting for her. The goslings averaged 15 pounds apiece in weight, but the hen still gave them her care and attention. Only time she ever left them was that brief spell to take care of the egg job in the house. Can't help but love an old hen like that, can you?

Ageless is the query, "Why does the chicken cross the road?" Believe it or not, chickens seldom do it any more. Those of you who remember when the motoring age dawned upon us may also recall that it was a routine thing to kill, run over or flatten out two or three chickens on every afternoon drive. Well, it has taken about 25 generations of chickens, says an ornithologist, for this severe and constant mortality among chickens to disappear to a comparatively small and negligible percentage. The chicken, the bird-behavior experts announce, has learned the lesson by experience and has passed the knowledge on to successive generations. Isn't nature wonderful? . . .

If it weren't for chickens, you wouldn't be wearing those soft French kid gloves. It takes 38,000,000 eggs a year to dress the leather used in the gloves.

The female **cockroach** lays her eggs by the sackful. The sack looks like a pillow with the slip removed and holds hundreds of eggs. The eggs hatch in a night, and the young cockroach, when a day old and not much larger than an atom of dust, can race across a kitchen floor with almost the same speed as its mother and father.

Two pleasant little thoughts: If you want to learn a little bit about insects, put a male and a female roach in your desk drawer, supply them with almost any kind of food, and a year later you will be able to count 125,000 cockroaches in the drawer. Now, if you're interested in how prolific the bedbug is, take a pair to bed with you some night, and a year later you'll have 85,000.

ONE OF LIFE'S COMPENSATIONS: Rarely do you find a house infected with cockroaches that also has bedbugs. Seems that cockroaches are very fond of bedbugs. On the other hand, a spider is a deadly enemy of the cockroach. Spiders eat the little cockroaches.

One more roach item: A cockroach has his sense of smell in his legs.

THOUGHTS WHILE SHAVING: Wonder who started calling a **cow** "bossy" and why?

Leave us not be unkind to our bovine friends: Nearly one-fourth of the food consumed by American families is supplied by the cow.

An official of the Hormel Packing Plant in Austin, Minnesota, says that among the strange things found in cows' stomachs are dog chains, dresser handles, coins, a diamond ring and perfume bottles.

Through error some Iowa cows were fed marijuana, and the animals stopped eating, lost interest in their work, seemed not to care whether they were living under a Republican or Democratic administration and finally lost consciousness.

Although sitting is the common posture of the cow, she'll almost always get up on her four feet when she's sick. But don't ask me why.

In a cow only the nose has sweat glands. . . .

Cricket Remedies: A university expert recommends sprinkling sodium fluoride on fresh slices of carrots or potatoes and then putting the slices where the crickets'll get at them. The chemical is available at all drugstores but it's poisonous. So keep the kids and pets away. And insecticide people have other products that do a quick job of killing the little squeakers.

Crocodiles are pleasant little jungle items. They average 24 feet in length, have a jaw that's 36 inches and a tail that's four-fifths of their body. They do their mean business with both ends—the jaws and the tail—but the tail is far more the vicious means of protection. Many times they've been known to slap a wild boar to death with a single swipe.

You can shoot at crocodiles all day long with a .22 rifle and not even puncture their outer hide. It takes a .45 or better to get under their skin. Their brains are about the size of a tomato, and sometimes crocs live to be a thousand years old.

Consider the Cuckoo Bird: If you think you work hard, extend yourself into his lot in life. He has to locate 225 worms a day just to keep alive. . . .

MAN'S BEST FRIEND

There are 100,000 show dogs in the country and 50,000,-000 that can't brag about their ancestors.

There are 166 breeds of dogs in the United States. Our country boasts the following purebred Americans—Boston terrier, American water spaniel, American foxhound, Alaskan Malemute, Chesapeake retriever. Fastest a dog has ever run is 37 miles an hour. A dog named Texas T. Weigel was actually listed in the Columbus, Ohio, city directory. It was Darwin who said, "A dog is the only thing on earth that loves you more than he loves himself." Porky, a small mongrel, yanked a 175-pound St. Bernard from the St. Clair River when the big pooch broke through the ice.

In spite of all that to recommend them, Beth Brown reported in her book, "Hotel for Dogs," the presence of her canine companion caused 113 hotels across the continent to refuse her admittance.

Here are a few dog bits from a dog show competitor: Show dogs are no more shy and nervous than actors or actresses. Too much temperament goes against a dog in the show ring. Because a dog is registered, it doesn't necessarily mean he's a quality dog. It's merely proof the dog's a pure-bred. Thoroughbred is a misnomer for dogs. Horses are thoroughbreds. To say a dog is pedigreed doesn't mean much either. The word pedigree means the record of the dog's ancestors, his family tree. A mongrel has a pedigree, too. The great majority of good dogs are produced from matings within the family. Dogs should have at least one common ancestor within three generations (14 years).

Cockers have been known to carry a block of butter without leaving a mark on it. Long-legged cockers are the English strain; short-legged, stocky cockers are American.

A chow dog never has to be housebroken, I've been told.

THOUGHTS WHILE SHAVING: I always feel a little bit sorry for our dog every time I let him out of a winter's morning. He jumps out of a nice warm bed and dashes out into below-freezing temperatures. It's worse than my running out in my nightshirt.

Dogs sometimes show they're smarter than humans. A friend had a pooch that was used to keeping cool at the lake in summer. Then she became a city dweller and the pet was confined to a sizzling-hot apartment. The owner wanted to help the dog keep comfortable one sizzling afternoon, so she fixed him a nice pan of drink water and then dumped half a dozen ice cubes into the dish. The dog's tongue was hanging out, red as fire, and yet the dog wouldn't touch the water until the ice had melted. A stunt which drew gratitude from the dog was this: The owner filled fruit jars with ice cubes and then placed the jars against the dog's belly and up near his head. Immediately he went into a luxury of relaxation, snuggled close to the cool jars and smiled. And dogs do smile.

When Father Charles Keefe was chaplain at Minnesota's state capitol, he had a dog that actually refused to eat meat on Friday. . . .

If you've got a pooch that persists in chasing cars, try this: Tie a small chain around his neck and to the loose end of the chain fasten a small block of wood. He'll step on the block, choke a little and give up his foolishness.

If ever you have to play nursemaid to a crying pup because the pooch is lonesome for its mother, remember this suggestion: When bedtime arrives, take a basket or a box, place an old sweater or a piece of blanket in it and place a mason jar of warm water (not too hot) on one side of the box. Cover the jar with a portion of the blanket and the dog'll curl up next to it and go to sleep immediately. . . .

You may have been under the impression that when your dog sneezes he has caught cold. Not so. Apes are the only animals that catch cold like humans.

Your dog is subject to the same kind of fainting spells that you are. The spells are due chiefly to cerebral anemia.

To de-flea your pooch try this: Sprinkle a half package of dry snuff over the dog's back and then brush it thoroughly into the hide. The fleas, they tell me, drop off immediately.

CLIP YOUR POOCH in the summertime, advises an animal doctor, for these benefits: It's one of the very best ways to handle the wood-tick problem on dogs, the coat will grow back by fall more luxurious and the sun and air are good for the dog's hide during the summer.

More information on how to keep wood ticks off dogs: Sheep dip does the trick, cleans off all that are on and keeps other ticks off for at least a month. Use it strong, just as the directions say, but either keep your dog off your bed or stay out of it yourself after you've applied dip to the pooch. The laundry tub and car sponge will suffice for equipment. And after the sheep dip has remained in the dog's coat for an hour or so, you may wash the dog thoroughly without minimizing the effect of the dip.

TIPS FOR making your muzzled pooch happier during quarantine days: If it's at all possible, build a runway for your dog and make it about three feet wide and 15 feet long. It can be made at very small expense out of chicken wire and a few stakes. As you might know, muzzles are most uncomfortable and should be used on the dog for as short a time as possible. The Animal Rescue League (and they understand dog problems) advises the runway and declares that if every dog owner does his part, health authorities will lift the quarantine just that much sooner.

THE SQUAWK LEGIT FROM AN ANGRY WOMAN: "I live next door to a gas station," the letter said. "Quite often cars stop there with dogs in the cars. While the women go to the rest room, the men take the dogs out for an airing. And what those dogs do to my yard. Oh, brother! I get so furious that I've been tempted (1) to take a shovel and when the dog gets back into the car, hike over and empty the shovel in the car and say, 'Your dog left this in my yard.' (2) Get the address of the violators, borrow a trailer and a cow and do exactly the same thing to their lawns. I'm sure the hundreds of us who are forced to live next door to filling stations will be ever grateful if you mention this. It may do something to halt the practice."

Flash: A baby dolphin can swim and keep up with its elders an hour after it's born. But who wants to be a baby dolphin?

The elephant isn't in it with a **dragonfly** when it comes to stowing away the grub. During the course of a day, a dragonfly eats three times its own weight. If a 150-pound man ate proportionately, he'd have to consume, for instance, almost 4 dozen 10-pound turkeys in a day. Would that be bad?

THOUGHTS WHILE SHAVING: A **duck** has a pretty eye.

Comes the sad word now that a **bald eagle** isn't really bald. Gray-white feathers on its head simply give the appearance of baldness.

Why the eagle became so popular as an emblem, I'll never know. Half the countries in the world use it and, to me, it's among the ugliest of all our flying creatures.

Bet you don't know what a baby **eel** is. It's an elver.

An **elephant** charmer from the circus told me that most people think an elephant drinks water through its trunk. 'Tain't the case. It uses its trunk merely to carry the water to its mouth.

Here's a little item we should have rushed to you long ago, I don't know what makes me so careless, at times. I hope you'll pardon my delay in telling you that an elephant's heart beats about 20 per cent faster when he's lying down than when he's standing up.

You have to hand it to the elephant. The big fellow can walk, shuffle, canter, gallop and lope. He can also eat hay.

Information carried around in the heads of newspapermen and women is, on occasions, startling. A reporter shouted across the newsroom one day, "A guy on the phone wants to know how long an elephant is pregnant." Another reporter answered, "Tell him two years." And it's the right answer.

FISH, FLEAS, FLIES, & FROGS

If you see a **firefly** blinking in the meadow tonight you might be interested to know that he's flirting or courting another firefly. Cute way of doing it, isn't it?

It's possible to serve a different kind of **fish** every day for five and a third months without repeating a single fish.

Anglers' Note: Fish, which have always had the reputation of being mute, are really vocal. They grunt, toot, chirp, click, rattle, hum and drum, say the experts.

Heavy rains had one curious result some years back down in Iowa. A farmer found **catfish** milking one of his cows which was standing knee-deep in water in a flooded pasture. What's more, the farmer said, the catfish milked the cow dry.

Fish don't sleep. They simply stop moving and that's the way they get their rest.

A famed fish expert tells us that he used to tie his own trout flies, paint his own plug baits, select colors with the utmost of care and deliberation. Then he suddenly discovered that he had been wasting his time. Reason: A fish cannot distinguish colors and is completely unaffected by them. Like a dog, a fish perceives all objects, whatever the color, in shades of gray. Also like a dog, the only factor in an artificial fly or plug bait that attracts fish is the motion. In other words, it doesn't mean a thing if it ain't got that swing. Apparently, the only advantage of color in flies and bait plugs is that it attracts—not the fish—but the customer.

Talk about **fleas.** In a letter to the column a woman once confessed she had them.

Comes word now from my exterminator pal that thousands of homes may be infested and the problem is a little more than something to laugh off. Take the fleabite, for instance. The bite is very serious as far as irritation is concerned. Generally it's not felt for a period of two or three days after Mr. Flea has taken his nip. It may not become evident for two or three weeks. But the itching and irritation may last for months.

A startling statistic about fleas is the fact that various types of fleas have caused more deaths than all the wars since the beginning of history. This is because fleas have spread such diseases as the bubonic plague and typhus. Cats and dogs are subject to infestation because of their contact with other infested animals or infested areas. Entire households may become infested through one pet. . . .

Fleas are pretty well satisfied to feed on the pet and rarely attack human members of the family as long as the pet's around. But remove the cat or dog from the house for a week or two, and the fleas come out in search of their normal host. Not finding the pet, they attack humans. Sending a pet to a hospital or taking the animal away on a vacation affords excellent incentive for the flea to seek a new feeding ground. Once fleas spread throughout the house, it's seldom they can be controlled except with chemicals. An exterminator can usually control flea infestation in a house with a single application. . . .

Life of a flea begins when the eggs are deposited in either the dust, dirt or bedding of the host or laid while the female flea is on the animal. These eggs may drop off any place the host walks through the house. The eggs are about a fiftieth of an inch long, and one female may lay several hundred. The egg stage lasts from 2 to 14 days, depending on the temperature. When the flea emerges from the egg it's a pale brown, is legless and has no eyes. The larva has chewing mouth parts and can be reared successfully on dirt scraped from most floors. When the larva is full-grown it forms a small oval cocoon of white silk. It may take from two weeks to three months for a flea to develop into maturity. Adult fleas can remain alive for a period of two years without any food. Thus it happens that a house or a basement where cats or dogs have lived may be closed for a long time and still be full of fleas, or the fleas may persist long after the animals are gone. Infestation of a house may start when stray animals sleep on doorsteps. . . .

Fleabites rarely occur from fleas that have been living outside. If you get your fleabite outdoors it's probably from a flea you carried out from the house.

Examine a flea closely, and you'll find him a streamlined

guy, but he's streamlined in reverse. High-speed motion picture studies of the flea reveal that when he hops he hops rear-end first. So nature obviously knows her streamlining. Many a housewife finds her legs covered with bites that eventually turn into a mass of sores, and the woman frequently doesn't know where the bites originated. Even physicians aren't always able to diagnose the sore as a fleabite once it has gone into an advanced stage.

This will probably bring no comfort to either you or your dog, in case you're afflicted, but most fleas have no eyes.

Note to dog lovers and flea haters: If the fleas that inadvertently hop from Fido onto your premises have become a problem, here's a way to corral the little rascals. Take a piece of ordinary flypaper and in the middle of it place a small piece of raw liver. In no time you'll find that the capture is almost 100 per cent.

Wonder why fleas don't drown when a dog goes in swimming? Surely they can't all congregate up around the pooch's nose.

An 8-year-old girl in our neighborhood was out sliding with her father one day when she noticed dozens of little black spots in the snow. "Look, Daddy," she yelled, "they jump." Investigation by the father revealed she was right. He gathered up 50 or 60 of the "leaping black spots," put them in a jar and sent them over to the University of Minnesota for analysis. Back came the report that they were **snow fleas.** They're about the size of a dog flea, jump by sort of curling themselves up and then springing. They breed in wooded areas usually late in the winter. May mean that we're going to have an early spring. Fear not, though, in case you run into a batch of them. They're perfectly harmless, can't even bite.

I'm beginning to feel itchy, so let's end this flea dissertation.

NATURE NOTE: If a male and female **fly** find each other attractive around your home sometime in spring, they may well have 191,010,000,000,000 descendants by August. Busy little creatures, aren't they?

A housefly is in its prime of life after five days. . . .

And a pair of flies starting in April might produce 5,000,000,000,000 tons of descendants by summer's end, if all survived . . . that's based on 20,000 flies to the pound. Isn't a pound of flies a disturbing thought?

Dope on the housefly that amazed and amused me:

If flies had the physical size in proportion to their harmfulness, they'd be bigger than rhinoceroses—and a lot more formidable-appearing. Seen through a microscope, a fly is a most fearsome-looking object. Scientists say the more we know about our enemy the better we can fight him, so . . . The fly gets its name because of its superior ability to do just that: Fly.

Man's most agile airplane is clumsy when you compare it with a fly. What plane can land upside down on a ceiling and stay there? As for quickness of take-off, dodging and ducking, you need only to swing a fly swatter to get some idea of the fly in those departments. The fly's landing gear —its six legs—presents a more intricate appearance than its wings, though, like flying machines, it uses the landing gear but little in getting about. It doesn't have to taxi down to the end of the air strip for a take-off. It simply squats down a little, hops up and is off. It's like a helicopter in that respect and then more like a fighter plane in complete maneuverability. Each of the fly's six feet is equipped with two little pads underneath. These have pores through which a sticky substance oozes, and the legs and feet of a fly are covered with an array of bristles, too. These serve as additional catchers of filth in which the fly delights to wade before it walks around on your butter or your pie or your baby's nursing bottle.

The fly often grooms itself by rubbing its legs together and then licking those legs in cat fashion. That may clean its feet but the germ-swarming stuff goes to its stomach. As a bacteria spreader, the fly can hardly be improved upon. You may have thought a housefly can bite. No, no can do. The flies that bite are not the housefly specie but are the stable fly or the horn fly.

There's another notable feature of a fly's head and that is its many-faceted, compound eyes. Under a strong magnifying glass, the surface of a fly's eye seems like honeycomb, and each eye is made up of hundreds of six-sided prisms tapering to narrow points at their inner ends where the sight nerves are inserted, each with its individual lens at the outer end. What the fly sees through these eyes, you'll have to ask him about, but it's probably the most tremendous field of vision we have in any life form today. Obviously, when you go to swat the fly, it can see in front, to the side and even behind. That's why they like to stay on the ceiling or hang on suspended objects. From the ceiling, too, the fly has a choice of flight directions. . . . In fighting the insect pest, DDT is now the best weapon against flies, but after you use one of those mist bombs be sure to leave the room for at least half an hour after you've used the spray. The five-percent solution should be sprayed on ceilings and upper parts of the walls and also on screen doors and windows.

How flies the housefly? How does he get on and off the ceiling? Does he fly upside down straight to his landing? Does he go into a barrel roll and skid in sidewise? Or does he go into a half-Immelmann and slide in backward? How does he get off after he's once on? Does he simply release his vacuum cups and let go? Does he take off and fly upside down? Does he hang on by his hind legs and swing down into an outside loop? Anyone familiar with the aeronautical maneuvers of the housefly?

This is a British scientist's answer to that old question: Does a fly turn over before or after he hits the ceiling? According to special high-speed movies, the insect does a half roll in the air and comes to rest at a slight angle off the original direction of flight. A fly really does walk with its head hanging down, however.

Flies may be smart, but here's one man's fooler for them. You know how it is when you're trying to sneak that little cat nap on the porch and Mr. Fly and all his relations start buzzing around you landing here and there all over your face, head and arms. Well, this guy says all you have to do is get yourself a fly swatter—or facsimile thereof—and hold it menacingly in your mitt while you snooze. Flies, it seems, recognize the bludgeon and keep away. . . .

Frogs and toads are the only creatures that close their eyes every time they swallow.

Farmers should never kill a toad, according to the experts on such matters. A toad's worth about $25 a year on a farm because of the large number of injurious insects he (or she) eats. Frogs are insect eaters, too.

The giraffe can see behind itself without turning its head.

If gnats are driving you gnuts, research shows that red lights attract the smallest amount of insects and especially the small gnat variety that gets through the screen. So, if you just want a glow on your porch, use a red bulb. Yellow is next in line.

BUSY LITTLE GIRL: A purebred **goat** will give its weight in milk every 10 days.

When collegiate goldfish gulping was in the news, this information on goldfish and their care was handed to me.

Goldfish should be fed once a week. Plenty of oxygen is important. Get this by using a glass tank with plenty of water surface—never a bowl. Water plants throw off oxygen and thrive on the carbon dioxide thrown off by the fish. Sudden temperature changes cramp goldfish. They'll even die if the change is too sudden. So use a thermometer. Don't worry about the green stuff on the glass. That's algae and the fish love it. Changing water isn't very important, either. Add a little Epsom salts to the water. It'll do the goldfish a world of good. Chinese originally developed goldfish from carp.

BETTER CHECK: It takes a gallon of water to sustain each inch of goldfish. Thus, if you have a five-inch goldfish, your tank should be at least of five-gallon capacity.

A pocket gopher has been known to dig an underground tunnel more than 600 feet long in 48 hours.

If you want to annoy your noodle a little tonight, ponder on this: What becomes of the sand or dirt that comes out of the hole dug by a striped gopher? He doesn't pile it up, so where does it go?

Goody, Goody: I found out why there isn't any dirt around the holes of striped gophers. Seems they use the old burrows made by the pocket gophers.

Is your wife taking on weight? Don't let it bother you. Consider the female **halibut.** She weighs 10 times as much as her mate.

The feet of Belgian **hares** are used in the manufacture of gold leaf.

Startling Statistic: The skin on a hippopotamus frequently weighs a quarter of a ton.

A HORSE I KNEW

Observation from a country editor: Horse sense is what keeps horses from betting on people.

Maybe you can dispute this, but a group of horsemen sitting at a hunt gathering agreed that never in their experience had they heard of a horse throwing an expectant mother. They called it a strange sixth sense or something like that.

You should be pleased to know that there is approximately one horse or mule in the United States for every 10 persons. Be a little crowded if we all decided to go riding at once, wouldn't it?

Horses have no eyebrows.

Information you should have had years ago: Horses can sleep standing up because their legs have a muscular mechanism which causes the legs to "lock," making a horse stand as though he were on rigid stilts.

If you have occasion to park your car in a farmer's yard where he has loose horses, have a care. The Rhode Island Insurance Company had to pay off a client who left his car in a farmer's yard while he hunted pheasant. On his return he discovered the farmer's horses eating the paint off the hood, sides and top of the automobile. Subsequent investigation revealed that the horses smelled salt, which comes from the soybean used in the manufacture of automobile paint.

I like this jockey's explanation for his racing success. Maybe you've seen it before. Said the jock: "When my mount is lagging, I lean way over and whisper this in his ear: 'Roses are red, violets are blue; horses that lose are made into glue.'"

If the horse does come back in cities, I hope the milk companies will teach their nags to walk on tiptoe during the early morning hours.

Hi, Horsey: The average workingman develops one horsepower of work in an eight-hour day.

A hummingbird eats four times its own weight in food every day of its life.

THEY'RE BUGS, MY BOY

Excerpt from a grammar-school examination paper down at Fairmont, Minnesota:

Q.—*What are insects?*
A.—*Insects are what you burn in the bathroom.*

Shudder items from a man who exterminates bugs scientifically. Humans in various parts of the world use insects as various types of food. Remember that the insect population of the earth exceeds in weight all other animal matter on land areas. Chemical tests have shown that certain grubs, May beetles, for example, compare favorably with tankage in food value for domestic animals. Birds and fish make good use of insects as food. In Mexico, the eggs of a large aquatic bug are regularly sold in the city markets. The eggs are about the size of buckshot and are obtained by sinking sheets of matting under water upon which the eggs are laid by the millions. They're fried, placed in sacks and sold by the pound. Used for making cakes, in fact. People in Jamacia consider a plate of crickets a compliment to a distinguished guest. Certain natives of Australia collect the bugong moth in bags, roast them over hot coals and claim they taste like nuts. They have a high oil content. Many Indians catch quantities of ants, grasshoppers and larvae and pupae of bees, moths, crane flies and wood-boring insects and eat them dried, roasted or raw. Testimony from insect-eating people bears out the fact that insects are palatable. Many of them can't understand why we can eat oysters, crabs and lobsters and then turn up our noses at nice, clean and palatable insects.

A baby kangaroo at birth is about one three-thousandth of its mother's weight; the human baby is about one-twentieth the weight of the mother. The newborn kangaroo's weight is only 1-350th of a pound, and the tiny one is but an inch long.

The minute a baby kangaroo is born, the mother begins licking a two-inch path through her own fur along which the baby kangaroo crawls to the shelter of the mother's pouch.

Lion tamers, in case you weren't familiar, have to watch their diets very carefully, but not for the same reason you and I should. It's to stay alive. The big cats know their trainers by body smells. And if a trainer changes his own particular odor by indulging in a dinner of, for instance, highly spiced foods, Mr. Lion might readily jump him as a stranger when he entered the cage.

The father had taken his offspring to the zoo. The pair stood in front of the lion's cage. "That animal is the king of the jungle," explained the father. "It's the most savage of our beasts. It could tear you apart."

The little girl stood by thoughtfully for a moment. "Daddy," she began, "if the lion got out of its cage and tore you apart and killed you, what streetcar would I take home?"

Next time you're in a spot that serves **lobster** and you want to amuse your friends, have the waiter bring a live lobster to the table, turn the lobster over on his back and gently rub his stomach. The lobster will actually doze off, claws tucked in and all.

A big cattleman from Miles City, Montana, dropped in with this odd information. It's about **magpies.** Every year in the western sections the magpies kill thousands of cattle. Their favorite place of attack is where an animal has been branded, and they begin by picking the scar. Frequently, says the cattleman, they bore into the critter's spine to cause paralysis. A cow's only escape is to retreat into some low trees or underbrush. When a reward was offered for magpie claws, this rancher brought in 2,000. He bored holes in boards, filled the holes with lard and a poison. The birds swooped down, partook, flew straight up in the air and dropped dead. . . .

If your summer resort owner has a **martin** birdhouse right next to your cabin, thank him. Martins are great devourers of mosquitoes. A doctor friend in Northern Minnesota once opened a dead martin and counted 2,400 skeeters inside the bird.

You girls with mink coats don't have to look down your noses quite so much. The mink's fur very closely resembles that of the English polecat. And that animal has a very disagreeable smell.

Every time you see a really perfect mink coat on a dame you may well assume that some fur expert had to sort over as many as 10,000 pelts to find enough to match up perfectly for a $10,000 or $15,000 garment.

LITTLE THINGS IN LIFE: Furriers have found out that female minks make a better mink coat than the males.

How womanlike: Mockingbirds have been known to change their tunes more than 80 times in seven minutes.

Pity the Moose: He must kneel when eating from the ground. His neck's too short and his legs too long for grazing.

Scientists have estimated that one mama **mosquito** between June and September can be responsible for 400,000,-000 offspring.

It's a neat trick if you can do it: One way to tell whether the Miss Mosquito that's stinging you is a malaria carrier is to take a quick peek at her hind legs: If they're up off the skin during the sting, watch out for the dread disease of the tropics. Domestic mosquitoes sting on all six feet.

Did you hear what the mosquito said when he bit into the preacher? "Yum, yum . . . divinity."

LITTLE THINGS IN LIFE: The adult clothes **moth** lives but a few weeks, but during that time lays as many as 300 eggs.

No wonder we have moth trouble. The government's

bureau of entomology reveals that, as newly hatched larvae, moths can squeeze through cracks only 4/1000ths of an inch wide.

STARTLING THOUGHT: Do you have a pair of **mice** around the house? Mice breed about six times a year and there are about six mice to a litter. The young mice breed when they're four months old. So, if a pair of mice have good luck, with no deaths in the family, they would normally increase in one year to 434 and at the end of the second year the little family could number 65,778.

Just in case you have a mouse around the house that you know has been there for two years, the little fellow has an age equivalent of an 80-year-old human, so you may hope that he'll be kicking off any day.

The ape and you aren't the only creatures who can focus the eyes. The **owl** has remarkable focusing powers and can dilate its pupils from pinhead size to a half inch in diameter. The owl, incidentally, can see better in broad daylight than any other living creature.

A side-knifer can open 100 oysters in three and a half minutes.

Show a **parrot** its reflection in a mirror and the bird'll toss every word in its vocabulary at its image.

You might cop a stunt used by the **penguins**—on long hikes they break the monotony of walking by tobogganing or pushing themselves along on their stomachs.

Learn something about **pheasants** from the proprietor of a pheasant farm. Ringneck pheasants, although bred in captivity for generations, never become domesticated but always remain wild. Eating quality of pheasant eggs is the same as chicken eggs. It takes 24 days for a ringneck pheasant to hatch—21 days for a chicken egg. A three-week-old pheasant can take flights of 50 feet. Ringneck cocks and hens all look alike for the first five weeks. . . .

Here's something you might want to make a note of in case a **pig** ever comes into your life. You can tell whether your pig is healthy by the way she walks. If she keeps up on the points of her feet, she's in fine fettle. Pigs have long, silky eyelashes, too. Did you know that?

I learned from a farm expert that hogs have more childhood diseases than children, among them such things as mange, lice, flu, bullnose, worms, elephant's hide and constipation.

A reader who says he has been a farmer all his life wrote that neither he nor his friends had been able to find out what a group of pigs is called. That item in the column one day brought an unusual reply.

"Regarding the farmer and his piggies," said the second correspondent, "and what a group of hogs is called, reminds me of a case down in Missouri some 30 years ago. The railroad was being sued for killing a number of pigs belonging to a farmer. The engineer was on the witness stand. Said he, 'As we rounded the curve, I saw a flock of pigs.' The judge interrupted at that point with, 'You mean a drove of pigs, don't you? A flock is a group of things flying through the air.' 'Judge,' continued the engineer, 'that's exactly where them pigs was when I saw them—flying through the air.' "

There isn't one of God's creatures that makes love with any more aplomb or *savoir-faire* than a male **pigeon.** We could all take lessons from that bird.

A carrier **pigeon,** when its ears are stuffed, can't fly.

City pigeons like to use nails as nest-liners, not because they can't find twigs, twine or other nest material but because the nails, inasmuch as they're metal, hold body heat and protect both the eggs and the little birds more effectively when Ma and Pa leave the nest for food. Comes spring and heat savers are no longer needed, so the birds shove the nails out until the next year's cold weather.

Just what good it does him, I don't know, but up in the Arctic regions a **polar bear** can sniff a seal a mile away.

Have you ever wondered, after you've come home from a hard day's work and you're sitting all alone with your thoughts, why some **rabbits** have long ears and other rabbits have short ones? Well, it's just too bad that you don't follow the meetings of the American Society of Mammalogists and the American Society of Ichthyologists and Herpetologists. Then you'd know. They've had learned papers reporting that it all depends on nature's system of wiring the rabbits for sound. In the southern desert and inland areas rabbits find more obstacles to the reception of sound than they do in the coastal and northern areas. Hence, the inland rabbits' ears stretch upward so they can hear better. Now, don't you feel better?

Live and Learn Department: W. A. Billings of the University farm informs us that when a doe (a female rabbit) gives birth to a litter, it's called "a kindling."

If you can spare the time, watch a jack rabbit at your next opportunity—every sixth stride he leaps a shade higher to get a squint at possible pursuers.

THEY'RE HERE, THE RATS

The American Chemical Society has estimated that there are two **rats** to every human in these United States.

What's so appetizing about carnations to a rat? Two stenographers reported they stopped in front of a florist shop at night and saw a rat swinging like the man in the flying trapeze from stem to stem on a couple of dozen carnations. The rat even went so far as to snip off two blossoms at a time, apparently in an effort to conserve energy. After carefully snapping a bud or a bloom, the rat would scamper down the base, scoot off into the darkness and then return in a moment or two for another flower.

Rat dope: In response to the item about rats eating carnations, a manufacturer of exterminants wrote the following: The only reason for a rat's stealing carnations is that it was probably using the posies for nesting material. The female of the species is the only one that will drag anything back to the nest. They'll eat almost anything except flowers. The major problem with rats, by the way, is not the disease they spread but the destruction they cause. They also carry fleas and lice that are known to carry plague, typhus trichinella-spiralis, ratbite fever, infectious jaundice, trench fever, foot-and-mouth disease and forms of influenza. Dominant species in much of the United States is the brown rat. Rats have killed lambs and pigs, they've caused floods, destroyed mail, and caused famines by destroying crops. They have caused more deaths among humans than all wars since history began. In the United States, even back in the fading days of depression and before our price structure had been boomed by inflation, it was estimated that rats cost each person six dollars a year. Rats have devoured full-grown humans and have been known to kill elephants, starting by gnawing at their feet.

Mother Nature didn't put those rattles on the end of a **rattlesnake's** tail for purposes of a warning signal to humans but instead so that reptiles might call to each other during the mating season.

Any time you get to thinking your job is tough, give this some consideration: Milking rattlesnakes for their venom is quite a business. An expert can milk some 150 of them in an hour. There's about a teaspoonful of venom in each milking, and the stuff's used for medicinal purposes. . . .

If you ever have to shoot a rattlesnake, don't worry about your aim—a rattler rears up, looks right into the muzzle of the gun and does your aiming for you.

A **robin's** smarter than you are at pulling angleworms out of the ground. Notice Mr. Red Breast next time he's worm hunting. He gives the worm one gentle tug and then waits. The worm relaxes and then Mr. Robin moves in for the kill. It's that bit of relaxing that releases the worm.

Average life of a **sardine** is approximately 14 years. That isn't in the can. . . .

Mother **seals** in distress cry with tears as flowing as any human's.
Skilled trappers always pick bachelor seals because the married ones usually have their skins scarred by teeth marks from family rows.

You mothers with tiny babes aren't the only inconvenienced folk in the world. Consider the mama **silkworm:** She has to feed her offspring at least five times during the night and more than twice that frequency during the daylight hours. . . .

Better be on the lookout for the silverfish. It's an insect that will cause considerable damage to nylon hose, rayon, Bemberg silk, and so on. A bug expert friend says the silverfish digests all synthetic materials and is considered the moth of the synthetic fabrics. Many a housewife finds unexplained holes in her nylon stockings or rayon undies which are probably due to the silverfish. The insect is peculiar to new homes and new buildings—those built in the last 15 years or so. The insect lives longer than any other household insect and also damages rugs, wallpaper, books, pictures and curtains. Moths seldom touch nylon, so if you are finding holes in nylon fabrics, it may mean you're under attack by silverfish.

If you want to go strictly polite, next time you smell skunk say this: "My, there seems to be some allyl mercaptan in the air."
A professional skunk raiser will tell you that the pussy is really not a malign little animal. Fundamentally it's a shy creature with an inferiority complex.
The skunk is not usually an aggressive creature. His

weapon is rather a defensive one. Carry a live skunk by the tail and there'll be nothing doing. Somebody else can test that theory, however.

A **slug** to you may mean a jigger of liquor, a counterfeit coin or the name of what you felt like on a morning after, but actually it's a land-living mollusk that has no shell. It's about six inches long and its head bears two pairs of horns, one for feeling, the other with eyes at the tips.

They've actually timed a **snail** and find that it takes the little fellow exactly 14 days to travel a mile. . . .

The next time one of your kids brings home a snail, try this performance: The creature will crawl over the edges of the keenest razor blade without inflicting any harm to itself.

The common **English sparrow** has twice as many vertebral bones in its neck as that long-necked fellow the giraffe.

To rid your premises of sparrows the easy way, simply give the feathered friends a lot of music. They hate it and will depart at once. A radio or a portable phonograph set up within their earshot will do the trick.

Spiders can go 17 months without food and snakes can fast for a two-year stretch, if they have to.

You may love dearly the **starlings** in your yard, but two Minneapolis residents have traced the disappearance of the tops of their tomato plants to this type of bird. A starling was making a nest out of the tops of tomato plants, peas, quack grass and roots. . . .

Maybe we should all turn toads. Toads are the only animal species free from cancer.

Broad-breasted turkeys are well-known now, but maybe you haven't heard of the trouble encountered when the type was being developed and perfected. In trying to improve the meatiness and breast weight of the birds, the turkeys were developed to too great a degree to a point where the front weight of the bird pulled the breastbone down onto the roost, thus bruising the meat at the front of the bird and ruling out as No. 1 choice a lot of the fowl. To correct this, instead of removing weight from the bird, the experts developed tail feathers to compensate so the breastbone was held off the roost. Complicated, this turkey raising, isn't it?

Go ahead and let 'em call you a weasel: It's the most fearless of all animals. It doesn't even have to be provoked to attack an adversary when it's in a scrappy mood.

A **whale's** right nostril is always larger than its left.

A good-sized whale, if it wants to do its darnedest, can attain a swim speed of 50 miles an hour.

If you want something to put you to sleep tonight start wondering how it is that whales can descend to depths where the water pressure would crush the sides of a steel submarine like an eggshell. The whales return to the surface later with the rush of a leaping salmon. Too rapid emergence is the terror, of course, of all deep-sea divers for fear of those deadly bends, but a whale has no trouble. Are you asleep already?

I suppose you've heard about the man who crossed homing pigeons and woodpeckers to produce a bird that knocks when he delivers the message.

Wood-tick Reminder: A dab of turpentine, ammonia or strong soapsuds on an embedded wood tick will cause the rascal to release his hold and make pulling him off easy. . . .

Another method of removing a wood tick is to put six or eight drops of chloroform into the palm of the hand and cup it over the tick. He'll let go.

WORM TURNS CONNOISSEUR

Tobacco worms that make a living by drilling into cigars won't touch a domestic stogie. They insist on imported tobacco.

Only the female of the glowworm is luminous.

When things get dull around the house, start an argument as to whether a **zebra** is white with black stripes or black with white stripes.

Part Six

S—E—X

Boys and girls are first taught the facts of life by tales about the birds and the bees, or so the story goes.

But nobody ever stopped to consider that maybe the little animals have to learn those things, too. This chapter is an effort to end that long-time neglect of our friends of the sea, the soil and the sky by explaining to them the facts of life about men and women.

Since we're the so-called higher animals, however, S-E-X isn't quite as simple as in the lower species that are used for instruction of little humans. So it's quite obviously necessary in the chapter that follows to go beyond the bare biological facts and discuss such vital matters as the nature of S-E-X arguments. We've also got to consider the S-E-X factors in clothing, and a lot of other human peculiarities in order to give the little animals a fair picture that won't scare them out of their natural functions.

The scheme used in classifying this section is to start with statements of simple facts that will be of interest only to males or only to females. Then, gradually, we bring them together with common desires. Finally, in the realistic recognition of life in the raw, we point out some of the common disputes that arise when S-E-X gets out of control.

If you have a pet poodle that seems to be going through an unhappy adolescence, or if your house cat seems to be a bundle of emotional conflicts, give them this to read. His dog's life will seem better after he knows about the sex practices of humans. The cover is beguilingly plain. No one need be embarrassed, and you may be doing some little creature a great favor at a most trying age by passing along this vital information.

On the other hand, if you're only human and want to read this yourself first, remember, you're on your honor. If you're a girl, no fair peeking into the section marked *"For men only,"* and vice versa. But I'll bet that's the first thing you do when you read about S-E-X.

FOR WOMEN ONLY

A teacher in the town of Fairmont, Minn., has produced a schoolgirl essay on the subject of men, written as an assignment in English composition. The penetration of the young authoress is obvious. Here's her whole essay:

"Men are what women marry. They drink and smoke and have many pockets, but they won't go to church. Perhaps if they wore bonnets they would. They are more logical than women but they also are always more zoological. Both men and women have sprung from monkies, but the women certainly sprang further than the men."

The Blow That Shocked Mother: The young daughter in this case, a girl in her teens, was browsing through a family trunk in the attic and found a packet of old love letters that her father had written to her mother in their courting days. The teen-ager took the letters downstairs, called to her mother and said, "Mom, I want you to listen to a letter I just got from one of my boy friends. See what you think of it." With that, she read the missive but substituted her own name where her mother's appeared.

"My stars and body," exclaimed the mother. "Such nonsensical stuff as these young boys get in their heads these days. You'd better find a more suitable companion. Such trash. Such mush."

The daughter then presented the mother with the letter.

Advice to girls: If you want to keep your youth, don't introduce him to anybody.

ODDS ON ENDING MARRIED

You girls still single after you're 22 have some cause for jitters: Half the feminine population of the nation is married by the time they reach that age. . . .

City gals, you'd better move. Statistics show that girls living in small towns are most likely to marry before they're 20, while those living in the cities are much less likely to marry that young.

Another item for the unwed femmes: A girl between 18 and 22 years of age and of average appearance and health will in those four years have as many chances for marriage as she'll get between the ages of 23 and 35. . . .

If you've reached 45 and are still single, chances are 9 to 1 you won't make the trip down the aisle, male or female. If you're single at 30, it's 50-50 you'll miss matrimony.

Single girls, if I were you I'd pack up this minute for Siam, or do you call it Thailand. There any girl unmarried by the time she reaches 30 has the right to apply to the government for a husband and, by golly, the government is supposed to get her one.

WHEN IN DENMARK: There's a flourishing club over there that insures young women against spinsterhood. If you're between 13 and 20, you pay low annual dues to the Anti-Celibacy Insurance Society. If you marry before 40, you lose all you paid. If you don't win a husband by then, you collect an income regularly.

Nurses will tell you that it's largely mythical—that business of their falling in love with a patient. After they've had them in a hospital, seen their feet, observed them at close range, the chances for romance are slim.

Rejoice, women, rejoice. The average life of a white woman in the United States is now 68.08 years. Males average on 63.39.

A court stenographer announces that women, on the average, talk 25 to 30 per cent faster than men.

And almost any porter will tell you that women are far more untidy than men in public washrooms.

Statistics indicate that women purchase 90 per cent of all men's handkerchiefs and 70 per cent of men's neckties and shirts.

NEAT TRICK DEPARTMENT

Men are not permitted to enter the ladies' bath. The male bath attendant under paragraph eight of the bath regulations is to be regarded as a woman.—PICK TIMES

Mrs. Osmore, proprietress of Sorority College on the River, promises moonlight rides galore for her fair young guests this summer, having leased Art Hully's big paunch for the season.—LANDING NEWS

Miss Alice Gresham, young Lattimore high-school teacher who was suspended for smoking cigarets in the building last week, tendered her resignation yesterday rather than be reloved by the school board.—FREELAND NEWS

Don't let your boy friend take a litmus-paper saliva test of your mouth. It tells whether you're sexy or not.

Another warning, Girls: Don't ever let your boy friend refer to you as being as "pure as the driven snow." A recent study of fresh snow that fell and melted showed that it contained about 125,000,000 bacteria to the ounce.

Take your choice, girls: College girls who drink have more dates but fewer engagements of the diamond ring kind. That's the finding of a survey among 336 girls in a coeducational college.

The girls were divided into five categories: women who never drank; infrequent drinkers; occasional drinkers; near-regular drinkers, and regular drinkers.

There were twice as many regular drinkers as non-drinkers. The infrequent drinkers had started in their 19th year, the regular drinkers started earlier. Average starting age was 17. The girls who reported little or no drinking attended church more often. Most of the girls who drank did so with the knowledge of their families. Also revealed by the study was the fact that the traditional tea party has given way to the cocktail party.

You drinking girls also had better bend an ear to this advice from a famed skin specialist. He advises that all young women who drink cocktails should absolutely sit down and eat quite a batch of food within half an hour of any alcoholic indulgence. The small blood vessels in a girl's skin, says the Wise One, lose their tone, the oil glands become disordered and a flabby, blotchy skin is the result if you swig without sending down some food also.

SKIN DEEP

Women usually look their worst when they hurry. With their faces fixed in a grim, fighting look they tighten up, hunch their shoulders, strain their heads forward, pound their heels into the pavement, bump into people, lose their

bundles and their charm. Deliberately assume a calm, self-possessed expression, it'll help you relax. Walk upright, eyes looking ahead. You'll cover territory and look handsome, too.

There's no easier way to set up complete self-consciousness in a woman than to mention a blemish she might have on her face. What spark she could have had fades immediately.

MALE OFFICE WORKERS, GET READY. Our offices are apt to be turned into women's dressing tables. There's a movement going to teach office girls "not to be caught short" at work. Idea is that any minute the average office girl is apt to receive an unexpected invitation to dinner with a romantic possibility. So the authorities who watch over our little frails are urging them to keep handy at the office a box that contains the following: a pair of fresh, sheer hosiery; a pair of immaculate white gloves; a dainty white kerchief; a toothbrush and powder, a clothesbrush, a suède-shoe brush, a small bottle of hand lotion, box of facial tissues, a make-up kit and a bottle of toilet water. Looks like such things as paper clips, carbon paper, second sheets, pencils and erasers will have to be tossed out in the alley.

Is it amazing to you that the average woman in this country uses three times her weight in cosmetics in a lifetime? No wonder they're such busy little creatures.

No shiny-nosed gals are our farm women. People who study such things report that average city families use 1.95 boxes of face powder annually, while the country girls are daubing on 1.85 boxes.

It wasn't too many years ago when every woman carried her powder puff tucked in her bosom. The custom seems to have died out completely.

Face Powder Test for You Girls: Sprinkle a little of your favorite face powder over a glass of water. If the powder contains filler, the filler particles will sink to the bottom of the water. Allegedly, it's the filler that clogs your dear little pores.

Actress Jane Wyman once attributed her perfect complexion to drinking parsley juice.

Every time you see a redheaded girl, don't you naturally assume she's Irish? The assumption's wrong. Scotland has more redheads per capita than any other country.

Here's a little item that will appeal: I know a girl whose eyelashes by actual measurement are more than half an inch long—and silky. They make her extremely alluring. Her technique is very simple. All any girl has to do, she says (the trick is probably hundreds of years old, but I'm a fall guy), is to massage the eyelids deeply with castor oil for several minutes each night. The lashes soon resemble Paul Bunyan's beard. She's living evidence of it, so maybe it isn't wrong.

What a change to the American scene a lipstick scarcity would make.

Only woman I've seen in years without her lips touched up was 84 years old.

SCENT—I—MENT

Don't look now, unless it's convenient, but a lot of you women have a blemish that I'll bet you weren't even aware of. If you're a perfume user and place the stuff behind your ear, you probably have what the cosmetic experts call a "perfume freckle." In reality it's a burn from the oils in the perfume. It's perfectly harmless so don't go getting all upset about it.

One perfume expert tells me the best place to put perfume is in the hair. There's something about the hair that mixes with the aroma of the perfume and sends it out in pleasant wafts.

Another who should know advises that your perfume will be more alluring if you put it in the crook of your elbow. That's especially so if you're going to dance during the evening.

A chemist I know stirs up batches of his own perfume as a hobby. Here's his idea for testing the full aroma: Put a snitch on your finger tip, snap your thumb over the moistened tip and then wave your hand in front of your nostrils. The snapping, he says, is what really spreads the perfume to bring out its fullest essence.

And never keep your perfume in a place where it's exposed to heat or light. Both weaken the essence.

As new to you as it was to me? The nail-polishing custom dates back to the aboriginals. The cave man went hunting and brought back the game. If the wife was a good cave woman, she'd personally dress the animal and prepare it for cooking. To let the world know she was a good cave woman, she'd allow the blood to dry on her nails and was very proud of red nails.

Had to look twice at this headline before I got it: "Women Informed of Need for New Support of Chest." It was a Community Fund story.

A small boy was writing an anatomy examination. This was one answer: "Your legs are what if you haven't got two pretty good ones you can't get to first base. And neither can your sister."

I don't suppose he actually counted that many while he collected the facts, but Earl Moran, the artist famed for drawing those lush girls, says that only one leg (feminine) in a million looks as good bare as encased in a silk stocking.

Before you let the sweet one conclude too solidly that she has beautiful legs, convince her of this little fact: Many a pair of pins which look good from the front or side fail to please the eye from the back. The rear view is the most trying test, according to the experts on those matters.

The term "show a leg," often used by boatswains' mates and masters-at-arms of earlier ship days to arouse sleeping men, has an unusual origin. It derives from the long ago when seamen were allowed to take their wives aboard with them. The women would merely put one foot out of the bunk at first call and thus were not required to turn out for identification.

Can't help but wonder who the gent was who had the bright idea that the female toe sticking out from the front of a shoe is an interesting or an exciting sight. . . .

Here's something to worry about: Female anklebones in the United States are getting larger and larger, due to the increased weight that high heels push onto feminine ankles.

SOUNDS LIKE S—E—X

Occasionally your Rotund Reporter does a little amateur speaking at banquets. For years I've noticed, when speaking in a hall full of women, that there's always an echo. But the echo rarely occurs at a stag affair. An acoustical expert finally gave me the answer—it's the silk in women's garments. It won't absorb the sound half as quickly as the thicker woolens that men wear.

CONFIDENTIAL TIP TO CO-EDS: Men like daring dresses on the other fellow's girl—not theirs. A male fashion jury rendered that verdict. It was the sophisticated, dreamy look they admired in their own dates, not the exposed look.

Surely you've seen the type who had this experience: This elderly woman went into a shop to buy a new hat. The clerk who waited on her kept bringing up headgear that simply didn't suit her. Finally, the woman eyed the clerk sternly and said, "Listen, dearie, I wear a corset and I wear drawers, and I want a hat to match."

If that Little Woman of yours is average, she'll spend about two hours shopping for a dress.

New high in catty comebacks: "My dear, what a stunning gown! Didn't they have it in your size?"

Linen suits give women about as fashionable a turn in summer wear as anything they don and the same material does just the opposite for men.

You girlies can save time getting into your girdles by applying a dash of talcum to the hips just before you begin the squeeze play.

Can you think of a human emotion any more gratifying than the pleasure a woman must get from the scratch she gives herself the minute she gets her girdle off?

A New York leather goods manufacturer has gone to the trouble of setting up handbag measurements that women are supposed to follow to make the purse fit the wearer. Half-pint women, those under five feet two, should use a handbag no longer than 10 inches. If women are from five feet two to five feet six, the purse can be 12 inches long. For the tall ones bags can be as long as 14 inches.

Women have carried cigarets in their purses since 1842. The smoking practice started in France that year.

Large-size women's shoes are always used in window displays in Denmark. Women with large feet then believe theirs to be average. Those with small feet are flattered.

Funny how sables do something even for the most unattractive women.

And you can stick just about the homeliest girl in town in a convertible coupé with the top down and invariably she looks like a pip.

Inconsistency, thy name is woman: The same dame who is always complaining that she has nothing to wear is the one who is always complaining that she hasn't enough closet space.

Maybe it's a swelling that comes in the night, but it looks

to me like the shoe salesmen of the country aren't doing their jobs. Look around under the tables in nightclubs and you'll see at least 40 per cent of the women customers with their shoes completely off or dangling.

WHAT PRICE VIRTUE

Pass along this suggestion to girls and women who must be out alone late at night—tell them to carry a good, strong old-fashioned steel hatpin, one from eight to ten inches long. Tell them not to put it in their purses but to carry the pin in such a way as to be able to plunge it deep at the first move of a molester. The hatpin was the natural weapon of the gals back in the Gay Nineties. It won't kill, but it's effective and leaves enough of a mark for identification for several days. Hatpins, if they can still be found, are not expensive, either. Every girl out alone at night should carry one.

And here's a hint from a woman who must drive her car late at night.

"After I have parked my car and am walking to the house," she says, "I take out my razor blade windshield scraper and carry it open. It makes me feel very well armed against any would-be purse-snatchers or attackers."

Shades of the Gestapo: A woman dancing in the state of Washington must not take more than three steps backward at a time, according to the state statute.

Women are greater smugglers than men, a survey reveals. Women go in for petty smuggling, however, while men who try it usually do it in a big way. Women consider smuggling a kind of innocent game and very often do it just to "put something over on a man."

In a scientific mood! You might as well know that surveys indicate women pay more attention than men to newspaper pictures of pretty girls with shapely legs.

If you're one who thinks publicity is essential to success, consider this: Eve's name is mentioned only four times in the Bible, and she's done pretty well in lingering in memory through the centuries.

WOMAN'S BEST FRIEND

In case your thoughts have been turning to diamond rings lately or may be soon, here are a few bits from a gemologist:

It takes a four-year course to turn out a trained gemologist.

A perfect diamond is one that shows no imperfections under a 10-power microscope. If a flaw shows up under a 12-power microscope, the trade still calls it a perfect diamond. It's an easy matter to have your diamond examined. You may even take a quick peek yourself and the gemologist will point out the flaws. Blue-white diamonds are one-in-a-million and are regarded as museum pieces. The "perfect" diamond is completely colorless. To see if your diamond is white, put it in the fold of a piece of paper and hold it up to the light. Let the paper diffuse the light before it reaches the stone. A diamond gets all its brilliance from the light it takes in. The light is refracted and diffused in a spectrum which makes it look as though the beauty comes from the inside. That's what makes cutting so important.

Unless a diamond is of unusual cut, it has 58 facets. Most diamonds have been cut that way since the beginning of the seventeenth century. So chances are you're wearing a "brilliant" cut if you're that lucky.

When that dame of yours peers into her diamond, the reason she sees brilliancy is because light which strikes the stone at any angle greater than 24½ degrees is reflected within the stone itself instead of passing through it.

Engagement rings take 80 per cent of all diamonds sold.

Last-minute advice: Hint to brides-to-be: If, just in the last few moments of your life as an unmarried woman, you'll sneak into a corner some place and do a few knee bends, you'll limber up enough to remove completely the possibility of having your bones crack audibly when you kneel at the altar. And that's something.

FOR MEN ONLY

Cute Custom from the South Seas. If a man seeks a woman he wears white flowers over his ear. If his love grows more ardent he switches to a red rose. When he cools off, if he does, he switches to some green thing instead of the rose.

Nose rubbing is more widely used by mankind as a greeting than are handshaking and kissing combined.
Heartbreaking note: In Samoa a kiss is merely a sniff.

AH, THIS IS BETTER

If you close your eyes when you kiss or get kissed, you may be interested in this scientific explanation as set forth by a Minneapolis M.D. whose name is withheld for obvious reasons: The dilation of the pupil is affected by fibers of the sympathetic nervous system, its contraction by vagus fibers. Everything that excites the sympathetic system dilates the pupil; anything that stimulates the vagus (parasympathetic system) such as fear, vexation or melancholy, contracts it. Assuming, then, that the person being kissed is stimulated with resultant joy and passion, pupils dilate and more light comes into the eye. A more pronounced example of this is going into a sunlit room from a dark one. Until the pupils contract sufficiently to diminish the intensity of light hitting the retina, one tends to blink the eyes. . . .

There's also another element, says the medico, the subconscious wish to blot out other events. Closing the eyes does that very well in most cases.

What a salesman, this guy! He persuaded 100 girls to let him kiss them purely in the interest of science. And after the "horrible ordeal," this is what he came up with:

While being kissed, 72 per cent of girls closed their eyes; three per cent closed one eye (may have wanted to see what was going on), four per cent started kissing with their eyes open but soon closed them, and 21 per cent kept both eyes open all the time. When asked (still in the interest of science) why they closed their eyes, these answers followed: She closed her eyes because his mustache tickled. She habitually closes her eyes because her regular boy friend is not very good-looking. She closed her eyes because a kiss is a serious matter and she likes to concentrate on it. She always closes her eyes because she likes to imagine she is being kissed by a movie hero. About the only conclusion you can draw from that series of answers is that it isn't wise to ask a girl why she closes her eyes when being kissed.

Male definition of Lipstick: A red menace that a girl can't keep on and a man can't wipe off. Or something that gives a new flavor to an old pastime.

MUST BE NICE WORK IF YOU CAN GET IT: Scientists are out now with proof that there is no emotional difference between blondes and brunettes.

Brunettes are easier on the eyes than blondes and redheads are still easier. It's an optical fact, say the experts, that red colorations are less fatiguing to the eye. Blondes produce a glare.

Yet blondes are not only preferred by gentlemen (going back to an ancient wheeze) but also by a manufacturer of weather instruments. A company making the instruments advertised for 2,000 strands of genuine human blond hair, 9 to 18 inches in length.

I've always wondered whether the good-looking doll or the tall, dark and handsome guy, as a result of their alleged good looks, got married any sooner than the homelier males and females. Now a couple of college profs have proved that being good-looking is very important if you want to get married at any early age. In the case of both men and women, these experts report, the average age of marriage increases as the attractiveness rating of either sex declines.

Ever notice in some of the major magazine and newspaper ads that pretty girls are frequently surrounded or accompanied by a male with a face that borders on the homely? There's design back of that. Artists figure that both characters should never ooze beauty. Men like to see pictures of beautiful girls with homely guys. It gives them hope. That's the psychology. . . .

NEAT TRICK DEPARTMENT

"Mr. Gilbert, inventor of the instrument, said the idea came to him while he was sitting on a park wench in Chicago."—BEND REPUBLICAN

"Lady, stranger in town, desires room and males in modern home near First National Bank Bldg."—Box 25, MODESTOR HERALD

BOSS TO SECRETARY: "Who told you you could neglect your office duties just because I make an occasional pass at you?"

SECRETARY TO BOSS: "My attorney."

A three-year-old was attending his grandpap's sixtieth birthday celebration. The old gent, in one breath, blew out the candles on the cake.

"Gee," gasped the kid, "you sure can blow out candles."

"Remember," piped up Grandma, "when your grandpa was courting me, there wasn't any electricity."

The frequency of petting activities, according to a pre-Kinsey scientific survey, is at its height between the ages of 21 and 25 in men. And 41 per cent of the men queried in another survey on the question, "At what age do you consider a girl most lovable?" agreed on 22 years as the best.

Once ran across the Venus de Milo measurements. I figured you might want to check your girl friend with them, so here they are: Height 5½ feet; neck 12⅞ inches; waist 28½; hips 36; thigh 19½; knee 13½; calf 13½; ankle 8½ and bust 34¾.

If you're a Lovers' Lane addict, you'll be interested to know that a half moon sheds about one-ninth as much light on the earth as a full moon dispenses.

BY ANY OTHER NAME

Go ahead and call your Sweetie Pie "my little blue rabbit." It's the finest bit of romancing they can do in France, so it should be okay here.

If you really want to flatter that dame of yours, though, tell her she's sweeter than oxime—the stuff is 2,000 times sweeter than sugar. . . .

Tell a girl she's camel-eyed and she'd probably sock you. Yet there isn't a movie actress in all of Hollywood with eyelashes as long nor expression as soulful as the humped beast.

Next time you masculines get into a woo situation, give her a little of this: "Ah, my pet, you have the eyes of a giraffe." It's really quite complimentary. A giraffe's optics are dark brown, large and lustrous, soft and melting, and are covered with long, sweeping lashes. But you'd better rush that explanation.

You swains casting about for a figure of speech for "her loveliness" also might try this: "Your face feels far softer to me than the shaved belly of a guinea pig." That's what face powders are tested on in cosmetic laboratories.

Or take a look at your girl friend, gents, and tell her that her kaolin, starch, siliceous earth, zinc oxide, zinc stearate, titanium oxide and magnesium oxide never looked better. It may stump her until you inform her you're talking about her face powder.

But never tell her that she's the cream in your coffee. It's the lactic acid of cream mixed with the caffeine citrate of coffee that causes sleeplessness or indigestion for some.

We've been making another common mistake in referring to feminine legs as gams. Mr. Webster lists the word in his dictionary, but the correct spelling is *gamb* with the alternate of *game*. Nowhere (except in Variety) could I find just plain gam.

It happened in a small town. A new male instructor in the high school started going around with one of the prettier females of the staff. Three prankster pupils thought they'd do a little spying on them one night, so the lads tucked themselves into the trunk of the coupé that belonged to the gent teacher, assuming he'd be taking his new affection out riding. He did, but somehow he found out the lads were in the trunk, which gives the tail end of the story an odd twist. The two teachers drove 12 miles out into the country that night, the driver got out, opened the trunk and said, "Now, boys, get home the best you can."

FIRST DATE

I GOT TO THINKING of an old girl of mine the other day and the first honest-to-goodness date I ever had in Minneapolis. My 14-year-old reminded me of it when I thought of the things he's going to have to go through pretty soon. . . . A strange mixture of pain and delight, with pain probably a little more pronounced.

Dagne Hansen was my date's name. She was Danish. A blonde with red cheeks and eyebrows that were darker than her hair. Her house was two doors from mine. Dagne was about eight months older than I was and had lived in Minneapolis all her life. That gave her advantages over me. I had done such things with her as swing her in a hammock. On many occasions I had swooshed up to her house on my bike, made a very spectacular stop by swinging one leg over the bike and riding up to the door with just one foot on the pedal. The time had come, though, in our lives when I figured it would take more than hammock swinging and bicycle acrobatics to hold her attention. . . .

I'll give Dagne credit for one thing. She made me fingernail conscious. After I had made up my mind that we should have a date, I began preparation for it by keeping my nails clean for at least a week ahead. I argued with myself for several days about whether it would be easier to ask her face to face or do it over the telephone. I rehearsed the telephone routine by the hour. Every time I found myself alone, I'd pick up an imaginary phone and start, "Hello, is Dagne there?" I even filled in the waits. "This is Cedric Adams. Could I speak to her, please." The voice on the other end would say, "Just a minute and I'll call her." Then my imagination took me to the point where she said, "Hello," and I said, "Dagne" and then another wait. "This is Cedric." I'd get over that part in fine shape.

From there on I had trouble. During some of the rehearsals I'd ask, "Are you busy Friday night?" Then I'd reason with myself: Maybe I shouldn't start out that way because if she didn't happen to be busy and told me so, it wouldn't leave her any out. Why wouldn't it be better to say, "I'd like to have a date with you on Friday night." That always sounded silly as an opener. So I'd change it to, "I'm going to a movie and someplace to eat afterward on Friday. Would you like to go with me?" That sounded a little on the stupid side, too, even in rehearsal. I finally agreed that the best approach, if it had to be on the telephone, was, "Could we go to a movie Friday night and maybe someplace afterward?" I remember I finally made one telephone call and she answered; and I was so startled because I didn't get a chance to use the wait I had rehearsed that I hung up before I could get out a single word.

At last I clinched it, though, and then my rehearsing began in earnest. We'd have quite a ride downtown on the streetcar and there'd be a lot of time that had to be filled with conversation. I couldn't figure out exactly what she would want to talk about. There'd be times in the movie, too, when we would want to converse, I told myself. I remember so distinctly that walk up to her front door. Just before my finger touched the doorbell button I wanted to run away. It wasn't going to be worth it, I feared. Some strange force made me push the button. . . .

We got through the streetcar ride and the movie. It was exciting having her next to me. If only I hadn't told her we were going somewhere to eat after the show. How I had the nerve to do it I don't know to this day, but we wound up at an old Chinese inn where they had dancing. She ordered chicken chow mein. I wasn't that hungry. Besides, I was a little worried about the check. I remember I took my cap in with me. I ordered a banana split—15 cents in those days. I'll bet the waiter thought he had a couple of live ones.

Dagne suggested we dance, which we did. When I suggested another dance she said she thought it was too crowded. I knew then that I wasn't cutting the mustard with her. I finished my banana split. She seemed to dawdle over her chow mein. We were in there about two hours, the longest 120 minutes I ever put in in my life. I recall having sort of planned on maybe a little good-night smack. I had even rehearsed that. It didn't happen. For weeks I looked upon myself as a social failure. I wonder what ever happened to Dagne. She had such pretty eyebrows.

- o -

If your dame insists on having you on the outside when you're walking down the street, give her this. It comes from an old Anglo-Saxon custom when upstairs tenants had the cute little habit of tossing their garbage out the windows into an open ditch that ran between the sidewalk and the road. The gent took the outside to lessen the danger of having his lady pal socked with a mess of refuse.

LOOK 'EM OVER

I'm going to take a day off sometime just to study women's eyebrows. They're no more uniform than their noses, but I'll bet it would be amazing to note the varying shapes, length and treatment of eyebrows.

Women are always changing the part in their hair. Wonder why men never do? Think I'll start a little survey to see which place is most popular for the part. I'll bet right now the middle would run third.

I don't know why they'd want the information, but a Washington organization made a survey among stenographers and secretaries and it revealed that 16.6 per cent of the girls put on their shoes and stockings before their scanties when dressing. About 75 per cent said they put their shoes on afterward. And (here's the laugh) 8.3 per cent of them said it was none of the investigator's business.

In all states the nightgown remains more popular than pajamas.

Your elbow, if you're a man, bespeaks your character while you're dancing, according to one of the nation's ace instructors. Those who hold their elbows down have no confidence; elbows-up people are cocksure of themselves, and those who dance with their elbows real high are both proud and vain.

The average man is more vain than the average woman. When about to be photographed, he preens before the mirror like a peacock, straightens his necktie, etc. And probably not more than 1 per cent of men are good-looking. Few have ears that are mates. The two sides of their face don't match. If a man is dark and hasn't shaved, he looks like a gorilla in a few hours, and if he's blond and just out of the barber's chair he looks like a big pink baby. . . .

Wonder why it is that a man can be dressed in his best outfit and yet look as shabby as a bag when he gets into one of those three-way mirror arrangements in a clothing store or a tailor shop? . . .

A POX ON OUR SEX: Librarians will tell you that invariably book thieves are men. Women almost never steal books from public libraries.

The statistics may be old, but they still should give us fellows food for thought: Women control 70 per cent of all private wealth; hold more than 65 per cent of all savings accounts; own 40 per cent of all real estate; 23 per cent of all stock shares; inherit half the money in estates and are beneficiaries of 80 per cent of all life insurance. Foolishly we still refer to them as "the weaker sex." Men must be nuts.

Did you know that more men than women go to the movies alone? A survey which revealed that fact stunned the big shots in Hollywood.

What price learning? In the extension division at the University of Minnesota students were surveyed on reasons why they were taking extension courses. Out of 209 who were questioned, 29 of them admitted they were taking extension courses "for matrimonial reasons." And 12 of the "confessors" were men. A guy taking applied psychology may have his laboratory sitting right next to him.

Nothing looks more awkward than a gent with a bay window trying to put his rubbers on by putting a leg up over a knee and then reaching. And there's nothing any more grunt-provoking, either—or more disappointing to many a damsel, who gets a new view of her swain.

IT GOES TO YOUR HEAD

I spent a whole morning in a millinery salon. (Please, Mr. Printer, be very careful on that last word, don't spell it with two "o"s.) That might seem like sacrilege—my fat frame in the brocaded elegance of a woman's hat department. My presence there was not completely a matter of choice, however. The Long-Suffering One had received an invitation in the mail to a showing of millinery.

"I'm going to attend that," wifey said as she tossed the invitation in my lap, "and you're going with me. I'm sick and tired of your perpetual scoffing at the hats I wear. You're going to select my next one. Meet me there at 10:30 in the morning." I said, "Look, I'll help you with the washing and ironing, I'll dust, I'll even put up a few mustard pickles next August, but I'll be hanged if I'll assist with your hat buying." I got there at 10:26.

A hat department in a women's store is no place for men, believe me. In the first place, the walls were all lined with mirrors. No matter where I looked I could see my William Howard Taft shape leering at me. An affable woman who introduced herself as Miss Benson greeted us. "May I show you some of our new models?" she asked. The three of us traipsed across the room. By that time I had seen enough reflections of myself to realize that I looked extremely shabby in the surroundings. The other women customers in the department let me know by their gazes that I was an intruder. I was given a stool on which to sit, a very frail stool. It was like balancing a lily pad on a mushroom, if you can get the picture. "My husband is going to select something for me," Madam A. began.

"Well isn't that lovely," Miss Benson responded. "You know, we don't get husbands in here very often. What would you like?" My first impulse was to tell her that what I really would like would be to get out of there, and fast. Instead I said, "Oh, I'd like something not too big, not too small. Something not too fussy and still not too plain. Something that will wear well." Miss Benson lost some of her affability.

But in order to make my mission seem a little more practical, I decided that there might be some material along millinery lines that would make a column and extend my tenure of office at the newspaper at least another day. Here are some of the notes I took: In buying hats, women should try to look as lovely as possible, rather than obey any particular trend. Some customers try on as many as 50 hats and then walk out without buying. The average woman tries on nine before she decides. Occasionally a customer will take the first lid she tries on. The saleswoman usually swoons at that. Seeing too many hats confuses a purchaser, too. The average woman buys three hats a season. Highest-priced hat in this particular department would cost me about a week's pay. Hat designers often go to museums for their inspirations. Others have been patterned after the old marriage headdress. Saw one topper called the "mother and daughter." . . . A hat with a miniature hat on it as part of the trim.

Women start asking for the first straw hats around Christmas. When you think you have a model you like, be sure to stand up for a complete look. Customers often think store mirrors are made to flatter, but it's the same glass as your home mirror. P.S. That hat I liked wasn't the one she bought. See the folly of it all?

Could you stand this, pardner? A North Carolina daily tossed out for one day all pictures of brides and brides-to-be from its society pages and instead ran photographs of grooms and grooms-to-be. Once was enough for the southern gentlemen. The gals were back in the next day.

Ponder over this one, gents, even though you'll probably go ahead and propose anyhow: From the time you were a kid of nine up till you're old and toothless, you've always had to explain to some woman why you didn't come home earlier.

ON WITH THE WEDDING

It takes two to make a marriage—a single girl and an anxious mother.

HINT FOR BRIDES: Lithuanian girls not only prepare hope chests for themselves, but on the wedding day they also turn over a pile of new duds to the groom.

Ever know how the custom of "best man" at a wedding developed? It started in primitive times when a fellow, deciding on a woman for a bride, called on his male friends to help in carrying her off—by force. . . .

Thoughts while shaving: Every time I attend a wedding

I always feel sorry for the mother of the bride as she sits so alone during the ceremony. Her daughter, of course, is at the altar; the brothers are usually ushers; the father is doing the giving-away, and there sits the mother all by herself.

But women apparently have the opposite view, as this letter shows: "Never, never, never feel sorry for the mother of the bride as she sits alone at the wedding. Sure, father may be up front giving the daughter away. But mother is just sitting there admiring her own handiwork, the beauty of the wedding, and she's purring to herself over the entire affair. For months, mother has planned every detail of that wedding, loved every second of it, fretted and fussed, of course, acted overburdened. But she has lived all her life for that moment. Don't deprive her of that glory by feeling sorry for her. She doesn't want any place of prominence in that wedding. Remember this—the ceremony provides her the first opportunity she's had in weeks to 'unlax,' rest her dogs and feel sure she shouldn't be bossing everybody."

Wedding ceremonies, it seems to me, would be more impressive if the minister stood with his back to and the principals faced the audience.

Get married by a minister rather than a justice of the peace and your chances of staying hitched are better. In a survey of some 600 couples who have been divorced, wedded life for the preacher-tied had lasted an average of 7.81 years; while those married by a justice of the peace had an average marital span of only 5.13 years.

NEAT TRICK DEPARTMENT

Georgianna Bouley and Maynard MacAdam were married Wednesday June 10. Mrs. Louis LeClair sang "Ave Maria," and "Mother, Dear, O Pray for Me."—SOCIAL ITEM

Among the many gifts presented by the bride to the bridegroom was a beautiful dressing down.—TIMMONS COURIER

The missing bride, who disappeared from her home last

Sunday, was 18 years old, slim and dark complexioned and had a bad scare just above her left knee.—ANNUAL TRIBUNE

MARRIED MEN TAKE NOTE: Married men live longer than bachelors. At the age of 40, for example, the death rate of single men is double that of husbands. And don't revive that crack, "They don't live longer, it just seems longer." The above is based on actual life insurance statistics.

Does this shoe fit in your family: A survey made by a Stanford University psychology professor among 300 married couples shows that the married men were happier than their wives.

When you women grow weary of putting down the term "housewife" on the forms you have to fill out these days, you can give yourself a lift and add some to the general confusion of the times by saying that you're an Oilologist. It's Greek to you and to anybody else, for that matter, for housewife.

The honeymoon is over when he suggests that she pay more attention to the frying pan and less to her own.

PENETRATING THOUGHT: The smile that over a cocktail looks so ethereal may not be so charming over a breakfast cereal.

The man who is much more careful about holding an umbrella over his wife after they're married than before probably does it because he's paying for the clothes.

If you're married to a wife who's a chatterbox or a little on the gabby side, you have a mate afflicted with logorrhea.

Attaboy, Hindus: Custom forbids a Hindu wife ever to utter her husband's name.

Husbands and wives may find peace and happiness in this little hint from a psychologist who says almost any marriage can be successful if both the husband and wife will completely forget just five words. And the five words they must forget are: "The trouble with you is——"

"I'll tell you how it is," remarked the young man as he finished his lager. "I met a young widow with a grown-up daughter and I married that widow. Then my father met our stepdaughter and married her. That made my wife the mother-in-law of her father-in-law and made my stepdaughter my stepmother, while my father became my stepson. Then my stepmother, the daughter of my wife, had a son. That boy was, of course, my brother because he was my father's son, but he also was the son of my wife's daughter and therefore her grandson. That made me grandfather to my stepbrother.

"Then my wife had a son. My mother-in-law, the sister of my son, was also his grandmother. My father-in-law is the brother-in-law of my child because his stepsister is his wife. I am the brother of my own son who is also the child of my stepmother. I am my mother's brother-in-law, my wife is her own child's aunt, my son is my father's nephew and I am my own grandfather and I can't stand it."

Here's one they told at a business luncheon. A client came to one of our lawyer specialists in divorce proceedings with a problem that could be solved in only one way— she needed a husband immediately. A man of action, the attorney got busy. Hurriedly he beckoned a truckster who had done some odd jobs for him. Arrangements were completed, and soon the truckster and the client were duly married. Afterward, the client went home happily protected in her legal rights to an estate. And the husband pro-tem was paid handsomely.

"That's sure an easy way to make dough," he told the lawyer.

"That's right," answered the lawyer, "but don't ever breathe a word about this. If it ever got out, it'd be pretty hot for you."

"Hot!" the truckster exclaimed. "Why, my wife would kill me."

This story is an aftermath of a flood that occurred in a small town in the mid-South. Two elderly people had been driven from their homes. Wet, weary and in a dazed condition, they were wandering the streets in the higher section. A kindly lady in the unaffected part of town spotted them in front of her own home, invited them in and gave them dry clothes, hot food and a place by her fire. . . . Not long after the old couple had eaten, their hostess observed that the old lady, in her comfortable chair close to the stove, was getting drowsy. "Come," said the hostess, "let me put you to bed till morning." The elderly lady agreed and she was trundled off to the spare room. A few minutes later the old gent was in the same drowsy condition and off he was trundled. Next morning, even before the hostess was up, the elderly lady was up and about fixing the fire. "Well," her hostess greeted her, "how did you sleep last night?" "None too well," answered the elderly lady. "That man next to me snored all night long. Who is he, anyway?"

VIVE LA DIFFERENCE

A new difference between husband and wife has been discovered: When a woman is resentful, angry or frightened her stomach turns pale, slows down and produces less acid and stomach juices. A man's stomach behaves exactly the opposite when he is angry, worried or resentful. This, the medicos think, might be why stomach ulcers afflict four times as many men as women. . . .

Sex-division stickler: Why, when a man comes inside from the cold, does he invariably stand with his back to the fire to warm himself while women usually stand facing the fire?

If you husbands are ever casting about for a reason why the Mrs. should get your slippers or perform some other little similar chore, give her this: Listen dear, my blood's thicker than yours, that's why you should wait on me more. And it's a fact. A man has an average of 500,000 more corpuscles per cubic inch than a woman.

Could it be woman's vanity or man's potbelly that makes it? A woman who has drowned always comes up face up, while a man comes up face down.

Strange the varying gestures men and women use to indicate any loss of weight. A woman will invariably stroke her hips with a downward motion, while a man will pull his pants out at the waistline to indicate a loss of girth.

A social worker took a little time off to extract from reports to the state social service department a few gems written, I suppose, unconsciously. Here are a few: "Woman and house are neat but bare." . . . "Couple breaking up home; friend helping." . . . "Until a year ago this applicant delivered ice and was a man of affairs." . . . "These people are extremely cultured and something should be done about their condition." . . . "Man is aggressive; family has nine children." . . . "Roomer pays no board, as he usually acts as 'godfather.'" . . . "Saw woman, she has seven children; husband is a veteran." . . . "Family's savings all used up; relatives have helped." . . . "Woman badly bruised; furniture man took spring. Applicant's wife is a lady and hardly knows what it's all about."

The Junior League girls of Minneapolis a few years back developed a novel gag. They secured a display model figure, dressed her in current fashions and used her as a symbol. She went to all their functions, even had dates, and used the name of Cynthia. The poor wax girl had an experience one week end, though, that put her in a hospital where her kind are patched. She was staying at a prominent architect's home and enjoying it, too. The architect had a house guest, a gentleman. So, for a gag, Cynthia was put in the guest's bed. What happened when the guest made the discovery hasn't been revealed; but poor Cynthia came out of the incident with a broken arm.

Sign on a photographer's window: "Candid Photos of Affairs, Babies and Weddings."

Tests made by a University of Iowa psychologist show that sex isn't always the best advertising lure.

The reason: Male eyes linger so long on a feminine figure or a shapely limb that there's no time left for the advertiser's message.

They've even brought sex into castanets. You know those little ebony oyster-shaped gadgets that Spanish dancers click between their fingers? Well, one's a male, the other's a female. The castanet with the treble tone is the female, the bass-toned one is the male.

Date trees are planted one male to 48 female trees per acre. Nice work if you can get it.

Wisterias won't blossom unless you've got a "boy and a girl" wisteria together.

NEAT TRICK DEPARTMENT

Thomas Bankell, the furniture man, delivered a lovely overstuffed ouch to Miss Alice Donies Monday for her new parlor.—MARTINVILLE TRIBUNE

We're going to have another joyful singspiration. It's generally recognized that sinning is about the best exercise in the world. You'll have a good time after you get there.—FROM A CHURCH BULLETIN

Mr. Jason stated that when he refused to pay the $5 the fortune teller became angry, called down the wrath of the gods and put a nurse on him. The séance then went on.—LEWISTOWN TRIBUNE

Several taxi dance girls told police who responded to the riot call that they thought the prize-fighter was simply pinch-drunk.—SAN FELICE TRIBUNE

Next time your Little Woman starts relating some small incident with 30,000 words, this may halt her: Simply remind her that Abraham Lincoln used only 265 words in his Gettysburg Address.

HINT TO WIVES: Next time your hubby comes home after a few nips and he says he's stone sober, give him this little test: Tell him to face you, stand erect with his arms at his side, close his eyes and then swiftly bring his arm up, hand extended, and touch his nose with his thumb. If he can do it three times in succession, he's got you.

This one comes from a couple of women who were discussing property settlements: "Lawyers, lawyers, lawyers, nothing but lawyers. I've had so much trouble with papers and abstracts and deeds and courts that sometimes I wish my husband hadn't died."

Either the British press is misinformed or else my home state is filled with lawbreakers. Here's a quote from a British publication called, **This Month:**
"In Minnesota it is against the law for men's and women's underwear to hang on the same line."

FAMILIARITY BREEDS

The Roman poet, Cato, asserted that the custom of kissing really came into being in order that husbands might more readily discover if their wives had been tasting wine.

North Carolina demands that there be at least two feet beween twin beds in hotels, and it's illegal to swear into a telephone in North Dakota.

If, with the last pass she made at you, she missed you by a hair's breadth, the actual measurement was 1-48th of an inch.

ALIBI FOR HUSBANDS: Tell the old gal you were merely exercising your brachialis anticus. It's the muscle that bends the elbow, but she'll probably never guess. . . .

Maybe it's older than the hills, but there was a laugh in it for me. Two women were chatting over the back fence. "How do you keep your husband from staying out late?" asked one.

"It's very simple indeed," replied the second. "All I do when he comes in after midnight is shout down to him 'Is that you, Jack?' "

The other woman was puzzled. "But how does that cure him?" she asked.

"That's easy to explain. My husband's name is Charlie."

Life in the smaller communities: The following ad appeared in a southern Minnesota weekly: *Personal*—Lady's purse left in my car while parked. Owner may have same by describing contents of purse and paying for this ad. If owner can explain satisfactorily to my wife how the purse got into my car, I will pay for the ad myself.

Jolt of a Lifetime in Coincidence: They had been keeping company for 11 years. And all through those years the woman had never had the slightest inkling nor suspicion that the man was married. Then one day the woman was taken sick and removed to a hospital. She was placed in a two-bed room with another woman. That night, the gentleman with whom she had been keeping company for 11 years came to the hospital to visit the roommate. It was his wife!

Why men leave home has been the subject of gagging across the nation since the first colonist jumped his home ies. The following are actual reasons taken from some county court records in abandonment cases. The allegations were made by wives whose husbands deserted them: "We had a very happy married life," one wife states, "until last October when my husband won a $50 jackpot on a football game. He left me the day he won it and I haven't seen him since." . . . Another one stipulates, "He ran away with my very best friend. She had a strange power over him. I went to her with tears in my eyes and begged her to let him alone, but she told me that I had had him long enough." . . . "We have always received aid from either the Family

Welfare or Public Relief ever since we were married," another wife complained. "Finally, my husband was offered a position. It was just too much—he left me."

I once collected newspaper clippings detailing the grounds listed by people in petitioning for divorce. From the sheaf let's examine a few to indicate the whimsical shoals that wreck the matrimonial tub. A wife at Grand Rapids, Mich., testified in her divorce suit that her husband was so stingy he used canceled stamps. . . . It took Hollywood to produce a suit where a wife complained that her husband shook his golf sticks at her canary.

In Los Angeles a martyr had the bonds severed because his wife insisted that he accompany her to Angelus Temple to hear Sister Aimee wrestle with the devil. In Chicago a judge dissolved the holy bonds of matrimony after the good wife testified that her husband objected when she slid down the banisters and tried, with considerable cruelty, to break her of that delightful habit. . . . Such are the records in black and white.

Do you really suppose that the divorce rate has anything to do with either canceled stamps, canary birds, evangelists or banisters? Might not the nub of the matter be found in the fact that since time immemorial married couples have become horribly bored, and that when they confront each other in this spiritual Sahara they seize upon any fault or habit of their mate and use it as a rack on which to hang their hatred? Canary birds and banisters are not the cause of incompatibility but merely the ventholes through which the steam of deeper fires explodes.

I can't figure out the case of the Seattle man who was granted a divorce on the grounds that his wife nagged him despite the fact they were both deaf and mute.

This is easier than the Reno routine: In Nepal, a Newar woman can divorce herself at any moment by placing betel nut under her husband's pillow.

Smart, these Chinese: An old penal code in China provided that a man could obtain a divorce if his wife was too talkative or if she had an envious or suspicious temper.

And if a Chinese woman can't get along with her in-laws, it gives her husband one of seven justifying causes for divorce.

THEM WERE THE DAYS: In early tribal times it was considered a serious breach of conduct for a man to see his mother-in-law, talk to her or have any association with her whatever.

You'll have to locate it yourself, but in Zululand you can obtain a divorce for $1.25.

ARE YOU HAPPILY MARRIED?

Ran across a little test that you wives can sit down and give yourselves tonight. It may provide some diversion for you—maybe for the entire family. Better give the test to yourself first and then work on it with the Old Man. The psychologist who whipped up the questions says if you can answer "yes" to eight of the 15 questions and are honestly trying on the others, your husband will be even happier 10 years from today than he is now. Thus you may consider yourself happily married. The test requires intellectual honesty, however, so don't go gypping on your answers. Pencils out, dearies, and you may write in the answers where I leave the dots:

Would your first reaction be, "Of course—I'd be happy with you," if your husband unexpectedly proposed moving to another town or even a foreign country? . . . Do you feel reasonably certain that if your husband got into serious trouble, he would turn first to you? . . . Do you get an instinctive feeling of happiness when you know he's in good spirits and feels fit? . . . Does he frequently discuss his business with you? . . . Do you enjoy talking with him about his business? . . . Does he frequently help you with the dishes or other chores in your department of the home? . . . Do you help him with the gardening, home repair work or other tasks in his department? . . . Do you participate together in any recreational sport? . . . Do most of his friends like you? . . . Do you like most of his friends? . . . Can you remember in some detail what you and he talked about last night? . . . Do you and he gen-

erally enjoy the same entertainment programs? . . . When
he talks to you about something that interests him much
more than it does you, do you really try to listen to what
he's saying rather than daydream about something else?
. . . Do you like your husband's company as much as that
of any girl you know? . . .

There's that self-examination. Count your "yes" answers
and then announce to him, if you dare, whether he's happily married—or not.

Inventory of the domestic side: "Is your marriage slipping?" asks another expert on that sort of thing. Then she
propounds 10 questions, personal ones, for the test. See
how you wives come out; and maybe the husbands had
better check their veracity in the answers.

Do you take him for granted?

*Have you made it easy for your husband to maintain the
chivalrous attitude of your courtship days?*

How are your at-home manners?

Do you enjoy poor health?

What really is your attitude toward your husband?

*Have you cleverly found means of getting along under
difficulties?*

Do you nag and quarrel?

*Publicly, have you built up your husband's self-esteem
and made private criticism tactfully and mercifully?*

Finally, have you lost the light touch?

Ask yourself those 10, answer them sincerely and a wife
can discern, says this expert, the faults in her own character
that may be causing a marriage to slip.

Part Seven

TO SATISFY THE INNER MAN

If you're reading this while eating, according to medical authorities, you're violating a pretty important eating rule. Few persons, say the doctors, can read at the table and enjoy their food at the same time. When you dive into viands without giving their appetizing qualities some attention, you're feeding rather than eating.

Food talk can be a lot of fun, however, and if you want to give it a lively start in some group toss this question at them: If you were allowed to eat but one single item for three days, what would you take?

The problem varies so much from person to person, that the talk will astound you. For a rotund one like me, food of any sort is a problem, and the worst part of the problem is that it's such a pleasure. An innocent little remark by me one evening, just my mentioning that I could down a full quart of ice cream at any time, regardless of what I had just eaten or what I was about to eat, touched off a series of reports on strange dishes and food preferences that I'd like to pass on to you.

Here are some of the reports of actual food combinations that amazed me: Hot pan gravy on chocolate cake; fruit cake and yeast; cream in ginger ale, half and half; Swiss cheese in a sandwich of angel food cake; and gin over cornflakes.

One in the party reported this favorite: A glass of buttermilk, a shot of bitters and an ice cream cone sprinkled generously with salt and pepper and topped with great gobs of mustard. He put the bitters down first, then nibbled on the seasoned cone and wound up with swigs of buttermilk.

I like to hear that kind of talk. It makes good copy, as do many of the world's food customs.

At Eskimo dinners, for instance, guests are expected by etiquette to carry away the left-over food as an indication that they enjoyed the meal. How would you stand up to finishing a meal of some of the foregoing combinations and then being expected to take more of the same home for a bedtime snack?

About all it really proves, I suppose, is that food generally is as fascinating to other people as it is to us eupeptic problem eaters. So we include a food department in this volume. Now it's not necessarily the last word, but it may have some words you never noticed before in cookbooks or other tomes devoted to the eating art. Unlike any other cookbook, this one racks up the foods in alphabetical order, the same simple scheme we used in the Animal chapter. That may seem a mixed-up approach, but what do you expect from a man in the kitchen?

THE APPLE AND ITS DERIVATIVES

Scientists have discovered that a container of charcoal helps keep stored apples fresh longer.

Keep apples away from your fresh-cut flowers. Apples give off ethylene gas that causes flowers, especially carnations, to wilt.

In case you're putting up any apple cider, and want to be sure the stuff does not turn hard, try this: After your cider has stood for 48 hours, add one and a half tablespoons of sodium benzoate to each five-gallon crock. This harmless preservative will keep your cider in perfect condition for six months. Incidentally, the small red Wealthy apples make the best cider.

Quick, what's a rasher of **bacon?** Well, it's three slices, and I'll bet you didn't know.

Sign in the market sector: "100 Per Cent Boneless Bananas" . . .

One reason why you're urged not to put your bananas in your refrigerator is because the fruit is actually 30 per cent water. Almost a drink, isn't it?

B IS FOR BEEF

Whenever there's a choice, always take beef from the right side of the animal. Tests indicate that it's more tender than cuts off the left side, but don't ask me why.

If your beef roasts haven't been as delectable as they might have been lately, try putting several brand-new nails —the four-inch variety—through the roast prior to ovening.

Next time a can of **beets** is opened at your house, save the juice, mix it half and half with pineapple juice for a mighty tasty and refreshing drink.

Back in 1889 **broccoli** was a pretty delectable dish, but they fried it in those days. . . .

Garden laugh: Brussels sprouts have been defined as cabbages with the withholding tax deducted.

Bun comes from the French word "bugne" which means swelling. Raised bread rolls were first called buns by the French.

Butter at a buck a pound isn't so bad, reasons an Iowa farmer who figured it takes 2,500 squirts from a cow to make a pound of butter.

CANDY & CAKE

MAMA'S HELPER: You can help keep the cake in your cakebox fresh by placing a freshly cut apple in the box.

Have you had trouble with your banana cakes? To remove the black spots that usually appear in banana cake, simply eliminate the use of soda in baking.

Has your angel food or sponge cake come out soggy or curdled lately? Take this tip and try baking them with old eggs. The military paper, *Army Times,* reports experiments carried on at the University of California showed that slightly aged eggs, those from two to four weeks old, make flakier cakes than the strictly fresh hen fruit.

And listen, dearies, icings won't run off your cakes if they're sprinkled with a little cornstarch first.

A cake chef I know has a dandy suggestion for holiday fruitcake: To slice your fruitcake, use a sharp, wet knife and a sawlike motion. It avoids breaking down the cake structure and reduces crumbling.

Candy goes back to the time of Alexander the Great when his soldiers brought back a sweet root called "kand" from India. The term candy stemmed from that sweet root.

The terms **cantaloupe** and **muskmelon** are interchangeable, although the name cantaloupe is usually applied to the small muskmelons.

Two carrots **a day will supply all the vitamin A you need, if you like carrots.**

CHEESE & CREAM

If you want to evaluate the sharpness of cheese follow this little table: Mild cheese is from one to two months old; mellow from two to six months; nippy from 6 to 12 months, and sharp anything more than a year old.

Wonder where the term cottage cheese ever originated? . . .

FOR AN EVENING SNACK: Make an ordinary cheese sandwich, dip in egg, milk and salt, and then fry it on both sides as you would French toast. Then pour hot chili sauce or maple syrup over it. Very yummy!

My personal kitchen laboratory hasn't tested it, but the suggestion sounds good enough to pass on: Try adding a small lump of Philadelphia cream cheese to your ordinary cream for vastly improved whipping cream propensities.

Little Things in Life: One of the prettiest sights for my money is cream dissolving in a tall glass of iced coffee.

A survey among our various chicken **parlors reveals this: 90 times out of 100, women ask for breast while men insist on the leg.**

ABOUT COFFEE

Americans annually consume a volume of coffee sufficient to keep Niagara Falls flowing for 67 minutes. The National Dairy Council says adding cream to coffee reduces by 40 per cent the flow of digestive juices caused by the caffeine.

Take a back seat, Norway and Sweden. America now has you licked when it comes to per capita consumption of coffee. We swig coffee to the tune of almost 20 pounds a year per person, while the Scandinavian countries are now way below that.

TAKE A LITTLE CORNY HINT: To keep **corn** fresh and better tasting, remove the husks immediately and wrap the ears in wax paper, then put them in the refrigerator. Husks left on sweet corn absorb a lot of the flavor.

Laugh not at the lowly corncob. Here are a few things cobs have been used for: They clean dismantled parts of airplane engines; they are important in the refining of lubricating oils; jewelers burnish jewelry with them; the cobs' woody portion is ideal for cleaning furs, and the cobs give up fermentable sugars of commercial value.

A **cranberry,** before it reaches the grocery store, has to be, of all things, an athlete. It has to bounce over a barrier before it passes final inspection. A top cranberry picker, by the way, can pick from three to four bushels a day.

Fellow named George Stephenson, inventor of the locomotive, was the first to insert a **cucumber** in a glass cylinder somewhat like a lamp chimney to start the vegetable growing straight instead of all curled up.

A housewife comes forward with a stunt that I've been waiting for for years. Slice your cucumber with a little bit of the skin left on it, and you remove the belch. If it works, it's wonderful.

AGE-OLD MYSTERY SOLVED

Have you ever wondered as you swooped your morning sinker into the coffee just how the hole in a doughnut got there? Well, the honor belongs to a sailor, a Captain Gregory who was in the China trade away back in 1847. And old logbooks prove it. Gregory, tired of the fried cakes or "twisters" his galley slave was turning out only half done in the middle, put his mind to devising a cake that could be fried through and through. He got the idea of cutting a hole in the cakes, thus permitting the hot grease to reach more of the surface. And that's how the hole in the doughnut was born.

From old New Orleans comes this suggestion for cooking doughnuts: Turn them twice on each side instead of just one flip.

Ten per cent of the doughnuts consumed in the United States these days are used as foundations for various kinds of desserts.

PARTING SHOT: A doughnut will supply enough calories for more than an hour of sweeping.

Wonder how **"duck soup"** ever came to be a slang phrase. Can't remember ever having seen it as a food item.

In case you ever do any **egg** packing, be sure to pack them with the large end up. They'll stay fresh longer. Seems that the air cell through which the egg breathes is almost always at the large end. When the egg is packed large end down, the weight of the egg content smothers the egg so it loses quality two or three times faster than when packed the other way.

If you keep your eggs in the refrigerator, you'll do better by placing them in the coldest spot in the box, and that's right under the ice-cube trays, as a rule.

But keep your eggs away from both lemons and onions. They'll absorb those odors.

If you want a job that's fairly safe from replacement by machine, get yourself lined up as an "egg breaker." So far, only the human nose and eye have been able to detect off-quality eggs, and the experts say it will probably always be that way.

Good thing we never went for ostrich eggs for breakfast or we'd have to get up a lot earlier. It takes about 40 minutes to hard boil an ostrich egg. . . .

RED ONES DON'T COUNT

Bet you didn't know that the world's most hunted fish is the herring. It's the most important food fish to man and probably the fish with the most natural enemies.

We're all engaging in ichthyophagy, I hope. It's the practice of eating fish. It's pronounced **"ick-thee-off-a-jee."**

You'll never in the world remember it, but it's something you should know: What produces that fishy odor in fish is the lactic acid in the fish muscles combining with trimethylamine oxide and water to result in acetic acid. Now are you happy?

IT SMELLS

A NOTE OR TWO ON GARLIC: Larger hotels use from three to five pounds of the stuff a day, and the United States gets rid of around 20,000,000 pounds a year, or 666 freight cars. About 75 per cent of the domestic garlic is grown in California. Garlic began growing on the plains of Siberia thousands of years ago and used to be offered to the gods on their feast days. When it was transplanted over here, cows used to eat it, but that made the milk taste of garlic and the settlers got pretty sore. Even if a cow just sniffs garlic, the milk may be tainted. Garlic helps the voice, is fine for worming pups and is considered a specific for insomnia, high blood pressure, acne, eczema and asthma. Best way to get the smell off of your hands is to wash them in cold water right after you've handled garlic. . . .

Scientists also hang a high vitamin content on garlic, and the stuff is now obtainable in capsule form which offers all the advantages without the breathy quality.

Garlic, alcohol and coffee are three common foods which produce perspiration of a special and particular odor.

Whoever it was that said everything in life you like to do is either fattening, illegal or immoral, forgot a category that would include garlic and onions. My, how those little green ones stay with you.

After you have your half a grapefruit in front of you, scoop out one wedge and fill that section with maple syrup. The sprup penetrates the rest of the fruit and adds a very satisfying flavor.

Please pass the grass: A scientist of the National Farm Chemurgic Council has evolved a grass pill that contains the proteins of grass, alfalfa and other green plants. It supposedly combats overweight, hardening of the arteries and other ills of advancing years. Maybe that guy Nebuchadnezzar wasn't so nuts when he started chewing up his front lawn.

Strange origins: The **hamburger** goes back to 780 A.D., when Italian physicians prescribed chopped beef, fried with onions, as a cure for colds and coughs.

I suppose you've heard about the college lad who got a part-time job in the meat market. At closing time the proprietor told the youth to be sure to hang up all the meat before going home. The next morning the butcher returned to find the lad still working haggardly. "I got the meat hung up fine," he explained, "until I came to this pesky hamburger."

From a bee raiser comes the suggestion that after a day's work or when body fatigue sets in, a tablespoon of **honey** will restore your pep. It's a great energy-giving food and revitalizes you almost instantly.

Horse-radish used to be called "harsh radish" (which it is) and the present name is an outgrowth. . . .

MANY PREFER VANILLA

Records show that ice cream has, since its invention, come in as many as 150 different flavors, including sweet potato and cantaloupe.

America is the only country in the world where you can get good ice cream sodas.

For the calorie-conscious: Two scoops of ice cream will give you enough energy for an hour of wood sawing.

I got a laugh from the gag about the hillbilly who came out of the mountains into the village for one of his rare visits and bought an ice cream cone. He went outside and ate the ice cream and then returned to the store, handed the cone to the clerk and said, "Thanks for the use of the vase."

Here's a little trick for better **ice cubes.** To eliminate the "smoke" they leave in a glass of water, simply rinse the cubes in warm water for an instant before dropping them into the glass. This takes the frost off and it's the frost that causes the "smoke."

Try this on your next leg of lamb. Place the leg topside up on the table and you'll note a fatty tendon which describes a "y" leading upward along the outside of the leg. Right at the intersection, make an incision, then run your finger down into the flesh at this point. You'll find a hard globule of fat. Draw it out and sever it. It's an oil gland which, when removed, will make your lamb much more enjoyable. Few cooks, even butchers, says our informant, know of the "oiler."

To improve the flavor of lamb, rub it before cooking with a mixture of salt, black pepper, garlic and marjoram.

For years I've wondered what that green stuff down the middle of a **lobster** was and whether it was edible. Recently I found out that it's perfectly okay to eat it. I'm glad that's settled.

Menus to the contrary, there's no such thing as broiled live lobster. Death comes to the lobster when it's split down the middle just prior to the heat treatment.

A FEW SQUIRTS

Farmington, Minnesota, a small community which celebrates an annual Milk day, has collected at least a gallon of information, some of which may be new to you, about milk. Have a few squirts:

The average American consumes 200 quarts of fresh milk and cream a year, compared with 160 quarts he used 10 years ago. United States cows give enough milk every year to fill a river 3,000 miles long, 40 feet wide and 3 feet deep. Milk produces more than 10 per cent of all cash income on farms—in most years, topping wheat, eggs, cotton and tobacco. A quart of milk, in case you've forgotten, has 675 calories in it. The cow has been domesticated for at least 6,000 years. Average individual uses about 20 pounds of butter a year.

Hope you haven't been leaving your morning's milk on the back stoop during the sunshine hours. Scientists reveal that a bottle of milk loses at least 40 per cent of its riboflavin content (whatever that is) if exposed to an hour of morning sunshine.

Of all kinds of milk tested, reindeer milk has been found to be the richest. Which is probably why Santa Claus is fat.

No wonder we say, "Slower than **molasses** in January." A cupful of spilled molasses requires three minutes and 41 seconds to travel a foot, compared with four seconds for milk, water or kerosene.

LINES TO AN ONION

A professional onion eater was booked once to appear in a movie short demonstrating how he ate as many as two dozen bulbs a day, with a little salt.

> *Oh, Onion, dear, how succulent thou art,*
> *How needful to the gastronomic art,*
> *Thy luscious taste!*
> *Thou dost with charm a tender steak imbue*
> *And lacking thee, a tempting Irish stew*
> *Is desert waste.*
>
> *But, Onion, dear, thou hast a fault—just one;*
> *Thy fragrancy doth linger on my tongue*
> *And breath o'erlong.*
> *So, after eating thee I dare not be*
> *In any sort of highbrow company,*
> *For thou art strong.*
>
> *They shun me if they get a whiff of thee,*
> *As if I were a leper do they flee*
> *From me pellmell.*
> *Though life without thee seems a dismal blank*
> *Yet we must part. Thou hast thyself to thank.*
> *Onion, farewell.*

A city ordinance in Waterloo, Nebraska, prohibits the barbers of that town from eating onions between 7 a.m. and 7 p.m. on working days.

The orange used to be a pear-shaped fruit about the size of a cherry.

This is a prominent hotel proprietor's very delightful orange-base breakfast drink, practically a full meal in itself. Take a full tumbler of orange juice, a jigger of fresh pineapple juice and a jigger of fresh lemon juice. Add one fresh egg. Beat the entire mixture to a creamy, golden froth in a mixer and serve. The creator calls it a "Sunny Smile," and the potion is well named.

From the Rio Grande Valley comes this culinary suggestion: Use orange or other citrus juice on your dry breakfast cereal instead of milk or cream, and add a little sugar. It's delicious to many.

AW, SHUCKS

In case you're the kind of optimist who goes into a café or restaurant broke and orders oysters hoping to pay for the meal with the pearl you find, here's a tip: The oysters which are most likely to contain pearls are those with shells that are irregular in shape, stunted, honeycombed by boring parasites or covered with abnormal growths.

A true New Englander never washes his oysters—he says it washes away their tangy flavor.

Make mine on rye, Charlie: Connoisseurs who have tasted it say the flesh of **panthers** has a rich and delicate flavor surpassed by few meats.

Don't be a lug. Eat the **parsley** with which your hostess has so carefully garnished the meat. It's very heavy in vitamin A.

Did you know that it's against the law to make a **pastry** reproduction of the White House?

Exactly 413 years ago, **peacock** instead of turkey was the popular yuletide dish in Europe.

It's an easy matter to hate the **peanut,** especially when somebody behind you in a movie is cracking shells and crunching throughout the show. Nevertheless, we have many reasons to love the peanut. Its oil lubricates tractors and watches, and its hulls are now used as a substitute for cork in the caps of beverage bottles.

SANDWICH SUGGESTION: Make a spread of **peanut butter** and whipped cream—half and half.

DON'T CONFUSE WITH PEASANTS

Had trouble with your pheasants being a little dry? Here's a suggestion for you. Before you roast the bird, rub it with olive oil mixed with salt and paprika, then wrap the bird in a towel for an hour or so while the oil soaks in. Before roasting, lay a thin strip of salt pork across the breast, too. Another added touch is this: Place an onion and some celery in the bottom of the roasting pan; after roasting starts add a pint of cream poured over the bird, baste with that sauce occasionally and then use it as gravy for your wild rice.

After you've tired of pheasant in the ordinary methods of preparation, you might give this man's recipe a fling, called "Breast of Pheasant Meat Balls." Grind up the meat of the breast, mix it with egg, milk, cracker crumbs and seasoning to taste and then fry the balls or broil them. Understand, too, that the meat doesn't have to be cooked beforehand. Treat the pheasant breast as though it were sirloin or hamburger. Saves all the work of baking the bird and adds new relish to at least one fowl serving.

Mother's Little Helper has an item for you if fresh **pineapple** is available. Once you have your fresh pineapple (the kind that has a stalk sticking out the top) cut it about an inch below that stalk and then bury the lower portion of the slice and some of the stalk in dirt in a flowerpot just as though you were planting any other kind of plant. In a matter of weeks, you'll have a plant that's a foot or two across. In a matter of more months, if you've turned out to be a good gardener, you'll have some pineapples, but they won't be too good to eat, so don't plan on going into the pineapple business.

At last I've learned why butchers leave the tail of the **pig** on after the animal has been butchered. It serves as a handle in lifting. Why couldn't I have figured that out myself instead of having to be told by a meat man?

Pork lovers should thrill to this: Among gags to make pork sweet and tender is a corset for pigs. The foundation garment, according to its inventor, allows the flavor of food and fat to permeate the meat more thoroughly.

TRY THIS PORK DELIGHT IN YOUR CASSEROLE: A layer of wild rice, a layer of pork chops, another layer of wild rice, cover with thick slices of Spanish onion, top with a layer of wild rice and cook her up. Season the chops pretty highly.

50,000,000 FRENCHMEN LIKE 'EM FRIED

Ask your wife how many ways she knows of cooking potatoes. If she can name more than eight she's better than average, and yet her recipe book probably lists at least 100 ways.

If you want to get the most food value out of those valuable potatoes, don't mash them. Even after as short a time as 10 minutes, hot mashed potatoes lose one-third of their vitamin-C content. At the end of 30 minutes 90 per cent is lost.

It's also the vitamin-C content you save when you boil your spuds with their jackets on. Peeling and then boiling the Murphys is the most destructive form of cooking them from a vitamin preservation standpoint.

Copy this for your recipe box: Next time you want to decide whether a spud is too mealy to bake, try a little launching party. Specific gravity does the trick. Put your spud in a bath of salt water. The mealy potatoes will not float to the surface. Those that do will be fit for baking and turn out the way you like them.

For frying potatoes, oysters or anything in deep fat, it's

best to have two kettles of fat and switch the stuff periodically.

Would you ever guess that more than 150,000,000 pounds of potato chips are consumed in this country annually? And think of the crunching involved in that bulk.

Heard of a farmer whose seed potato plants were set next to a field of tomatoes and popped forth with potatoes at the roots and tomatoes above the ground. Just another evidence, I suppose, of the postwar breakdown of morals.

Pretzels, says a brewery executive who's made a study of them, date back to the time of the Caesars. I can see Julius munching on one right now.

If you're a borderline **prune** lover (I mean if prunes are just so much prunes to you), add to them a stick of cinnamon and a slice or two of lemon. It jumps them into the yum-yum class immediately.

Big laugh for me came from the story of the workman who sat down to eat his noonday meal and started unwrapping a parcel about 20 inches long.

"What in the world is that?" asked one of his fellow workmen.

"Well," explained the man, "my wife's away and I made a pie for myself."

"A bit long, isn't it?" inquired the other.

"Sure it's long," the man countered, "it's rhubarb."

Your salt intake should be increased in hot weather, as you know. One good way to up the quantity is to add salt to your orange juice. What a fine job it does for both the salt and the orange juice.

BY PRESCRIPTION

"Sauerkraut is rich in vitamins." So says a magazine advertisement.

Now that is more like it; the sauerkraut concocters
Have picked the right road to success and to wealth;
They have lined up their trade on the side of the doctors
And they dish out their stuff in the interest of health.

Sour cabbage as food is a scourge and a blight—
But to list it as medicine—maybe they're right.

To mention its taste would be clearly an error,
And no one, of course, would refer to the smell;
But the notion of sickness fills people with terror—
And what they won't eat in their zeal to stay well!

For wan hypochondriacs sauerkraut is brewed,
But down with the varlets who use it for food!

About 70,000 tons of sauerkraut are canned each year in the United States. Think of the burps in that tonnage.
Men working in sauerkraut factories wear rubber boots.

Any Latin student can tell you that the word **sausage** which we use today is derived from the Latin "salsus," meaning salted or preserved meat.

Next time you're serving canapés and are stuck for something to stick the **shrimp** in, remember this idea: Hew out a red cabbage, making a hole in the top that will hold about a cupful of dressing, and then stick toothpicks with the shrimp into the cabbage. Makes a very colorful addition to any canapé tray. Or have you been doing it all your life?

Spaghetti was invented in 1831 by an Italian named Prati.

If your tots rebel at **spinach,** you can hand them such dandies as dried lima beans, liver, oysters, or an egg yolk. All of those things have three times as much iron content as the overpraised greens.
Cream your spinach and add a hearty pinch of nutmeg. The kids'll go for that combination.
Or just a dash or two of chives to the spinach will make junior gobble up the iron food.

Next time you sink your knife into a porterhouse **steak,** think of this: The steak was named from the many porter houses of Colonial times. Porter was a heavy malt brew featured along with a meat dish of a toothsome steak.

Next time you feel the need of quick energy food, try this old favorite of athletes. It's a tartar steak. But don't let the chef give you ordinary hamburger. Be sure he grinds up a small steak, pour the yolk of an egg over it, top that with a Bermuda onion slice and eat the whole thing raw. It's non-fattening, too, if that helps any.

To serve strawberries at their best, first dip them in scalding water, then plunge them quickly into icy water, then add a touch of lemon juice to cancel the berries' acidity and to add a certain tartness.

Mucilage used on postage stamps is made from **sweet potato** starch. No wonder it's yummy.

Cooks will have to check this one, but I've been told that a teaspoonful of tapioca (cooked) will keep any soufflé from falling. . . .

Haven't had any **French toast** for a long time. Wonder if the French actually originated it? Or if Turks ever take a Turkish bath?

If you get into an argument on whether a **tomato** is a fruit or a vegetable, stick to the vegetable side and you'll have the United States Supreme Court with you. They arrived at the decision on it back in 1893.

Add a tablespoon of vinegar to the water in which you boil a fowl and it'll make the bird far more tender.

Ah, a recipe for **turkey dressing** sent out by the University of Minnesota farm and okayed by the Duchess of Windsor, so it must be good. Most dressing comes out a soggy mass and lies like brick in your stomach. Not this. It's light as air and a child can make it. Take enough day-old bread and cut off the crusts. With a fairly coarse grater, crumble the bread finely into a dishpan. It takes about three loaves for a 15-pound bird. Chop a good-sized Bermuda onion into fine particles, not hunks, and stir this in evenly. Add powdered sage and a little salt. Melt up a pound of butter and have your helper stir this in as you pour, and then spoon or pour the dressing into the bird but don't pack it in. Sew up the incision and it's ready for roasting.

They tell this about a woman who hired a country girl for a maid. About the first thing she cooked was a **turkey.** The housewife had to be away during the cooking of the turkey, so she left complete instructions. Among them was this, "Be sure to take the bird out of the oven and baste it every 20 minutes." Well, the bird came out beautifully. Later the maid left for another job and it wasn't until a year later that the two saw each other. Then came the confession. "Remember that turkey I cooked?" the maid said. "Believe it or not, every 20 minutes I took it out of the oven, removed the old thread and put new back in. But I know now what you meant by basting it."

Next time you have **waffles,** add about a teaspoon of lemon juice to the batter.

Would you believe that each person in a family uses 40 gallons of water daily? That a cow will take 25 gallons; a steer or a horse 12 gallons; a hog 2 gallons; a sheep 1½ gallons, and each 100 hens 5 gallons daily? The figures vary in hot and cold seasons, but only a little. Check these statistics with your guess on the subject. It takes 1½ gallons to fill the average lavatory bowl; 6 gallons to flush the toilet;

7 to 15 gallons to service each faucet in the kitchen sink, and 30 gallons to fill the average bathtub. Important, isn't it, water?

This is supposed to be an infallible method of telling whether a **watermelon** is ripe. Place atop the melon an ordinary broom straw. Adjust the straw so that it balances on the melon in a crosswise position. If the straw twists, the melon is ripe, according to the belief.

And for eating watermelon it's been suggested that the thing to do is trim off the rind and then eat from the outside toward the middle, thus leaving the most juicy part till last.

That bottle of Sir William **Worcestershire** sauce in your pantry really has a little romance behind it. The sauce originally was used freely by the ancient Phoenicians and also the early Romans as a self-starter following a tough night. The Worcester tag was given it after it reached England. Incidentally, the sauce represents the cooking, blending and steeping of more than 100 separate ingredients.

AFTER DINNER

One of the world's most universal excuses for drinking, I'll wager, centers around the idea of washing down a heavy meal. It's every man to his own tastes, I say, but take a few notes that I don't think you'll find in the average bartender's manual:

You have to hand it to the primitives for a literary style. In a certain part of Africa the tribesmen make their **beer** out of honey, and here's what they say about it: "One who drinks beer made from honey may sleep on the ground all the next day and say nothing." Which is pretty prose for passing out.

Gin was first distilled in Geneva, and the name of the liquor is a contraction of the name of that Swiss city.

In case you're a **sherry** wine addict, you might as well know the origin of the term. The English corrupted Jerez de la Frontera, the town that forms the center of the sherry-producing district of Spain, to "sherry."

Any gourmet will tell you that **wine** doesn't go well with eggs or salads and here's why: Eggs contain sulphur which dulls the sense of taste; and salads, as a rule, contain vinegar, the traditional enemy of all wine.

Bourbon whisky has been made from popcorn in areas where corn was short. Probably not safe to sit near an open fire after a couple snorts of that.

Whisky, rather curiously, played an important part in the abolishment of capital punishment in my home state of Minnesota. In the governor's office I once examined the entire 1905 transcript in the case of William Williams, last man to be hanged in Minnesota.

Williams had been convicted of a first-degree murder charge and was sentenced to hang in Ramsey County. The sheriff of Ramsey County at the time decided to make the execution quite an affair and set about immediately to invite 50 of his intimate friends to the hanging. Prior to the execution, the guests staged a drinking bout, appeared at the hanging a little more than half stiff. The crowd gathered on the hanging platform with the result that the structure sagged. When Williams' body was suspended from the noose, the sagging floor caused slow strangulation instead of the customary quick hanging. In fact, it was necessary for the sheriff to pull the body back up and start the actual hanging a second time. Gov. Johnson heard about the orgy, the error, the spirit of the occasion, and at once set in motion the legal steps that subsequently did away with capital punishment in the state.

STARTLING STATISTIC: **Milk** as a mix for a highball is in many cases cheaper than charged water.

Origins: Drinking a toast goes back to a custom in vogue in old water-front taverns. It was common practice to put pieces of sugared toast in the bottoms of tankards of hot toddy, hot grog, mulled wine and other drinks favored by seamen. The sugared toast made a toothsome morsel, hence the expression.

BACCHANALIAN AFTERMATH

When you munch on a clove to keep the Little Woman from knowing that you snatched a quick guzzle on the way home, you're really chewing the undeveloped, dried flower of an evergreen tree which grows in the Dutch East Indies.

A good-sized dish of cottage cheese, says a drinking pal, will tame a morning-after stomach and kill what little edge you might have left.

If you want to avoid that "Aw, lemme alone" feeling the next morning, drink a cheery toast out of this and your mood will change completely: Two well-beaten eggs in a glass of tomato and grapefruit juice.

Another hang-over remedy is celery tonic and tomato juice—half and half.

Part Eight

MOTHER'S LITTLE HELPER

Don't you sometimes long for the simple life of your early married years when all was happiness with a parlor, bedroom and sink existence? Maybe it was just the continuation of the honeymoon, but that seems to be about as nearly perfect a living pattern as I can imagine. Wonder what it is, then, that makes so many of us drive all the time for a bigger or fancier house, a bigger mortgage, bigger headaches in taking upon ourselves increasing tasks of keeping a household running smoothly? It must be more than just the matter of raising a family. Three-fourths of the world manages to live and grow with a minimum of space per family.

No matter how stately one's mansion, however, the business of living is pretty much centered, you'll have to admit, in parlor, bedroom and sink. There you have the real essentials, even though the parlor has undergone transformations and is combined with the bedroom in some of our efficiency units or becomes inseparable from the sink (kitchen) in others.

In a way the problems of the household, no matter how big and complicated they eventually become, are just an extension of the little difficulties in the parlor, bedroom and sink. Change a fuse or electrical fitting without getting the shock of your life. Fix a dripping faucet without flooding the kitchen. Stop the squeak in a hinge without splitting the door. Taking care of those things seemed like a pretty good accomplishment for the young homemaker, male and/or female. But pretty soon the challenge wasn't there. It took a bigger house, a yard, a furnace and countless gadgets to preserve the good old state of *status quo*. And the *status quo* for householders is probably universal—a little behind on the mortgage or rent, a little behind on things you intend to fix and a little behind the eight ball.

So Mama's Little Helper is including a whole chapter of household hints and assorted words to the wives that should help keep the honeymoon glow in your physical surroundings. The Old Man can read these, too, because he'll end up doing most of the chores anyway, or paying to have the Little Woman's whims done and undone. There are plenty of pitfalls and short cuts in living to go around for the whole family, anyhow. In fact, you've probably had some pretty hot arguments right in your own home about whose job is the hardest, the husband's or the wife's. The issue is as old as the hills and at times as bumpy. The husband's attack usually sounds something like this: "You can stay in bed every morning or nap when you feel like it. You can dress easy and don't have any boss prodding you. Your afternoons are pretty free if you want them. You can postpone chores. You've got a cinch, if you only knew it." Then wifie sings back with a tune built around this theme: "Compare a pan of dirty dishwater or a stack of soiled clothes or digging out filthy corners or ironing all day with your schedule. You work in a nice clean office. You meet different people. You lunch with your pals. Your days vary." And so on into the days and nights, the months and years.

Well, I once raised that argument with a remark in my column and for the first time heard from a woman who admitted beautifully that there are compensations in the life of a wife. Here's what she said:

"What reimbursement does a housewife get?" Under my breath I wanted to answer 'none.' That's how I've felt at times. Work, work, work—all day long. Kids under your feet. Cracker crumbs, toys all over, a tricycle making its dizzy rounds. I don't know what it's like to fix a meal without interruptions. Two chubby hands toying with the gas stove. A toddler making a pool of cream on a clean tablecloth. Pudding tossed at walls. . . .

"What reimbursement, you ask? You can't measure it in dollars and cents. Part of the reimbursement comes when Friend Hubby gets up from the table, gives you a kiss and says, 'Darling, that was a wonderful dinner.' Some more reimbursement comes when you see little cheeks filling out, little legs growing sturdier. Yes, more reimbursement is yours when you tuck the little shavers into their beds with a teddy bear clutched by their side. Then you feel the clasp of their arms around your neck and the good-night kiss on your cheek. The final reimbursement comes when you breathe a prayer for them and, as you tiptoe out, you hear a child voice cry, 'Mommy, you forgot to say God bless you.'

"Indeed, I'm beginning to feel that housewives and mothers are pretty well paid."

Husbands, I suggest all of you copy that and save it, it's part of your compensation, too, and will halt many spats. But don't let those poetic thoughts sidetrack you from the endless things you have to do to keep life rolling smoothly around the old parlor, bedroom and sink.

PRESSING MATTERS

The arguments could go on endlessly about whose work is most important in the house, but let's give the Little Woman her due for what she does. Especially since she gets quite a high score from some pretty substantial scientific observations of her daily effort. There's really quite a compliment, for instance, in this seeming complaint from a Purdue University prof who teaches time and motion studies. He says the women are wasting too much time and making too much extra work for themselves.

There's no reason, says the prof, why all women shouldn't be seated while washing dishes or ironing. He also points out that a woman uses the vacuum cleaner, then goes over the same territory again with the dusting cloth. If she wore a Dust Mitt, she could vacuum and dust on the same household tour. The prof really goes at you, girls, about the way you handle the washing and ironing. First, he notes, you wash the clothes, then hang them out to dry, bring them in, dampen them again, roll them up, unroll them, and finally iron them. Why not, he suggests, just watch your line and bring the stuff in while it's still damp enough for ironing?

Before you rise up in righteous indignation, girls, remem-

ber that those views are not mine—they're an expert's who studies such matters with the cold eye of science.

Another statistician has figured out that a housewife's arm travels approximately 6½ miles while ironing a normal week's wash and that in ironing seven shirts she lifts a 3½-pound iron for a total of 490 pounds.

Are we men or are we mites? One of our sex points out that a bricklayer in an eight-hour day lays from 400 to 500 bricks and each brick weighs six pounds. But a woman lifts a 3½- or 4-pound flatiron more than 1,000 times during an average weekly ironing, and she does it in four hours instead of eight. In other words, the woman ironing lifts at least a ton and a half in half the time that a bricklayer does.

PITY THE WIVES OF PHYSICIANS AND SURGEONS: They have to be as particular about ironing their husband's shirt-tails as they are about any other part of the shirt. It's due to the fact that the medicos remove their shirts in hospitals before operating. The shirt hangs exposed to the view of nurses and attendants, and no surgeon wants to admit ownership of a wrinkled shirttail.

For best results in pressing the old gent's neckties, cut a piece of cardboard that'll slip inside the tie and put it there before you iron over the damp cloth.

WISDOM FOR WASHDAY

Some of this may be old stuff, but here's what the experts advise for washing silk stockings: First, plenty of frothy suds and lukewarm water of an even temperature for both washing and rinsing. Turn the hose inside out before washing and do as little handling as possible. If the stockings have stubborn mud spots on the ankles, plunge them into another batch of suds but avoid rubbing. Rinse at least three times in lukewarm water and squeeze out as much water as possible by rolling them in a Turkish towel. Never hang stockings in bright sunlight or over a radiator. It's best to place them on a towel to dry after stretching gently lengthwise and smoothing out the feet. It you use a wash line or a rack for drying hose, always hang them by the toes.

The Minnesota Writers' Project of WPA days dug up this little household silk-washing hint from an early newspaper: "To clean silk—a quarter of a pound of soft soap, one ounce of honey, one pint of gin. Put on with a flannel or a nail brush and afterwards brush with cold water, then dip in cold water five or six times and hang out to drain and then iron wet on the wrong side with a hot iron." Gin must have been cheaper in those days.

Now the dear old department of agriculture comes up with a suggestion for adding wear to your hosiery. (Those guys get around for a department like that, don't they?) Rub a piece of candle wax or paraffin on the heels and toes of stockings before each wearing and it makes them last four times as long before holes appear. Laboratory tests show a thin film of wax does the trick and doesn't interfere with appearance or laundering qualities.

PASTE THIS INFORMATION ON YOUR LAUNDRY WALL: Wet laundry on the line will not freeze in winter if a handful of salt is used in the rinse water.

Before washing any garment with a zipper, close the latter and take care in pressing the garment that the zip's teeth aren't knocked out of alignment.

While we're on the subject, here's the origin of Monday as wash day: When the Pilgrims had anchored in Provincetown Harbor, Monday was the first day they were able to go ashore for laundry work, and that day was kept as wash day thereafter.

If it's grease you get on your gabardine, try rubbing a little ordinary school chalk on the spots, let it remain there for an hour and then dust off the chalk. The grease often goes with it.

And when it comes to washing windows on our cars or houses, I wonder why more of us don't adopt the trick used at many small-town filling stations, where they clean bug-spattered windshields with a corncob. A cob lasts a long time and functions far more efficiently than some of the scrapers or cleaners.

Watch your chimney.—If there's black smoke belching out it means that fuel's being wasted, and that can be more costly than spoiling a line of fresh wash.

Before coal is delivered, be sure there's no foreign matter in your coal bin—no oily rags, waste paper, old overalls or other discarded matter. Your coal delivery man will be very glad to check it for you. Most of them do it as a matter of safety, anyway, so if the driver-salesman asks to look over your basement, don't think he's an old snoop. He's trying to give you some necessary protection against fire.

TIP TO PROSPECTIVE BUILDERS (this came from a lock man who should know): Put three hinges on every door in your home and you'll save money. The middle hinge upholds the lock area and prevents sagging.

There may be some special architectural reasoning behind it, but I can't figure out why keyholes weren't always put on top instead of beneath the doorknob.

A cork of the proper size inserted under a door makes a perfect and inconspicuous "keeper-opener."

If your house has windows that rattle, there's nothing better than breaking one of the prongs off a wooden clothespin and using it as a wedge between the window and the casing.

Handy with a paintbrush? Slap a coat or two of colored paint on your garbage cans. You'll be amazed at what it does for your premises. And if you're really skilful, add a little floral pattern or some kind of design. Makes taking out the garbage half the chore.

Keep the oil off the floor of your garage if you want to get the maximum mileage out of your tires.

To de-skunk your car, in case you meet one of the smelly little rascals, try this: Most of the skunk's oil sticks to the wheels and under the fenders of a car, so after you've hit the animal drive on a gravel road for about half an hour. The dirt shot up under the car will carry a lot of the skunk oil off with it.

A woman once told me she sticks her knitting needles into a pencil sharpener when the ends get dull, and a few gentle turns repoint them beautifully.

You may not be trying it today, but the next time the occasion presents itself, remember this—you can drive a nail into a plastered wall without crumbling the plaster for a square yard around the nail hole if the nail is dipped in hot water for a few minutes or into some melted paraffin before it's used.

A postman advises that on rainy days or nights if you address your letters in pencil you'll get less smear. Rain on ink-addressed letters often is responsible for getting them to the dead letter office.

COME INTO MY PARLOR

If you ever have to junk an automobile, be sure to save the headlights. Two of them installed above a ping-pong table in an amusement room provide excellent light for the game.

Amusement room dampness or basement mildew, incidentally, can be cut down a lot by placing an electric fan in your basement and letting it run for 24 hours.

You know what happens when you hang a picture and then maybe two or three months later move it to another spot. A dust line indicates exactly where the picture had been in the first place. To eliminate that dust line, insert a thumbtack on the reverse side of your picture at the bottom of the frame. Let the thumbtack protrude just enough to keep the picture frame away from the wall and you're all set.

PARTY LINES

To prove that hostesses never listen to excuses given by late-arriving guests, a psychology prof went to a dinner party and apologized with, "Sorry to be late, but it took me longer than I expected to strangle my uncle." "Yes, indeed," replied the hostess. "So nice of you to come."

Getting a permanent wave before some special occasion? Well, save those little gadgets the beauty operator puts on the ends of the curls (they have that silver paper covering) and toss one or two into your fireplace. They create brilliant rainbow color effects in the fire that add a truly festive note.

And instead of incense for your next party, sprinkle a drop or two of your favorite perfume on a heated electric light bulb—one that will be lighted throughout the evening. M-m-m-m.

The smell of onions on your breath is actually given off by the lungs, if that'll do you any good as a social alibi.

To cut down the entertainment overhead, supply each party guest with a rubber band, the ordinary office type. Let the guest hold his right hand out, palm down. Loop the binder over the little finger, pull the band over the back of his hand and then loop the other end around his thumb. The band should be well below the knuckles. The gag is to remove the band without using the other hand. Get a group of people so engaged and you're set for the evening.

If I were asked to voice one complaint against the average hostess I'd say it was her failure to provide adequate ash trays—dinky little things that fill up or spill, and not enough of them.

And while on the subject of social protest, I think the average home movies should never be exhibited to anyone but members of the immediate family. To me they've always seemed like sure killers for the fun spirit of any party.

Unpopularity trick to scare the daylights out of your hostess. Puff hard on a cigaret to be sure it's glowing, then press the lighted end smack against her linen tablecloth. But be sure you have a coin underneath the cloth at the point where the cigaret touches. It'll work on everything but velvet and never leave so much as a smudge.

MAMA'S HELPER: Roses are gathered better late than early. Late afternoon is the best time to cut roses if you want them to keep longer.

To keep those cut posies strictly fresh, if you want to go to the bother, try tying a small rubber balloon filled with water at the end of each stem.

Don't blame me if your petunia won't take it. I'm mentioning this merely as an experiment that has worked, but before you try it, consult your florist or your greenhouse expert. A gardener put an infinitesimal portion of vitamin B-1 powder in water with which he sprinkled a dying plant. In a month the plant had not only snapped back to life but had sprouted two new branches. The recipe: Enough Vitamin B-1 powder to cover the head of a pin for each 25 gallons of water. Sprinkle on the soil once a week for outdoor plants and once in two weeks for indoor plants.

And don't throw away the water used to rinse your milk bottles. Put it on your house plants. It'll help them grow and keep them healthy.

Let the man of your house dump all the cigar ashes he wants to on your plants. The ash contains lime, potash, small quantities of phosphorus, manganese and magnesium —all good plant foods.

ANOTHER SUGGESTION FOR BETTER HOUSE PLANTS: Leave a slice of bread in your electric toaster until the piece is burned to a crisp. Then pulverize it and sprinkle the black ash over your potted plants. The burned bread makes a form of charcoal and really zooms the growth and condition of the green things.

For an added decorative touch drop a grapefruit seed or two in your potted plants. They'll sprout and furnish a neat little bunch of foliage around the base of the plant.

Housekeepers, this is for you: After you've sat around all afternoon playing bridge and smoking, or if the old gent has had a group of poker players doing the same thing the night before and you want to rid your premises of the stale smoke odor rapidly, simply place a soup bowl or two filled with vinegar on the floor, and presto, the old odors leave like mad.

But be sure to take the bowl out at night. The fumes will raise heck with your plants.

You won't look pretty doing it, but here's another method of ridding a room of cigaret smoke: Walk through the room and wave a wet dish towel through the smoke. The stuff collects or does something, and three or four swipes of the towel will make your room fresh as a daisy.

Next time you find the coffee tables, window sills or even your piano sticky from the night-before party, try squirting a little of that leftover charged water on the sticky areas and then wiping them with a dry cloth. There's something about carbonated water that does a miraculous cleaning job.

Oil of peppermint rubbed on those white rings on tables or other furniture also will remove the spots.

If you didn't know it all along, scratches on your walnut or fumed oak can be covered with a touch of iodine.

BED SORE-POINT

Why is a sheet so thin and cold
When Autumn is our portion?
Why doth it chill our shrinking feet
And drive us to contortion

> To keep our forms from freezing stiff
>   Congealing in the middle,
> And yet, when Summer comes along,
>   Is hotter than a griddle?
> How can a sheet at one time be
>   So white and light and wispy
> And other times be thick enough
>   To cook us till we're crispy?
>
> What is it makes the same thin thing
>   Enact with such persistence
> A dual role, a two-faced life,
>   A Jekyll-Hyde existence?
> Oh, drat the flat contrary things,
>   They have no sense of fitness.
> As victims of their fickleness
>   May absolutely witness.
> It's time somebody took the things
>   And made their habits vary
> So sheets, in June, would keep us cool
>   And warm in January.

Strange what an unmade bed can do to a bedroom in making it look untidy.

YOU HOUSEWIVES MIGHT CHECK YOUR OWN EFFICIENCY: The average hotel chambermaid can strip a bed in three minutes and make it up completely in seven.

Pajamas could stand a little change in design. That knotty string around the middle and the up-creeping jacket, one would think, could be remedied.

Always willing to help. The following space is gladly devoted to a "cause." Read it carefully, you may be a violator. Your own neighbors may be whispering. And you may be very innocent through it all. The warning came to me on a postcard saying: "Won't you please give a friendly tip to users of Venetian blinds. Inform the folks that they are NOT blinds unless completely closed. Neighbors on the first floor seem to forget that the second-floor occupants from across the way get a different slant and often an eyeful." Well, from now on, don't say that I didn't warn you.

Papa helps Mama: After you've washed your Venetian blinds in a lukewarm soapy water, rinsed them in a clear, cold water and allowed them to dry, give them a little rubbing with a rag moistened with linseed oil. It'll bring the shine right back.

You might want to try the stunt of making old drapes useful by sewing them together for a bedspread. Very fetching.

Tip to you Ladies: Your husband's humidor is a dandy place to store silk stockings—if the old man doesn't have it full of stogies, of course.

Wonder how many women remember the old curling iron and how they used to heat it by sticking it down the chimney of a kerosene lamp in the sleeping chamber?

REMINDER TO YOUNG PARENTS: Don't put soiled diapers on your varnished bedroom floors. The floors will turn black and the stain is one that won't come out. Ask Pa, he knows.

And if your wee one has a stuffy nose, a pressure cooker makes a very fine humidifier for his sleeping room. Fills the room with steam and much-needed moisture.

Are you guilty, too? Every time I go into a strange bathroom, I can never resist a tiny peek into the medicine chest. And in more than 20 years of peeking I've never found one in perfect order.

The old roller towel wasn't such a bad invention after all. Wonder how it happened to vanish from the American scene?

CLEANLINESS IS NEXT

If you weren't in one last night, you probably will be today, so bathtub talk is always timely. The first tub as we know it made its appearance in Cincinnati in 1842 and was exhibited by its designer, Adam Thompson, to a group of Christmas-party guests. And jumped on he was, too, by the public press. The tub was referred to as "an example of epicureal luxury, evidence of an undemocratic tendency and a dangerous departure from the virtue and simplicity of honored ancestors." In 1843, the bathtub invaded Philadelphia and an ordinance prohibiting bathing between Nov. 1 and March 15 failed of passage by two votes. The legislature of Virginia laid a $30 yearly tax on tubs, other eastern cities hiked up the water rate on bathtub owners.

Boston's puritanical ire reached a point once where a city ordinance was passed to make bathing in a modern tub unlawful except on medical orders.

HOSPITAL PEOPLE CALLED UP WITH THIS WARNING: You should take particular caution in your use of porcelain handles on faucets. When too much pressure is exerted on porcelain and it cracks, it leaves the ugliest of wounds. There's something about the sharp way in which porcelain cracks that not only cuts the skin but also tears tendons, and that's what does the damage. So—be careful with your porcelain handles.

Better call a plumber if one of your bathroom taps drips. At the rate of one drop a second it will waste 2,299 gallons of water in a year.

That drop per second, if it comes from the hot water faucet, also may up your hot water bill by 5 to 10 per cent.

Science clicks again to inform us that the ring around your bathtub (and mine, too) isn't dirt after all. It's caused largely by calcium and magnesium in hard water. They draw a precipitate from the water that forms the ring. There's a sulphated soap out, though, that leaves no ring.

Next time you're down on your hands and knees scrubbing your tile bathroom floor, think of this: Scrubbing the Holland tunnel under the Hudson River in New York is equivalent to scrubbing 3,000 tiled bathrooms. The job's been boiled down to a seven-hour performance, is done once a week at night and takes 1,500 gallons of soap and 20,000 gallons of water each time.

IF YOU BATHE AT NIGHT, YOU MIGHT TRY THIS LITTLE

TRICK FOR KEEPING YOUR CLOTHES FRESH AND DAINTY: Just before you start your bath water, hang up your suit or your dress in the bathroom. Let the bath steam seep into the garments and then let them hang there overnight. By morning you'll have given them a good steam and they'll have a freshness that will amaze you.

One for your think tank that should be a pushover. A gent goes into his bathroom. It's built like a vault. One door, no windows, and a three-hour time lock on the door. He enters the bathroom, turns on the water, fills the tub and both handles jam so he can't shut off the water. The level is up to his neck at the time this scene begins. How does he make his thrilling escape? (*Answer at end of this section.*)

An old toothbrush is the world's best safety-razor cleaner.
Instead of throwing away your scrap pieces of soap, girls, run them through your meat grinder. They come out as soap flakes.
WELL WELL, here's a very practical idea. The little cardboard tube inside a roll of bathroom tissue makes a slick mailing tube for any medium-sized newspaper or small magazine. A gummed label can be pasted on the outside for the address.

Here's the answer to the problem of the gent with the overflowing tub: He plunges under for an instant to pull the plug or release the stopper that lets the water drain out of the tub.

EVERYTHING, INCLUDING
THE KITCHEN SINK

It costs more to furnish the average kitchen than it does a dining room or a bedroom.
Here's a little statistic for you housewives to toss at friend husband, especially if he's a furnace tender: In a normal

household, the weight of the dishes a wife washes in a year is greater than the weight of the coal the Old Man heaves into the hopper. And think what a showing you wives make over the husband who has nothing more to do than twist the thermostat on an automatic heater.

What would we do without them? The average housewife washes nine piles of dishes as high as the Empire State building in her lifetime.

Too bad our wives can't take a little lesson from the dining-car workers. The dishwasher, in a sink that's less than two feet square, washes more than 900 dishes a day.

MOTHER'S LITTLE HELPER: When you're cleaning your silverware for some gala occasion, boil the silver in an aluminum pan with plain salt water. The salt does the same job as soda, only you get no scum. That's the advice of a woman of science.

Most people, warns a diamond expert, handle their gems too tenderly when cleaning them. Best way to wash diamonds, he advises, is in a granite dish of water with any good soap or soap powder. And, he adds, boil the precious stones as you would goulash.

Girls, if you want to add to the life of your linen tablecloths, change the folds and creases constantly when you put them away, folding them in thirds one time and quarters the next. It'll save strain on the same threads.

Another stunt eliminates the creases entirely. Cut off an old broomstick a little longer than the tablecloth is wide and then roll the cloth smoothly on the broomstick. A clean piece of tissue paper wrapped around the rolled cloth will protect it.

Women in distress get me. This should help somebody: If, by some odd turn of Nature, you've worn out one rubber glove and now have a collection of them for the same hand, you can make a right-hander out of a left-handed glove simply by turning it inside out. (*Isn't he a blessing to us, girls?*)

Here's a solution for what I'm sure is one of your vexing household problems. To prevent lime from forming in your teakettle, place a square of clean muslin in the bottom of the kettle. All the lime will adhere to the cloth.

Our Household Problem department also pops up with this: You can make whipping cream or beating an egg a spatter-proof job by doing it in a small, round goldfish bowl. And please don't postcard me with, "Yeah, but what'll we do with the goldfish?"

If you ever want to lubricate your egg beater or your meat chopper (and it'll surprise you what a little lubrication will do) use glycerine.

To boil a cracked egg, drop a little vinegar in the water. That will keep the albumen from seeping through the crack in the shell. But you won't remember it.

And you can avoid smelling up the house when you boil cabbage, cauliflower, and the like by placing a small piece of charcoal in the water.

Better toss out your old can opener. Use of a worn one will drop slivers of solder in your food. The solder contains a dangerous poison which accumulates in your system even though the amounts from any one can are trivial.

ANNUAL WARNING: Pressure cookers should be examined carefully once a year to see that everything is working properly and fitting tightly. Canning season, I suppose, would be the most logical time for the check-up.

Should your milk happen to freeze any time during the winter, don't thaw it out in a hot place. That flattens the milk, makes it sour more readily. Place the bottle in a pan of cold tap water and it'll thaw out just as soon and it keeps the milk better.

Those who have tried it say that storing cigars in the deep freeze is the best method of keeping them fresh.

Bet you housewives who do home canning didn't know that the phrase "hermetically sealed" comes from the use of the seal of Hermes, the pagan god. Alchemists of old placed the seal on their vessels. Hermes was reputed to be the inventor of the arts and sciences, and alchemists called their work "the hermetic art." Or didn't you care?

Warning to husbands: Don't come home and, in trying to be Mama's Helper, give the lids on her freshly put up vegetables an extra turn to tighten them. You'll break the air seal on the jar if you do.

When your screw-on jar lids stick, however, a piece of sandpaper used as a "gripper" makes removal a cinch.

Safety hint. Keep matches where mice can't get at them. I know of at least one case where a blaze in a bureau drawer was started when mice nibbled on matches. Had the fire started when the woman who reported this was away, her whole house might have gone.

Don't throw away your old candle ends. It's easy to turn them into a very beautiful giant candle that looks like the big ones you buy in the novelty shops. Use an empty tin can (coffee cans, if they haven't ridges around the top, are dandy), place one short candle in the center of the can to provide a wick. Then melt all your old candle ends and pour the wax into the can. The wax will harden around the candle in the center. When the can is full, you've got your big, decorative candle. The more candle colors you mix, the better-looking your giant candle's going to be, too.

Be sure to look under the sink every time you change maids. Housewives in many cities have discovered that household employes, upon termination of a job, have taken to writing candid opinions of their employers beneath the sink, where the next girl could read it and get the lowdown.

Part Nine

PUZZLES & GAMES

Have you ever been to a party where the drinks and the guests didn't seem to mix properly for an interlude of fun? It could happen to anyone, so here are some tricks, puzzles, games and other assorted stunts that you can use when the going gets dull.

Mental acrobatics is not a new exercise by any means. Some of history's leading wits and biggest brains are credited with having originated catchy little puzzlers that you can use to liven up a party or to sharpen your own mind.

If you're a card player, for instance, did you ever stop to figure out how your favorite game fits into the national picture? Rummy is the card game that most people have known. Forty-six per cent of the people in the United States have played a form of rummy at one time or another. Next in order of popularity is solitaire—43 per cent have played that. Poker comes next with 37 per cent; pinochle follows with 36 per cent; hearts with 33; contract bridge with 31. The survey, conducted by a playing-card manufacturer, also revealed that when asked what game they played the last time they played cards, contract bridge was on top with pinochle, rummy, gin rummy and solitaire following in that order.

And I don't know who figured it out, but a single bridge deck has more than 690 billion different combinations. If the deck is shuffled properly, each bridge player can count on a singleton about once every three hands.

No wonder husbands are frequently late in returning home from poker parties. There are 2,598,960 different possible poker hands. You wouldn't want the old man to come till he'd tried them all, would you?

If you are a poker player and don't bluff more than 6 per cent of the time, your opponents can't judge whether it's your policy to bluff or not. Hike up your deception more than that, though, and your chances of being caught are multiplied.

You can pick up a little spare change by betting you can throw every double with a pair of dice in 10 minutes. It's a gambling chestnut and usually takes less than four minutes to accomplish. But don't blame me if the darned things don't pop.

AND REMEMBER I WARNED YOU, GUYS. A series of experiments conducted at Duke University showed that indulgence in alcoholic beverages tends to retard crapshooters in tossing their desired point.

If card or dice playing is too strenuous for your system, a crossword puzzle may be just the thing. But did you know that the first crossword puzzle published in the United States was run only as far back as 1913 in the old New York World?

When it comes to exciting games, however, I admire the nimble brain that thought up the hotfoot.

Beyond something really inspired like that, however, I like mental calisthenics on the simple side, and preferably without an answer.

THIS IS A FAVORITE: If a man were to stand at the equator and walk completely around the earth, I wonder how much farther his head would travel than his feet.

That's a sample of the kind of puzzles and games that appeal to me, and frankly I don't know if any of them would qualify for the $64 question. But in my own way, I've put together at least 64 questions that ought to be worth a dollar apiece. However, don't send me an answer sheet and claim any money. For the most nettling ones of the group, the answers are printed in a separate section at the end of this puzzle chapter.

NOODLE ANNOYERS

1. Bounce this around in your bean. Two apple vendors went to the market daily with lots of 60 apples to sell. The first vendor sold his at the rate of two for $1 and realized

$30 daily. The second sold his at the rate of three for $1 and realized $20. Together, then, they collected $50. One day the second vendor was ill and said to the first, "Will you sell my apples for me today? Since you sell at the rate of two for $1 and I sell at the rate of three for $1, you can combine the lots and sell them at five for $2 and receive the same return as both of us selling individually." The first vendor agreed and sold the combined lots at five for $2. At the end of the day he counted his receipts and discovered he had only $48. What happened to the missing $2?

2. For that agile noodle of yours, try this annoyer: We (you and I) both have some apples. If I give you one of mine, we'll both have the same number. But if you give me one, I'll have twice as many as you'll have. How many do we each have?

3. A farmer has three sons. He sends them out to gather eggs. The first one comes back with 15 eggs; the second returns with 50 eggs, and the third comes back with 85 eggs. Says the farmer to the boys, "I want you to go to town now and all sell your eggs for the same price." They came back with 10 cents apiece. What was the price of the eggs?

4. We got a university's mathematics dean going on our Noodle Annoyers and he suggests the following problem: Diophantus passed one-sixth of his life in childhood, one-twelfth in youth and one-seventh as a bachelor. Five years after he was married a son was born who died four years before his father at half the age at which his father died. What was the age of the father when he died?

5. How high is a tree that's 15 feet shorter than a pole three times as tall as the tree?

6. And another old one: "Mary is 24 years old. She is twice as old as Ann was when she was as old as Ann is now. How old is Ann?" You still may have trouble in figuring it out. Here's the background, anyway: The puzzler reportedly started in the New York Press back in 1903, touched off nationwide debate and remained the country's No. 1 puzzle for years. . . .

7. A simple Noodle Annoyer that's short and sweet: A brick weighs six pounds and half a brick. What is the weight of the brick? And please don't say nine pounds.

8. There were two barbershops. In the first shop haircuts were 40 cents and shaves 20 cents, total 60 cents. In the second shop, haircuts were 35 cents and shaves 25 cents, total 60 cents. A customer studied the prices and then discovered that by getting a shave in the first shop he saved five cents and by getting a haircut in the second shop he saved another nickel.

"I've saved 10 cents," says he to himself.

But 20 cents plus 35 cents makes 55 cents, in spite of the fact that he had saved 5 cents on each item. How come? asks Charlotte. I know, let X equal the first haircut and so on.

9. Here's a real Noodle Annoyer: If it takes seven cats to kill seven rats in seven minutes, how many cats will it take to kill 100 rats in 50 minutes?

10. A fish's head is five inches long. Its tail is as long as its head plus half its body. Its body is as long as its head plus its tail. How long is the fish? Simple, huh?

11. Here's one that a department-store executive tossed at me. A blind man goes into a store and buys 100 pairs of black socks with clocks on and 100 pairs of white socks with clocks on. On the way home he drops the bundles and gets the socks all jumbled up—whites mixed with blacks and blacks confused with whites. Have you the picture? Then, in his own way, he starts sorting them. How many socks would the blind man have to select from them all to get a pair?

12. Now that you've toyed with the sock problem, here's a similar Noodle Annoyer from a professor of psychology, only he uses gloves. There are 100 pairs of black gloves and 100 pairs of white gloves. How many gloves would the blind man have to select from the jumbled pile to assure himself of one matching pair? And the answer isn't three this time.

13. Another tough one: What four consecutive odd numbers will add up to 80?

14. Give a friend a dollar's worth of change in 50 coins using only halves, quarters, dimes, nickels or pennies. There are two combinations. Get them both. . . .

15. Identical cups of tea and coffee are filled to the same level. A teaspoonful of tea is transferred to the coffee cup. The mixture is then thoroughly stirred, and one teaspoonful of it is transferred back to the teacup. Is there more tea in the coffee cup than there is coffee in the teacup? Maybe it's too easy.

TONGUE TWISTERS

TRY YOUR ENUNCIATION ON THESE. And remember, they should be read slowly and distinctly at first and then speeded up as much as possible without the tongue becoming twisted: Five wives weave withes . . . A school coal scuttle . . . A shot-silk sash shop . . . Some shun sunshine . . . The sixth sick sheik's sixth sheep's sick . . . Shingles and single; shave a single shingle thin . . . I snuff shop snuff; do you snuff shop snuff? . . . Thirty-six thick silk threads . . . Coop up the cook . . . She says she shall sew a sheet.

Roll your tongue over these: Frank threw Fred three free throws . . . Old oily Ollie oils old oily autos . . . Bob bought a black back brush . . . Chop shops stock chops.

Here's one for your thorax: A phrase in which six different pronunciations of "ough" occur: Though the tough cough and hiccough plough me through.

Here's a tongue twister that needs to be tried only once. "The sea ceaseth, but it sufficeth us."

If you want to give that yap of yours a real workout, try saying this fast: "Such slipshod speech as she speaks." *Now repeat it several times.*

THIS TRIPS MANY ON THE SECOND TRY: "The clothes moth's mouth closed."

No matter the amount of rehearsing, even the smartest boys in radio can't repeat fast three times this simple little tongue twister: "Red leather, yellow leather."

Repeat four times: "Blue Broadloom rug."

Say this fast five times: "A big mixed biscuit tin."

QUICKIES IN
COMMON THINGS

Which direction is the face of Abraham Lincoln facing on a Lincoln penny?

Try this little test in observation: On a piece of paper, draw a replica of a telephone dial and see if you can insert in complete detail the numbers and letters for every hole.

Choose a word in this line of type that you think a dime will cover completely, then take out a dime and see how far off you were.

I'll lay you college graduates five to one that you can't give me the Latin phrase represented by the initials of your A.B.

Oh, you want to do a little figuring, do you? Well, starting at 6 a.m. today and ending at 6:30 a.m. tomorrow, exactly how many times does the minute hand lap the hour hand?

You men, without counting, try to guess the total number of pockets in your clothing, including those in your topcoat, and see how close you come.

Do you know what Mrs. Cannonball said to Mr. Cannonball? "I'm going to have a B-B."

QUICKIES WITH ANSWERS

Want to stump your Sunday-school teacher? Ask him or her (or even the parson) what kind of wood Noah used to build his ark. It was made out of gopher wood, just so you'll know.

Next time you get a group going on guessing games try them on how much a ton of pennies would be worth. The answer is $2,750.

See how smart your family is and ask them right now to guess the area of the Pacific Ocean. It's 68,634,000 square miles, covers more than a third of the surface of the globe, adds up to half the water on the surface of the earth and is half again as big as the Atlantic.

Here's one for you old disputers and you may hop on it with all your might: There are approximately 556,000 grains in a bushel of wheat.

YOU CAN STICK YOUR FRIENDS ON THIS ONE: Which state has the most shore line of any in the country? California with 1,350, or whatever it is, will loom as No. 1. Michigan has about 30 per cent more. . . .

Have you ever gazed at a locomotive and wondered how much it weighs? The average steam locomotive will tip the scales at 144 tons.

You college students might toss this one at your instructor tomorrow: "How, my good man, did you get along with your pogonotomy this morning?" It's the manly art of shaving, in case you stump him.

Can you think of a word with three pairs of letters all in a row? Bookkeeper.

Do you know what language Jesus spoke? It was Aramaic, a language related to both Arabic and Hebrew. And not too long ago a community of some 3,000 people still speaking it was discovered in Iraq.

PLAY IN ANY PARLOR

You may find a little fun in this pastime the next time you get a group together. It's a test to determine if a subject is predominantly masculine or feminine. Ask each guest to light a match, drink out of a glass, look across the room and look at his or her nails. One of dominant masculinity will scratch the match toward him, look into the glass while drinking, stare directly when told to look across the room and cup his hand to look at his fingernails.

The dominant feminine will scratch the match away from herself, look over the rim of the glass while drinking, let her glance wander while looking across the room and raise her whole hand to look at her nails. Give it a whirl on your family.

GIVE YOURSELF A LITTLE COLOR TEST: Preferences, according to a recent survey, are as follows: Intellectuals of both sexes go for blue; athletes prefer red; egotists pick yellow; convivial persons have a yen for orange, and the lovelorn, bless their little hearts, revel in crimson.

Add this to your parlor tricks: Pick out a subject, particularly a fat woman if there's one around. On the floor you make a pretty good-sized loop with a string. You suggest to her that when the loop made by the string approximates the size of her waistline, she tells you to stop expanding the loop. After you've extended the loop to the point where she thinks it resembles her waistline, take that amount of string and see how it actually measures around her waist. Some of the guesses will amaze you.

For a little mild hilarity blindfold two or three of your guests and then ask them to light cigarets with the blindfold still on.

If you have a fiddle player in your home and want to pull a gag on him, rub the strings and bow with soap. It'll mute the violin almost to complete silence.

A meanie is this newest form of "hot foot": Take an eye dropper loaded with oil of mustard and squeeze a drop or two along the sole of a victim's shoe. It whips a lighted match all to pieces for effect. And the more one stamps, the hotter the hot foot.

Give these a whirl. I guarantee they're easy. Arrange the following letters into common English words: e-s-c-u-a-r and h-y-s-t-e-c.

For some mental acrobatics, try your pronunciations of the following and then check with the dictionary. I'll bet you don't go better than 50 per cent correct. Percolator, poinsettia, pretense, caramel, sinecure, chiropodist, lamentable, neuralgia, nonchalant, resource, gondola, impotent, incognito, indisputable, grimace.

A diction expert claims that not one person in a hundred can pronounce the following 11 words correctly: Data, gratis, culinary, cocaine, gondola, version, impious, chic, inquiry, acclimate, and respite. Give them a whirl, then look to Webster.

Open your mouth wide and then think of the word bubble. Did you feel the impulse to compress your lips?

FAMILY SPELLING BEE

LET'S PLAY SPELLING GAMES, SHALL WE? I'm assuming you're the first member of the family to read this department. So ask the others to spell the following: kimono, rarefy, battalion, guerrilla, picnicking, ukulele, diarrhea, renege, charivari, embarrass, pyorrhea, catarrh, shillalah, connoisseur, queue, Philippine, paraffin, acqiesce, cirrhosis, benefited, rhythm, liaison, siege. Spell 20 of the 25 correctly and you should be on a newspaper copy desk.

They'll give you odds of 10,000 to 1 that you can't spell all 10 of the following words correctly: Sacrilegious; supersede; privilege; exhilarate; indispensable; rarefy; liquefy; ecstasy; hypocrisy, and irrelevant. How did you come out?

Want to slow down that wife of yours? Give her this; "All right, you think you're so smart, spell 'erysipelas.' " She missed it, didn't she?

Stick the members of your family with these spellings: "Phlegm" and "sieve." Bet they missed them both.

To pass an idle hour or two sometime, try to think of words that begin and end with the same two letters. Here's a start: periscope, iconoclastic, amalgam, enliven.

ANSWERS TO ANNOYERS

1. To come out even in making lots of five apples, he sold only 48 apples at the rate of two for $1 (total $24) and 72 apples at three for $1 (total $24). The ratio of apples sold at each price was different.

2. One has seven apples, the other has five to start.

3. They sold the eggs for a cent a dozen and three cents apiece for the odd eggs.

4. The father died at 84. The son died at 42, when the father was 80. Diophantus' life: childhood, 14 years; youth, 7 years, bachelorhood, 12 years; married at 33; son was born when father was 38.

5. Tree: 7½ feet; Pole: 22½ feet

6. Ann is 18. When Mary was 18 (six years ago) Ann was 12, or half of Mary's present age of 24.

7. The brick weighs 12 pounds.

8. He would have saved 10 cents only from the maximum prices of both shops—the 40-cent haircut and the 25-cent shave—for a total of 65 cents. Now don't ask me where to find the barbershops with those prices, I've heard about inflation, too.

9. It takes 14 cats to kill the 100 rats in 50 minutes. It takes seven cats to kill one rat in one minute. If they worked 50 minutes they'd kill 50 rats. Double that for 14 cats to kill 100 rats in 50 minutes. . . .

10. Head of fish, 5 inches; body, 20 inches; tail 15 inches. Total, 40 inches.

11. Pulling any three socks out of the pile would result in a pair of one or the other color.

12. He'd have to pull out at least 201 gloves, enough to get all of one color or all for one hand, plus one more glove, to be assured of a proper pair.

13. 17—19—21—23

14. A.—40 Pennies, 8 nickels, 2 dimes; B.—45 pennies, 2 nickels, 2 dimes, 1 quarter.

15. More tea in the coffee cup.

Postscript

Postscript
by
Bob Hope

Who ever heard of a beautiful blonde cuddling up for an evening with a newspaper column? But cuddling up with a good book, that's different. It's so different that the very thought of it drove Cedric Adams to publish a book.

In real life Adams is what they call a newspaper and radio personality. He has half a dozen secretaries, each more beautiful than the next, and private offices at the newspaper, the radio station, and in his home. But he lives on a cabin cruiser all summer and does his work from the boat. The rest of the time he spends getting acquainted with everybody in Minneapolis, which is the supply source of his secretaries.

It's pretty important for Adams to know everybody in Minneapolis—in the whole state of Minnesota, for that matter—because he really runs the state and has to keep in touch with his constituents. Just like the politicians who *think* they run the state. Only the politicians have to be elected every couple years; while Adams has the housewives' vote sewed up and goes on forever. I know, because I once made the mistake of not buttering up to Adams before a Minneapolis show and my audience consisted of just three people—my aunt, my cousin, and a girl usher with buck teeth. Since I learned what a good word from Adams can do, I've been packing them in up there.

So with that kind of power, a regular newspaper Svengali, Adams takes time to turn out a book. A big fat book it is, too. Which gets us back to that juicy picture of the slim blonde cuddling up with a fat book for an evening of fun.

The psychiatrists have a word or two for that, but I wouldn't dare print them here because this book is bound to fall into the hands of innocent children. But you grownups know what I mean if you've still got all your marbles.

Those deep-forehead (and I don't mean receding hairline) psychologists could make your hair stand up telling you what Adams is *really* thinking when he thinks about that beautiful blonde cuddling up with his book. Her smooth fingers caress the pages one by one as her dreamy eyes drink in his words. Then sleep finally comes near. She closes the book lovingly, hugs it to her bosom for a second before putting it down on the bedside stand, where it will be the first thing to catch her eye at morning.

Wow! Hand me a typewriter, quick. I'm going to write a book myself!

Next time you wonder about the thrill of being an author, just remember those little paragraphs. It's the old story that makes the world go round—*book* meets girl. And it explains why Cedric Adams, whose newspaper columns and radio programs have Minnesota feeding out of his hand and at the same time feeding his family in style, just had to write a book. It was boiling in his blood and had to come out. He can't get that kind of thrill from writing a newspaper column. Nine times out of ten somebody just forgets the sheet on a bus and it gets sat on by a squashy fat dame going home from shopping. Ouch!

But that book and that beautiful blonde, they both got something enjoyable, cuddled up together like that. And so has Adams in one of the most enjoyable books I've ever cuddled up with.